Poetry Therapy

The Use of Poetry in the
Treatment of Emotional
Disorders

*Like the sun that breaks his arrows
On a dark river*

Poetry Therapy

The Use of Poetry in the Treatment of Emotional Disorders

Edited by
JACK J. LEEDY, MD

Cotherapist, Poetry Therapy Group, Project Teen Aid,
OEO, Brooklyn, Associate Attending Psychiatrist,
The Brooklyn-Cumberland Medical Center,
Director, Poetry Therapy Center, New York

Philadelphia & Toronto
J. B. LIPPINCOTT COMPANY

TO

NORMA LEEDY

For her understanding help

Poetry Therapy

is dedicated

Copyright © 1969 by J. B. LIPPINCOTT COMPANY

This book is fully protected by copyright and, with the exception of brief abstracts for review, no part of it may be reproduced in any form without the written permission of the publisher.

Distributed in Great Britain by
Pitman Medical Publishing Company, Limited, London

Library of Congress Catalog Card No. 67-15033
PRINTED IN THE UNITED STATES OF AMERICA
SP-B

Foreword

Ne t'es-tu fais mal, mon enfant?

I RAN INTO DR. LEEDY LAST YEAR on West 86th Street—he and I were neighbors—and learned that he was editing a book, *Poetry Therapy*. It appears that I have been "pioneering" in poetry therapy.

Two of my clinical experiences come to mind. More than 30 years ago, in Vienna, I attended a performance by the world-famous Yvette Guilbert. (Both Freud and I admired her greatly; Freud's letters to Miss Guilbert were recently made public.) When this distinguished artist read modern French poetry aloud, one could visualize her in many roles. She transformed herself in a moment from a grandmother to a young girl to a Parisian apache. One of the poems moved me most profoundly. It tells of a young man in love with a girl who only toyed with him, and asked more and more from him as proof of his love. Then she requested that he bring to her as food for her dog his mother's heart. The young man murders his mother and cuts out her heart. On his way back to his mistress, he stumbles and falls. His mother's heart rolls into the dust. Tenderly the heart solicits of him, "Did you hurt yourself, my child?"

I have never forgotten that poem. There was a time I knew it word for word in French. I am still haunted by the line, "Ne t'es-tu fais mal, mon enfant?"

One of my Viennese patients was then a young college lecturer in French. He hated his mother. He asserted that she had never loved him, but had given all her affection to his brother, five years younger than he. He had spent many psychoanalytic sessions with complaints about his mother and accusations against her. I once said to him: "I am convinced that your mother has loved you and that now you no longer recall this period." When he complained again about his mother, I recited the poem that I have just mentioned. On hearing that last line, my patient commenced to sob, and continued to do so for a long time. Following this session, his relationship with his mother progressively improved and the change persisted.

I remember another experience, less dramatic but significant. I had begun a new book, yet I doubted that I would be able to finish it. I had just passed my 78th birthday, and for some reason I felt depressed. By chance I came across a sonnet of John Keats:

> When I have fears that I may cease to be
>   Before my pen has gleaned my teeming brain,
>   Before high-piled books, in charactery,
>   Hold like rich garners the full ripened grain....

I remembered that Keats died when he was only 26. I suddenly felt consoled and courageous again. I am at work on that book, which I would like to entitle *Living Is Learning*.

I have always championed a poetic approach to depth psychology. The psychoanalyst should be like an actor who learns technique in order to forget it once he is on stage. I did not deliberately try to utilize the technique of the artist. In my work I listened, assimilated, and responded in a highly subjective way, allowing my own unconscious a maximum of influence and restraining the impulse to bring conscious criticism to bear on my observations. It was only after the observations had taken inner root that I allowed consciousness to turn on my own psyche. In so doing, I tried to produce a poetry of psychoanalysis. I wrote in *Fragment of a Great Confession*:

> The metaphors of the poet are often more meaningful than technical scientific language with all its precision and clarity. The psychologist is perforce content if he succeeds in expressing the processes of the unconscious approximately, even by an awkward and uncertain phrase. He must be satisfied if he somehow succeeds in capturing a little of the life of the mind while the poet has created and given embodiment to this life even as he thought to conceal it.
>
> Poets and psychologists alike try to grasp the last secret of the human soul. They agree finally: This last is unsayable.[1]

Gustav Mahler once spent several hours with Sigmund Freud.[2] The analytic insights obtained in that long session had a deep and lasting effect on the composer; they removed his doubts and inhibitions, restored his capability for love and strengthened his self-confidence. Mahler wrote a poem to his wife on the train back from Leyden, to prove the emotional effect of the long conversation with Freud. Its first lines may be translated:

> They melt, the shadows of the night
> What always tortured me as fright,
> Is blown away by power of one word,
> My feeling, pressing to the height,
> My thoughts, in danger of the glide,
> They flow together into one accord:
> I love you. . . .

I consider Dr. Leedy's *Poetry Therapy* a significant and timely contribution to all of mental health. Each reader will recognize its tremendous value. Its publication should stimulate the establishment of poetry therapy in mental hygiene clinics, mental health centers, hospitals, guidance and counseling centers, self-help groups, rehabilitation centers, the private practice of psychotherapy, and training centers in psychiatry, psychology, social work, nursing occupational therapy, pastoral counseling, mental retardation, and penology.

Inside the school system, I believe that the efficacy of poetry as therapy for disturbed youngsters may make a crucial contribution. Universities will do well to train prospective teachers and psychologists in the techniques of poetry therapy, this promising new approach in psychotherapy.

THEODOR REIK, PHD

November 20, 1968
New York

REFERENCES

1. Reik, Theodor: Fragment of a Great Confession, New York, Farrar, Strauss and Company, 1949, p. 211.
2. ———: The Haunting Melody, *ibid.*, 1953. See also p. 8, and Of Love and Lust, *ibid.*, 1949, pp. 52–53.

Preface

The Vacuum

THE SURPRISING THING about the publication of *Poetry Therapy* is that the vacuum it so appropriately moves into now has remained empty so long. Poets have revealed themselves and have analyzed man's condition long before human behavior was conceptualized as a science, but the task of consciously exploring how poetry operates therapeutically has awaited the deliberations of the contributors to this volume. The truism that the source of the poetic imagination lies close to man's innermost hopes and fears would have led, it seems, to an earlier coalescence of interest in the relationship between poetry and therapy. The ancillary art-therapies based on music, drama, and painting have been, for some years now, an integral part of a comprehensive treatment program. Poetry, a relative newcomer to the adjunctive program, has interesting potentialities.

Just as the patient in psychotherapy reluctantly yields his secrets to his own awareness, so does human nature only grudgingly allow itself to be scrutinized and systematized into the formulations of the various behavioral sciences. On the other hand, the poet entices participation. In effect, he says: "Here are my sorrows and my joys, my hopes and my fears. It pleases me to share them with you. If you see yourself in the mirror of my art and feel comforted or strengthened, follow me." The emotional impact of a patient's sudden and dramatic insight during an analytic hour resembles the effect that the reader experiences when he seizes upon what is for him a particular revealing intuitive communication from the poet. It is similar to what Keats describes:

> ON FIRST LOOKING INTO CHAPMAN'S HOMER
> Then felt I like some watcher of the skies
> When a new planet swims into his ken;

> Or like stout Cortez when with eagle eyes
> He stared at the Pacific—and all his men
> Looked at each other with a wild surmise—
> Silent, upon a peak in Darien.

The contributors to this book have been actively seeking the therapeutic principle that resides in the nature of poetry. Just as poetry reflects the many faceted moods of man, so can we expect that the contributors will see different therapeutic values in different elements of poetry. Above all, they are to be commended for their insistence that the poet's intuition be accorded its rightful place among our methodologies for understanding and treating the ailments of human nature.

The range of possibilities for using poetry therapeutically in different settings—clinics, hospitals, schools—and with different kinds of patients—neurotics, psychotics, retardates—has only been outlined in this volume and has yet to be fully explored. Most important, we are shown here how the vast reservoir of human feeling recorded in poetry may be tapped for therapeutic purposes, and the approach bears watching like a new planet swimming into our ken.

LEWIS R. WOLBERG, MD
*Dean and Medical Director, Postgraduate Center for
Mental Health, Clinical Professor of Psychiatry,
New York Medical College*

November 24, 1968

Introduction
The Healing Power of Poetry

POSSESSED OF INTUITIVE WISDOM, the Greeks recognized the healing power of poetry. They worshipped Apollo, the personification of the sun and the father of Asklepios, as a dual god of medicine and of poetry. Centuries later, by crediting the discovery of the unconscious to the poets, Sigmund Freud linked modern medical insight to the psychological intuitions of the past. According to the founder of psychoanalytical thought, the poets were the first to "salvage from the whirlpool of their emotions the deepest truths to which we others have to force our way, ceaselessly groping among torturing uncertainties." Other seminal theoreticians, such as Adler, Jung, Moreno and Reik, also confirmed that poets originally charted paths that science subsequently followed. Poets, then, were here to reveal and analyze the human condition long before the study of man's behavior was conceptualized as a science.

Today, bibliotherapy (which has been defined as the process of assimilating the psychological, sociological, and aesthetic values from books into human character, personality, and behavior) holds a firmly established position with such other modes of healing as occupational therapy, art therapy, music therapy and dance therapy. In many mental hospitals, the library plays a significant role in the total recovery program.

It has been exciting to help nurture poetry therapy as an important added dimension in treating the emotional disorders, and to introduce its practice as a new profession. The Postgraduate Center for Mental Health in New York, the Institute of Pennsylvania Hospital in Philadelphia, El Camino Hospital in Mountain View, California, Project Teen Aid, OEO, in Brooklyn, Crownsville State Hospital in Maryland, Langley Porter Institute in San Francisco—these and other institutions throughout the country have incorporated poetry therapy into their design for treatment.

Poetry therapist Joy Shieman's design for the construction of the ideal Poetry Therapy Room has been approved by El Camino Hospital.

In 1959, a Poetry Therapy group was organized at the Mental Hygiene Clinic, Cumberland Hospital, Brooklyn, and directed by our late associate Eli Greifer, assisted by Dr. Samuel Spector and myself. Georgia L. McMurray, my cotherapist of the Poetry Therapy Group, Project Teen Aid—now promoted to Project Director, Committee for the Education of Pregnant School Age Girls, Public Education Association, New York—has incorporated the principles and techniques of poetry therapy in the program for these girls throughout New York, to be followed hopefully in programs for these and other patients throughout the world.

Poetry Therapy indicates how poetry has been employed in private practice as well as in mental hospitals, research and counseling centers, and among self-help groups, in school guidance and in individual and group settings. It is our intention to clarify the specific role that poetry, because of its special nature, can be called on to perform in psychotherapy.

Our contributors are a group of practicing psychiatrists, clinical psychologists, psychiatric social workers, a literary critic and philosopher of note, a semanticist and university professors. Dr. Kenneth Burke and Dr. Aaron Kramer have written distinguished poetry of their own. *Poetry Therapy* itself is a compendium of comments on the theoretical underpinnings of poetry therapy along with discussions of its practice drawn from the records of the therapists. Because of its eclectic nature, this book should prove useful not only to members of the psychiatric profession but to all who wish to play a more active role in dealing with a major contemporary problem—the widespread and accelerating incidence of psychogenic disorders.

My appreciation goes to Dr. David V. Forrest, now in Vietnam, for his useful criticisms and for going beyond the call of duty to help design the excellent dust jacket for our book, and to Professor Morris R. Morrison of the City University of New York for his faithful and percipient assistance. Henry E. Manning, Assistant Commissioner, Affiliation Administration, Department of Hospitals, New York, and Joseph B. Mann, Assistant Commissioner and Executive Director, Cumberland Hospital Division of The Brooklyn-Cumberland Medical Center, have encouraged me greatly. For her help, I thank Elizabeth Fontaine, who 22 years ago founded the Hospitalized Veterans Writing Project, Inc., an organization of volunteers who encourage the patients in the 170 Veterans Hospitals to write poetry as part of their rehabilitation. My deepest gratitude is extended to Carter Harrison, of J. B. Lippincott Company, whose suggestions have been invaluable.

I now defer to Apollo. May his medicinal arrows continue, as always, to wing their way into the enigmatic areas of man's troubled soul.

JACK J. LEEDY, MD

November 1, 1968
New York

Acknowledgments

THE EDITOR of *Poetry Therapy* gratefully acknowledges the kind permission of the following publishers and persons to reprint poems and prose:

Kurt Adler, for short passages from *The Individual Psychology of Alfred Adler*.

Farrar, Straus and Giroux, Inc., for a brief passage of T. S. Eliot, *On Poetry and Poets*, copyright 1957.

John Dewey Society, for a sentence from Louise M. Rosenblatt: *Literature as Exploration*, copyright 1938.

Harcourt, Brace & World, Inc., for the passages from Cleanth Brooks: *The Well-Wrought Urn*, E. E. Cummings: *Poems 1923–1954*, T. S. Eliot: *The Cocktail Party*, copyright 1950, and *Four Quartets*, copyright 1943, S. I. Hayakawa: *Language in Thought and Action*, and I. A. Richards: *Practical Criticism*.

The Trustees of Amherst College from Thomas H. Johnson, Editor, *The Poems of Emily Dickinson*, Cambridge, Massachusetts: The Belknap Press of Harvard University, copyright 1951, 1955, by the President and Fellows of Harvard College, for three poems by Emily Dickinson.

Holt, Rinehart and Winston, Inc., for the passage from "The Figure a Poem Makes," from *The Complete Poems of Robert Frost*, copyright 1944 by Robert Frost, and the poems "The Road Not Taken" and "The Secret."

Alfred A. Knopf, Inc., for the several passages from Kahlil Gibran: *The Prophet*, copyright 1923 by Kahlil Gibran, renewal copyright 1951, and Wallace Stevens: "Which is Real?" from the *Collected Poems of Wallace Stevens*, copyright 1954.

Liveright, Publishers, for Louis Ginsberg: "Hunger and Thirst," from *The Everlasting Minute*, copyright renewed 1965.

Scott Foresman and Company, for a passage from Paul Engle and W. Carrier: *The Introduction to Reading Modern Poetry*, copyright 1955.

Bernard Tassler, Executor, for "A Poet Wants a Sepulcher in the Form of a Book for His Works," from Eli Greifer: *Philosophic Duels*, New York, Academy Publications, copyright 1938—with special gratitude.

The Viking Press, Inc., for an excerpt from Aileen Ward: *John Keats, The Making of a Poet*, copyright 1963, pages 137–138.

Contributors

MILTON M. BERGER, MD
Fellow, American Psychiatric Association, Past President, American Group Psychotherapy Association and Association for Group Psychoanalysis and Process, Associate in Psychiatry, College of Physicians and Surgeons, Columbia University, New York

SMILEY BLANTON, MD
Cofounder and Director of Psychiatry, American Foundation of Religion and Psychiatry, New York

KENNETH BURKE, LITT D
Poet, Novelist, Critic

CHARLES CROOTOF, PhD
Psychotherapist, Postgraduate Center for Mental Health, New York

KENNETH F. EDGAR, PhD
Clinical Psychologist, Indiana County Guidance Clinic, Professor of Psychology, Indiana University of Pennsylvania

DAVID V. FORREST, MD
New York State Psychiatric Institute, New York (Now Military Psychiatrist, Vietnam, Visiting Lecturer in Psychiatry, University of Saigon)

JOSEPH H. GELBERMAN, DD
Rabbi, The Little Synagogue, Director, Mid-Way Counseling Center, New York

SAMUEL ALVIN GREENBERG, MD
Founder of AFTLI and The Institute of Theopsychosophy, Brooklyn

HAROLD GREENWALD, PhD
Director, Group Therapy, Center for Creative Living, Faculty, Metropolitan Institute for Psychoanalytic Studies and Community Guidance Service, Private Practice, New York

S. I. HAYAKAWA, PhD
Professor of English, Acting President, San Francisco State College, California

RICHARD HAZLEY, MA
Associate Professor of English, Indiana University of Pennsylvania

W. DOUGLAS HITCHINGS, MB, BCh, BAO
Fellow in Child Psychiatry, Postgraduate Center for Mental Health, New York

ROBERT E. JONES, MD
Clinical Director, The Institute of the Pennsylvania Hospital, Department of Psychiatry, University of Pennsylvania School of Medicine, Editor, Transactions and Studies of The College of Physicians of Philadelphia

DOROTHY KOBAK, MSW
Psychiatric Social Worker, Bureau of Child Guidance, Board of Education, New York, and Associate Director, Mid-Way Counseling Center

AARON KRAMER, PhD
Associate Professor of English, Dowling College, Oakdale, Lecturer, Queens College, Flushing, New York

JACK J. LEEDY, MD
Director, Poetry Therapy Center, New York, Associate Attending Psychiatrist, The Brooklyn-Cumberland Medical Center, Private Practice, New York

HERBERT I. LEVIT, EdD
Director of Psychological Services, Woodville State Hospital, Carnegie, Consultant in Psychology, Office of Mental Health, Commonwealth of Pennsylvania, Clinical Field Supervisor in Psychology, Duquesne University, Pittsburgh, Consultant Clinical Psychologist, Laughlin Childrens Center, Sewickley, Private Practice, Pittsburgh

JOOST A. M. MEERLOO, MD
Associate Professor of Psychiatry, New York School of Psychiatry, now living in Amsterdam, Holland

MORRIS ROBERT MORRISON, MA
Teacher of Special Education, Board of Education, Instructor Remedial English, College of the City of New York

JEAN K. MOWBRAY, MS
Guidance Counselor, Bryn Mawr Hospital, Assistant Professor, Harcum Junior College, Bryn Mawr, Pennsylvania

ROLLAND S. PARKER, PhD
Formerly Consultant, The Police Athletic League, Inc., Private Practice, New York

THEODOR REIK, PhD
Professor of Clinical Psychology, Adelphi University, Garden City, New York

S. SUE ROBINSON, MSS, ACSW
Director of Social Service, The Institute of Pennsylvania Hospital, Philadelphia

LEWIS R. WOLBERG, MD
Dean and Medical Director, Postgraduate Center for Mental Health, Clinical Professor of Psychiatry, New York Medical College

Contents

CHAPTER	PAGE
Foreword: *Ne t'es-tu fais mal, mon enfant?* THEODOR REIK, PhD	5
Preface: *The Vacuum* LEWIS R. WOLBERG, MD	9
Introduction: *The Healing Power of Poetry* JACK J. LEEDY, MD	11
1 *Treatment of a Psychotic Patient by Poetry Therapy* ROBERT E. JONES, MD	19
2 *Poetry Therapy with Hospitalized Schizophrenics* KENNETH F. EDGAR, PhD RICHARD HAZLEY, MA HERBERT I. LEVIT, EdD	29
3 *Poetry Therapy for Psychoneurotics in a Mental Health Center* CHARLES CROOTOF, PhD	38
4 *The Universal Language of Rhythm* JOOST A. M. MEERLOO, MD	52
5 *Principles of Poetry Therapy* JACK J. LEEDY, MD	67
6 *Poetry as Therapy—and Therapy as Poetry* MILTON M. BERGER, MD	75
7 *Poetry Therapy with Disturbed Adolescents* MORRIS ROBERT MORRISON, MA	88
8 *Thoughts on the Poets' Corner* KENNETH BURKE, D LITT	104
9 *Validation of Poetry Therapy as a Group Therapy Technique* KENNETH F. EDGAR, PhD RICHARD HAZLEY, MA	113

CHAPTER		PAGE
10	Poetry, a Way to Fuller Awareness W. DOUGLAS HITCHINGS, MB, BCH, BAO	124
11	The Psalms as Psychological and Allegorical Poems JOSEPH H. GELBERMAN, DD DOROTHY KOBAK, MSW	133
12	Poetry as Communication in Psychotherapy HAROLD GREENWALD, PHD	142
13	Poetry as a Therapeutic Art ROLLAND S. PARKER, PHD	155
14	The Use of Poetry in Individual Psychotherapy SMILEY BLANTON, MD	171
15	Poetry Therapy in a "600" School and in a Counseling Center DOROTHY KOBAK, MSW	180
16	Why Poetry? S. SUE ROBINSON, MSS, ACSW JEAN K. MOWBRAY, MS	188
17	The Use of Poetry in a Private Mental Hospital AARON KRAMER, PHD	200
18	AFTLI and/or Poetry Therapy SAMUEL ALVIN GREENBERG, MD	212
19	The Double Door ROBERT E. JONES, MD	223
20	The Patient's Sense of the Poem: Affinities and Ambiguities DAVID V. FORREST, MD	231
21	A Curriculum Proposal For Training Poetry Therapists KENNETH F. EDGAR, PHD RICHARD HAZLEY, MA	260
22	Postscript: Metamessages and Self-Discovery S. I. HAYAKAWA, PHD	269

In Memoriam: *Eli Greifer 1902-1966*   273

Appendix: *List of Poems Suitable for Use in Poetry Therapy*   276

Index   280

CHAPTER 1

Treatment of a Psychotic Patient by Poetry Therapy
With a Historical Note

ROBERT E. JONES, MD

Clinical Director, The Institute of the Pennsylvania Hospital, Philadelphia

AT PENNSYLVANIA HOSPITAL, THE NATION'S FIRST, founded by Benjamin Franklin in 1751, mental patients have long participated in many activities designed to alleviate the pains of mental illness. Franklin himself introduced occupational therapy, and Dr. Benjamin Rush, called the Father of American Psychiatry, introduced music and literature as ancillary treatments for psychiatric patients.

The oldest known poem written by a mental patient in an American hospital is recorded in a leather-bound memorandum book written by Samuel Coates, a Manager of the Pennsylvania Hospital from 1785 to 1825. Mr. Coates always carried this diary with him, in which he noted in ink his reflections upon madness and his deductions drawn from his observations of the interesting patients and incidents that came under his notice in the cells and wards for the insane. The poem was written by Richard N., whose lunacy Coates ascribed to "misfortune and disappointment." Born in England and educated at Oxford, the patient had had a series of five failures in business and farming. Coates wrote:: "To be disappointed Five times was more than he could Well bear; he became low spirited, and to cut the Climax short, he became crazy, & *Now* a poor Lunatick in the Pennsylvania Hospital in Which it is expected he

Will End his Days." Soon after admission, he wrote the following touching lines to his wife:

RICHARD TO FRANCES

Depriv'd of Liberty, and left to prove,
The bitter want of Frances & her love,
(That love, which wert thou present to bestow,
Woo'd sweetly sooth thine hapless Richard's Woe,)
As burden'd with my Grief, I sat to mourn,
Thy letter came—Ah why not thy Return?
Why shou'd the fold, which pleas'd I took, contain,
The Tale of Absence, which encreas'd my pain,
While I a double weight of Sorrows bear,
Sever'd from thee, and kept a Pris'ner here!
Yet if Through Anguish of a tortur'd mind,
My thoughts, my Acts were faulty or unkind,
Though great my errors, great has been my Grief,
And Richard looks to Frances for Relief.
Think then in Pity, Love and tender care,
Upon the sufferings I am led to bear
And seek to set a wretched husband free,
Who loses but too much, in losing thee.
To our Dear Children now let me return,
To use a Parents labour and Concern,
Long have I felt both able and inclined,
To try the powers of Body and of Mind,
In fit employ to pass thy tedious stay,
Til hap'ly I may see the favor'd day,
When I may weep for Joy & own me bles't,
To hide my Anguish, Frances, on thy Breast.

In 1843, mental patients at Pennsylvania Hospital began publishing a hospital newspaper, *The Illuminator*, which they themselves wrote, edited, and hand-copied. It contained articles about current events, editorials on national policies, jokes and anagrams. Because it was done in beautiful manuscript, its production provided useful labor to a number of patients. A visitor, John M. Galt, superintendent of the asylum at Williamsburg, Virginia, said that its "leading articles would compare favourably with much of the periodical literature of the day."

Pennsylvania Hospital was a model institution, and it had

raised the use of milieu therapy to its highest peak of achievement. Under the leadership of one of the great psychiatrists of the 19th century, Dr. Thomas S. Kirkbride, a founder and president of the American Psychiatric Association, it provided milieu therapy in all forms: gardening, riding, work, sewing and occupational therapy, museum, sports, and the like. Dr. Kirkbride even provided a herd of tame deer within the hospital grounds.

Here is another quite early poem written by a mental patient at Pennsylvania Hospital, published in *The Illuminator* in 1843. It describes Dr. Kirkbride's deer park and, like many poems written by patients, has notes of sadness and nostalgia.

> Ye free, ye nimble pretty ones
>   As o'er the mead ye stray,
> Ye mind me of departed joys
>   Forever fled away.
>
> You're happy in your little sphere
>   With pasture rich and green,
> With water from the limpid springs
>   And sunshine o'er the scene.
>
> But we, the tenants of these grounds,
>   The prisoners of these walls
> May view you resting in the shade
>   And sigh as it recalls
>
> Our lost estate, our very love,
>   Our mind's sad overthrow,
> Our friends, our family, our homes,—
>   And sink beneath the blow.

Poetry therapy has been used at Pennsylvania Hospital for nearly two centuries.

THE ROAD NOT TAKEN *

EVERY choice involves a loss. Whenever we make a decision in life,

---

* This part of Chapter 1 received the first Kenneth E. Appel Award in Psychiatry, presented by the Philadelphia County Medical Society in May, 1965. Here it has been somewhat edited and enlarged.

we must give up something, surrender an alternative. Whenever we decide *for* something, we decide *against* something else. Whenever we select one possibility or pathway, we relinquish another. When we make a decision, in our optimistic aggressive culture, usually we think that we are making a gain, picking the best alternative; and we soon forget the pessimistic aspect of decision-making: the object lost, the alternative not chosen, the road not taken.

It is my belief that emotionally fragile persons, especially psychotic patients, find that the most distressing and tormenting part of making decisions is giving up the alternate choice, longing for the course not chosen, clinging to the object that inevitably must be lost.

A psychiatrist might consider that a patient is experiencing ambivalence when he remains rooted at a crossroads. Or he might believe that the patient is experiencing anxiety when he holds fast to a person or way of life that obviously is not so healthful a choice as some other person or way might be. And undoubtedly, he would be right. But nonpsychiatric language often conveys an idea in better words. One of the best expressions of the human decision-making predicament is Robert Frost's poem

THE ROAD NOT TAKEN [*]

Two roads diverged in a yellow wood,
And sorry I could not travel both
And be one traveler, long I stood
And looked down one as far as I could
To where it bent in the undergrowth;

Then took the other; as just as fair,
And having perhaps the better claim,
Because it was grassy and wanted wear;
Though as for that the passing there
Had worn them really about the same,

And both that morning equally lay
In leaves no step had trodden black.
Oh, I kept the first for another day!

[*] *Complete Poems of Robert Frost*, New York, Holt, 1949, with permission.

Psychotic Patient and Poetry Therapy

Yet knowing how way leads on to way,
I doubted if I should ever come back.

I shall be telling this with a sigh
Somewhere ages and ages hence:
Two roads diverged in a wood, and I—
I took the one less traveled by,
And that has made all the difference.

The purpose of this chapter is to relate how this poem helped a psychotic patient. The story will be told not as a case history but as a narrative, in the way it became known to me.

The Encounter

I first met Mrs. H in the Occupational Therapy shop of The Institute of the Pennsylvania Hospital. A small woman with graying blond hair and an intense stare, she approached me quite unexpectedly and asked, quickly, furtively, "Are you Dr. Jones?"

"Yes," I said, hesitant about getting involved with a patient I did not know.

"May I speak with you in private?"

"This time," I replied, "is set aside for working. Although I'd like to be able to talk with you, I'd be more interested now to see what you're doing in the shop."

Mrs. H looked around suspiciously and led me to a loom, where she was weaving a set of place mats. I admired her handiwork and asked how long she had been weaving the mats. But she didn't wish to talk about her work; she asked again if she could talk with me privately. I explained that it was not possible then for me to interview her, but that I was sure her own resident would be glad to discuss her problems with her. At this second rebuff, following her two requests, Mrs. H lowered her head onto the loom and cried.

The Assignment

Several weeks later, Mrs. H's resident went on vacation, and Mrs. H was assigned to my care for one month. My interest in her had already been awakened, because in our one brief encounter I had been impressed with her intensity and sensitivity. Reading her case record, I learned that she was a lawyer by profession and the mother of two children. This was her fourth hospitalization for a paranoid schizophrenic reaction. After her three previous hospital visits, she had returned to her husband and family in a Southern city.

My eagerness to work with Mrs. H led me to present her case to my preceptor and to tell him that I had a plan of therapy in mind. After interviewing her, my preceptor instructed me to obtain the permission of Mrs. H's private therapist before undertaking my program. The private psychiatrist granted permission for me to change the type of tranquilizing medication that Mrs. H was receiving, then said: "Doctor Jones, we haven't been able to do anything for or with Mrs. H for several months. You may try anything you like with her."

Formulation of the Case

I began my association with Mrs. H with a series of three visits to her ward, during which I attempted to establish some kind of rapport with her. On these visits, she was restless, hallucinating, angry. She believed that there was a plot against her in the hospital and that her two children were being held as patients on another ward. She thought that our conversation was being recorded. She demanded her own discharge, but could not state her future plans. Her expression was rigid, flattened, her conversation blocked. But she clenched and unclenched her fists, and behind her immobile face I thought I detected a well of emotion. However, our meetings were fruitless. The nurses complained that Mrs. H was untidy and careless about her dress and would not eat properly. Mrs. H continued her endless demands to leave the hospital. I wondered whether I could be of any value to her.

Through these visits, however, and a daily reading of her chart, I became impressed with two factors: her strong wish, which had reached delusional proportions, to be with her children, and her heightened distress whenever we discussed her husband. With these impressions, I formulated the theory that Mrs. H was in the throes of attempting to decide whether or not to leave her husband, and that under the stress of making the decision, her ego forces had been fractured and her psychosis had developed. Her psychosis, I reasoned, was a reaction to her anxiety about so momentous a decision. I speculated further that Mrs. H was ambivalent about giving up her husband, with whom she had so many arguments, who put her under so much pressure, who placed his own mother ahead of her. She wanted to choose freedom, to return to her law practice, to give more time to mothering her children instead of bickering with her husband; but she had not been able to reconcile herself to the loss of her husband, to surrendering the father of her children, the builder of their home. She was on the horns of a dilemma, and she was paralyzed into inaction by her psychosis.

The Therapy

Her therapy should take the form of learning how to make decisions. I felt I had to teach her the wisdom of Frost's poem. I designed a simple project: making a small blue daisy by gluing ceramic tiles onto a rectangular piece of wood. Carrying the colored tiles, the glue, and the small board, I went to Mrs. H's room and locked us in. Very firmly I told her about our project. I would put glue on the backs of the tiles and direct her where to place them. I made all the decisions: the background was to be white, the leaves green, and the petals blue. However, Mrs. H would have a single decision to make: to decide whether the center of the daisy would be a white tile or a yellow. Mrs. H sighed deeply a few times as we went to work. She did not speak, but eyed me suspiciously.

When we were half finished, Mrs. H selected a white tile and placed it in the center of the daisy. I complimented her on her choice. A few minutes later, however, she removed it and placed a yellow one in the center. Her perplexity mounted and she began to frown. Then I told her that I noticed that she was having trouble making a decision and sticking to it. "It makes me wonder," I said, "if you are having the same trouble trying to decide whether to stay with your husband." I told her that it didn't matter which tile she chose, that this was a minor decision—either tile would be suitable—but that I was going to remain with her until she decided. If she chose the white one, she would have to give up the yellow one, and vice versa. I would see her through this first small decision.

Mrs. H became markedly distressed: she cried; she threw tiles on the floor; she tried to escape from the room or to lie on her bed. She tried to fit both tiles into the space; she tried to throw away both tiles. Always I insisted that she return to the task. I repeated that I knew she was probably trying to make major decisions in her life; she must learn first about making unimportant ones. I pointed out that if she chose one, she would have to give up the alternative. Two hours later, Mrs. H made the final decision. At the end of the time, when she had finally placed a white tile in the center of the daisy, she collapsed onto her bed exhausted. I told her that I would return on the following day with another decision-making task.

On the following day, I brought two birthday cards, which said "Happy Birthday, Son." I knew that she missed her children and would want to send a birthday card to her adolescent boy. The cards were very similar; her job was to choose between them. The decision was agonizing and time-consuming, and again, after two hours, the patient was exhausted. But at the end of the time, she had written "Love, Mummy" on one of the cards. This was the first message that she had written to her family in four months.

On the third day, I brought two gifts for her son, and demanded that she choose between them. When she was able to choose, after an hour of deciding and revising, I congratulated her heartily on her growing ability to make a choice. I repeatedly pointed out that whenever she chose one thing, she had to surrender the other.

On the fourth day, we began another tile project, more complicated than the first, in which she was permitted to choose all the colors of a multicolored bird. With more conviction at each choice, she began to fill in the design. Also, we began to converse about other things. She told me that she had been unable to eat for several weeks because she could not select foods from the menu, as she had delusional ideas that the various foods had special meanings for her—for example, that spinach was a message from her son that she could not decipher. She confessed that she had believed for several months that microphones were concealed in the air vents. On that day, when she began to tell me her unrealistic, paranoid fears, I presented her with my volume of Frost's poems. I asked her whether she were really trying to decide to leave her husband, to choose a more independent course in life. She became silent, but nodded her head in assent. I read to her "The Road Not Taken," and left the volume with her.

On the fifth day, I handed her a book about birds, thinking that she could refer to it in selecting colors for her tile project. But she hurled it across the room. Then she explained that her husband was a bird watcher, that the book reminded her of him, and that she was angry at him. She confessed that she had indeed been considering a divorce, and that it was during the process of weighing the decision in her mind that she had become ill.

When, on the sixth day, we walked outside the hospital, she was jubilant. She explained that for months she could not go outdoors, because if she saw a bird or an airplane, she thought it meant that she had to run in that direction in order to get home to her children. This explained why, to the distress of the nurses, she had tried to climb over the hospital wall so many times. On our walk, she made no effort to escape. She was happy, smiling, appropriate in her affect, rational in conversation, and without delusions. She explained that she had approached me on that first day in OT because she had the delusional belief that a Dr. Jones in her native city had sent me to rescue her.

It was exactly one week after she began making decisions again that Mrs. H joined a group of patients on an excursion to the city art museum, the only patient from the disturbed ward who was permitted to go. Thereafter, she was quickly transferred to an open ward, granted grounds and town privileges. All medication was diminished, then stopped. She began to make a dress in Occupational Therapy. In a series of considered interviews, she decided to divorce her husband. She remained free of psychotic symptoms.

Often in our discussions, we mentioned Frost's poem. It became a text. Mrs. H memorized it. When I presented her to my preceptor again, she recited it for him and stated that she believed that she had recovered from her illness because of it. We both agreed that her therapy had consisted of learning how to make decisions, of reconciling herself to the loss involved in every choice, of studying both pathways as well as she could—then choosing one of them.

Six Years Later

Mrs. H returned home to the same family situation that had precipitated her psychosis. She did not feel a need to consult a psychiatrist on a regular basis, but made a plan to return in six months and again in a year to see her Philadelphia psychiatrist for two or three visits. Now, six years later, Mrs. H is still with her family and still free of psychotic symptoms.

Her final decision was a surprise. When she left the hospital, her plan was to obtain a divorce, but she chose, instead, to remain with her husband.

It was the *awareness* that she could make a choice that enabled her to remain with her husband and keep her family intact, trying to improve some aspects of their relationship, accepting other aspects. She had used her hospitalization to look down one path as far as she could—then chose the other.

CHAPTER 2

Poetry Therapy with Hospitalized Schizophrenics

KENNETH F. EDGAR, PHD   RICHARD HAZLEY, MA
Indiana State University of Pennsylvania

HERBERT I. LEVIT, EDD
Woodville State Hospital, Office of Mental Health, Western Pennsylvania

IT IS THE PURPOSE OF THIS CHAPTER to demonstrate the effectiveness of poetry in therapy with chronic schizophrenic patients at Dixmont State Hospital, Pittsburgh, employing matched groups, one receiving poetry therapy and the other conventional hospital treatment.[1,3,4]

Procedure

Seven patients were selected for their interest in participating, ability to relate verbally, and average or higher intelligence. A control group of five patients was matched with the experimental group in age, education, marital status and hospital diagnosis (Table 1). Therapists Edgar and Hazley visited Dixmont every Thursday for eight months. The seven patients sat at a large round table with the two therapists in a room designated for poetry therapy. Poems were chosen according to Leedy's isoprinciple—i.e. poems that symbolically represented feelings that the patients were unable to deal with successfully[4]—and were used as levers to involve the patients in discussing their feelings.

Evaluation. Pretest batteries were administered to both groups: the Rorschach, WAIS, HTP, Bender, and a psychiatric interview. Although the same battery was intended for the post test, its ad-

TABLE 1. *Experimental and Control Groups*

PATIENT	AGE	STATUS	EDUCATION	DIAGNOSIS*	ADMISSION	HOSPITAL-IZATION
Experimental Group						
Mrs. S	28	Mar	HS Grad	Par Schz	1st	7 yr
Mr. J	33	Sep	HS Grad	Schz (U) Pas-Ag	1st	4½ yr
Miss H	30	Sng	HS Grad	Par Schz	1st	1 yr
Miss C	51	Sng	HS Grad	Par Schz	3rd	8½ yr
Mr. P	29	Sng	HS Grad	Cat Schz	1st	9½ yr
Mr. R	29	Sng	Col 2 yr	Chr U Schz	3rd	4 yr
Mr. M	31	Sng	HS Grad	Cat Schz	1st	7½ yr
Control Group						
Mr. A	30	Mar	Col 3 yr	Par Schz	1st	6 yr
Mr. C	36	Mar	HS Grad	Par Schz	1st	7 yr
Mr. L	21	Sng	8th Grd	Ac S Schz	1st	4 yr
Mr. E	24	Sng	HS Grad	Sxl dev Chr	1st	4 yr
Mr. S	40	Sng	Col 2 yr	Heb Schz	2nd	8 yr

* Ac, acute. Ag, aggressive. Cat, catatonic. Chr, chronic. Heb, hebephrenic. Par, paranoid. Pas, passive. Schz, schizophrenic. Sxl dev, sexual deviant. U, undifferentiated.

ministration was impossible: all except one patient in the experimental group were either discharged or going home on visits by the end of the experiment.

Results

The average patient was 31 years old, single, and a high school graduate, with hospital residence of just over six years. They came from within 50 miles of the hospital, usually from small industrial towns, and had received medications, EST, traditional group and individual therapy. All had at some time hallucinated and/or been delusional, and several had been aggressive. Table 1 indicates the chronicity of their illnesses.

In their usual attitudes, all of these patients were relatively unresponsive to the hospital programs; they showed little or no enthusiasm from day to day. At the conclusion of eight months of therapy that included poetry therapy, hospital personnel noted a decided change. Of the original group of seven, three had been discharged and four were making visits home. Of the control group, one had been discharged; the four others were not permitted home visits, nor were their attitudes more enthusiastic toward hospital routine, Occupational Therapy, Recreation, and the like.

HYPOTHESES

From observing the effect of poetry therapy on the experimental group, one may state certain hypotheses. Poetry is a means to and a vehicle for therapy. It can help to create a mood in which emotions can be shared and responded to by the group, and so can stimulate interpersonal relationships. The participants' writing poems may be viewed as both sublimation and, more important, a means of symbolic externalization closely associated with dreams.[2] Such projected externalizations may circumvent repressive barriers and break through resistances in the group, since the poem appears to be objective. With its apparent objectivity, it can be dissected and used for the acquisition of insight more readily than personal symptoms or behavior. Patients can feel free to be more spontaneous and even critical, and thus there is more verbal and emotional responsiveness with subsequently less repression. Several patients who had previously both avoided and denied their own problems, and certainly could not verbalize them, were able to react to poems by such comments as "That's just how I feel!" This not only was cathartic but also permitted a sharing of common fears that were secret, personal, and festering until this point. With such objective externalization, they found that others shared their torment, and this brought about a common bond. Further, with the vehicle of poetry, interpretations could be made more easily and quickly and with more safety to the individuals and the group, yet with therapeutic results. Clearly, with a minimum of threat, poetry can put a wedge into the pathology and defenses of the psychotic and provide for relatively unthreatening interpersonal relationships, a structured therapy setting without rigidity, and a means of understanding without pressure.

Discussion

1. SIGNIFICANCE OF THE POEM

While the members of this particular group had been chosen from the hospital population because of their ability to relate verbally and their average or higher intelligence, they had had no exposure, with one exception, to poetry beyond the public school level. It was necessary, therefore, to avoid "difficult" poetry with extensive literary allusions, where the effect of the poem might be lost between the reading and the explanation, or where the interest of the patient might be deadened by the presence of material that he could not grasp. The therapist, then, must take into consideration the structure of his group and its literary level in his choice of poetry, otherwise the efficiency of the tool will be reduced or even destroyed.

As the therapy progressed, the significance of choosing the "correct" poems for each occasion became manifest. Several examples may suffice. After several meetings it appeared to the therapists that certain secondary gains provided by hospital life were perhaps affecting the patients' desire to get well. Within the confines of the hospital, the patient was freed from the ordinary exigencies of life. One patient, asked to describe his day, provided the therapists with a picture of total freedom from responsibility.

I get up in the morning, shave and dress. If I feel like working I go down to my job. If I don't I go back to bed. After lunch I have a Coke, go down to the barbershop, then go back to my room and lie down and listen to the radio.

What was apparent in this account was that the patient enjoyed his routine enough for that enjoyment to operate as a significant deterrent to his wish to get well. The therapists therefore decided to use a poem that expressed the patient's dependence on these secondary gains, "A Prison Gets to Be a Friend" by Emily Dickinson. The discussion following the poem was lively and provocative and seemed to provide the patient and others with some insight into how, at least to some extent, their confinement was a means of avoiding the normal pressures of life. The poem also served as a valuable referent when this particular symptom manifested itself, as it did from time to time.

Another patient, R, had been completely dominated by his father, an officer in the US Army, whose practice it had been to have R stand at attention after meals and narrate completely the events of the day. If R hesitated in his account, his father would strike him sharply on his forehead with the heel of the hand, and call him "Stupid." He used the same "technique" when he attempted to "help" R with his lessons. He demonstrated no affection for the boy, his most common interaction being that buffet against the forehead. R had been in three mental hospitals, a patient at Dixmont for four years, and had attempted suicide three times. All of his behavior indicated a massive repressed hostility against his father, which R refused to admit. In conversation he praised him, insisted that he had been a good father though a "perfectionist," and refused to admit of even normal failings that a son would attribute to a father. To attempt to demonstrate to the patient the difference between his conception and reality, a poem, in this case again by Emily Dickinson, was chosen. The poem describes a bird struck by a stone thrown by a boy, and concludes:

> Magnanimous as Bird
> By Boy descried—
> Singing unto the Stone
> Of which it died—

Once again the poem, which seemed to fit exactly the needs of the patient, appeared to provide a valuable insight that began the erosion of the false image of the father that was obstructing R's progress. Shortly after that, R wrote a poem of his own, the last line of which is "Illness is the fuehrer." Through simple word association he equated "fuehrer" with "father," and then, when asked to provide a grammatical analysis of the sentence, said, "Fuehrer is the predicate nominative which means the same thing as the subject, so I guess I am saying that illness is my father." This was the first occasion in which he had been willing to admit such a possibility; it demonstrates not only the effect that a poem may have but the importance of the patient's own writing in demonstrating that effect. One thing further should be noted. In post interviews, patients commented that "it made them feel good" when a poem was brought in especially for one of them.

2. TRANSFERENCE: TWO THERAPISTS

The presence of two therapists rather than one appeared important in the experiment. The manifestations of transfer indicated that patients tended to identify differently with each of the therapists. In the case of a woman patient S, one of the therapists came to be a father figure ("I feel that I can tell you my troubles"), the other assumed the role of her lover and possible husband ("I'd like to take him home with me. We would pack up my clothes, buy a ring, and go somewhere"). With *S*, whose record showed domination by the father and latent or perhaps overt incest, it was felt by the therapists that this dichotomy of lover-father was beneficial. *S* came to regard one of the therapists as a boyfriend, the other as a father figure. It should be noted that in practice one of the therapists tended to involve himself with the patients, sharing his own feelings and anxieties, and the other did not. Thus the differences in transfer made by the patients correspond to the roles played by the therapists, and, in the situation of this experiment, it was felt that the differences made by the members worked to their benefit. It should also be mentioned that those sessions that were conducted by only one therapist were judged significantly less successful. Not only was the group feeling impaired, as though one parent figure were missing, but the therapy could not be maintained at the same level. The pace of the sessions tended to flag, a situation that did not arise when both therapists were present.

3. IMPORTANCE OF MEMORIZATION

Eli Greifer advocated for some time the importance of memorization—what he has termed a psycho-graft—as an important adjunct to poetry therapy. The experiences at Dixmont indicate that memorization is indeed of value. *H* suffered from auditory hallucinations; particularly when working in the laundry, voices would admonish her, saying that she was a bad girl and should have led a better life. It was suggested to *H* that she memorize the last stanza of Henley's "Invictus" whenever she felt the voices might begin. While the memorization did not entirely banish the hallucinations, *H* reported that she was better able to control them and felt less powerless when they did occur. Postinterviews indicated that the patients attributed more to memorization than the therapists had realized. *R* reported in post interviews that he had memorized many of the poems and that he "was having important words pumped into him." *M* reported that "memorization helped him from being depressed." Even with the members of the group who did not show an inclination to memorize, copies of the poem used in each session were nearly always requested and the patients reported that they enjoyed reading them. It is the conclusion of the therapists that memorization should be encouraged and that the poems used should be available. Repeating or reading particular poems appeared to have a beneficial effect on the patients in that they provided occupation for their minds and relief particularly during depressed periods.

4. POEMS AS OBJECTIFICATIONS OF THE ILLNESS

One of the premises underlying this experiment—that poetry could be used as a means through which the patient may objectify his feelings—was utilized in several ways. First, the poem, when correctly chosen, provided an immediate incentive for discussion. Thus the warm-up period, which so frequently takes up a significant part of group therapy sessions, was bypassed. Immediately after the brief salutations, the first poem for the session was distributed, read and discussion begun. Even when it served only as a jumping-off point, the poem was the subject for discussion; there was no need to begin with the customary "Well, what shall we talk about today?" Better results are obtained, it should be said, when the poems are so chosen that they provide a continuity and a progression. Second, the poem provides a means for the patient to begin talking about himself indirectly, that is, via the poem. Through this device, disclosures are made that the patient might be reticent to make in direct discussions. The device also, it was felt, brought about a group cohesiveness more rapidly than conventional group therapy does, and the point at which the patient might reveal himself personally arrived sooner than it does through conventional means.

Most important, the therapists felt that poetry has long been a reservoir for the expression of human feelings. It was hypothesized that in the poetry the patient would find both direct and symbolic expression of his own feelings. It was believed that this discovery would accomplish two things: first, the patient would realize that he was not alone in his particular feelings. Thus, the sense of strangeness and alienation that is so much a contributing factor to mental illness would be alleviated. The alleviation would be furthered by the patient's realization that he was encountering feelings not only that he himself had experienced, but that had also been a part of the lives of men who were recognized and of some eminence. Second, seeing these expressions and talking about his response to them, the patient would be enabled to objectify, via the poem, his own personal feelings. Once that was accomplished, then, through discussion, a catharsis and self-realization would begin that would be less possible so long as the patient's feelings remained internal and were dependent on projection for their expression. In this regard, the therapists soon realized that there was a tendency on the part of some of the patients to intellectualize the poem, to talk about the poet's intention rather than their own feelings, or to make references to world history, cultural epochs, and so forth, thus keeping the poem at arm's length. This, of course, is a defensive maneuver that the therapist should curb. Therapists should make an effort to avoid abstractions and to encourage the patient to talk about the specific relationship between himself and the poem.

5. THE IMPORTANCE OF THE PATIENT'S OWN WRITING

One of the most significant and useful features of poetry therapy is the patient's expression through his own writing. Our general procedure was to discuss a poem and then ask the patients to write a few concluding lines that expressed their own feelings, either in opposition to or in agreement with the poem and the discussion. As in the experiment at Slippery Rock College, the poems were judged not on their literary merits, often few, but as an expression of the patients' parapathy. The discussion of the patient's poem was conducted in somewhat the way that a dream would be analyzed. The significance of these poems has already been mentioned in the case of R, who wrote "Illness is the fuehrer." Another significant example is V, a woman of 28 who had regressed in voice, mannerisms, and attitude to preadolescence, and who had no realization of where she actually was. She wrote, after a discussion:

> In this interior decoration
> There is some congestion
> That squanders in the mind.

In previous sessions, V had demonstrated the ability to tap the unconscious and to write highly symbolic and effective lines. In the context of the discussion, the therapists felt these particular lines to be important. Following *V*'s reading of her "poem," she abruptly looked up and said in a voice that was, for the first time, unchildlike, "Where am I? Is this some kind of a nut house or something?" From that time on she showed a heightened awareness and insight, and progressed from a closed to an open ward to an outpatient basis. It was felt by the therapists that the lines she wrote were critical in her progress and were perhaps the precipitating event that brought about her initial contact with reality.

Summary

Seven patients diagnosed as chronic schizophrenic and with an average hospitalization of six years were treated two hours a week for a period of eight months with a group therapy technique involving the use of symbolism in poetry as a lever to release feelings and, hopefully, to bring about catharsis and insight. Three of the patients were discharged within the eight-month period and the other four began making home visits. Those remaining in the hospital were observed to participate more enthusiastically in hospital routine. Of the five controls, one was discharged, four showed no signs of improvement.

REFERENCES

1. Greifer, Eli: Poetry therapy, The Brooklyn Psychologist, September, 1964.

2. Guthiel, Emil A.: The Handbook of Dream Analysis, New York, Grove Press, 1951.

3. Hazley, Richard, and Edgar, Kenneth: Validation of poetry therapy as a group therapy technique, *in* Poetry Therapy, Chapter 9.

4. Leedy, J. J.: Poetry and Medicine, MD Med Newsmagazine, 1964.

CHAPTER 3

Poetry Therapy for Psychoneurotics in a Mental Health Center

CHARLES CROOTOF, PHD
Postgraduate Center for Mental Health, New York

A POETRY THERAPY GROUP has been functioning for a year now at the Postgraduate Center for Mental Health in Manhattan. The patients of the group join by first becoming members of our Living Room Club, in the Social Rehabilitation Department under the direction of Dr. Maria Fleischl, psychiatrist. The members of the therapeutic club may avail themselves of one or another kind of adjunctive therapy almost any evening of the week. Dance, art, music, drama, poetry therapy, arts and crafts, and vocational counseling are offered them for a nominal monthly fee. This arrangement creates a supportive atmosphere for the members, many of whom live alone and welcome the companionship of the others. Though most of them are employed, they are troubled by psychoneuroses of varying severity. Some are borderline; some have been previously hospitalized.

Poetry sessions are held once a week for an hour and a half. Attendance ranges from 12 to 20, and during the year 9 or 10 members have attended almost every session. Many of the patients are constantly struggling against the encroachment of feelings of isolation and against slipping into a loss of communication with other people. During a recent session, the intensity of the reaction to the lines

> Today I met a stranger—
> Though for ten years I have lived with him

gave clear indication of the fear of isolation that the patients are struggling with.

Having been the therapist and leader of the poetry group for this year, I have tried to form some answers to the question: How can poetry contribute to mental health?

The extent to which poetry has provided solace and comfort to humanity through the ages is buried in the history of mankind. We will never know how many hearts and minds have been stirred to feel less alienated and more human by the quiet beauty of the Song of Solomon, by the tragic suffering of a Job or an Oedipus, or by the derring-do of a Beowulf. The imagination of each generation is captured by its own poets. Homer, Chaucer, Shakespeare, Tennyson, Longfellow, and Whitman spoke to their contemporaries in the idioms and the symbols of their day. Where Bob Dylan sings the language of today's youth, their parents were moved by Robert Frost and Carl Sandburg. Just as the classics are best understood through a fresh translation for every succeeding generation, so does each popular poet arouse and intensify the feelings of his contemporaries by means of the current symbols of love and hate, hope and despair.

Once we begin to deal with effecting changes in feelings, we have already moved close to the purposes and intent of psychotherapy. When we consider further that words and language are the means by which those purposes and intentions are to be realized, we have already enumerated two basic ingredients of both poetry and psychotherapy—feelings and language.

It is not at all surprising that in his day the amazing Aristotle had something to say of poetry therapy. Writing in reference to a particular species of poetry—tragedy—he observed in the *Poetics* that the passions pity and terror could be corrected and refined. *Katharsis* is the word he used. Butcher states that Aristotle's use of the word implies the "expulsion of a painful and disquieting element"[1]; it is a homeopathic cure in that pity and fear are first aroused by poetic tragedy and then purged together with the latent pity and fear that were brought to the poetic experience.

Poetry of one kind or another has in fact been such an ancient and universal nostrum for ministering to hurt minds and baleful moods—from the earliest incantations of the tribal priests and medicine men to the vast outpourings of Tin Pan Alley and our modern rock and folk minstrels—that we have been even less consciously aware of its restorative powers than of nature's subtle way of healing a cut finger.

One can only speculate how it came to pass that the ancient Greeks conceived Apollo to be the god of both poetry and medicine. Somehow in their ancient wisdom they must have perceived the relationship between poetry and the art of healing. Thousands of years later, in the middle of the twentieth century, Smith and Twyeffort [2] assert that literature may be used as an aid in treating mental illness by helping the patient obtain a better knowledge of himself and his reactions, thereby improving his total life-adjustment. Between Apollo and the *Cyclopedia of Medicine*, we can only guess at the untold number of souls that the bards have comforted and at how much insight and hope they have given to those perplexed in spirit. The long parade of gleemen, skops, minstrels, balladeers, folksingers and sophisticated poets ministered to the despondent and the defeated, comforted the lonely and the lovelorn, and understood the hostile and the hateful. With venom and rancor drawn off, love and hope could move in.

The belief that a therapeutic essence resides in the nature of poetry has, in recent years, stirred some mental health practitioners to seek out and explore more highly conscious and organized uses of poetry in the service of psychotherapy. On the contemporary scene, the first to search actively for the healing principle in poetry was the late Eli Greifer, who, about 35 years ago, began to write therapeutic poems, later published as *Psychic Ills and Poemtherapy* and *Poems for What Ails You*. In 1959, Greifer used poetry therapy at Creedmoor State Hospital, Queens Village, New York, and subsequently formed a poetry therapy group at Cumberland Hospital in Brooklyn, together with Dr. Jack J. Leedy, psychiatrist, Director of the Mental Hygiene Clinic at Cumberland. Greifer used poetry to help patients develop a philosophy of life that would help them adjust to their misfortunes.

Patients help to select poems, read them aloud individually or in unison, in some cases memorize them; they carry on group discussions of the poet's life and work, are also encouraged to write poems for the group. Combined poetry and music therapies are developed in group singing of psalms, hymns and poems set to music.[3]

Greifer rejected the cynicism and obscurantism of "modernists" like T. S. Eliot and his followers and exhorted his poetry groups to dispel gloom and depression, to seek out joy and happiness through constructive attitudes and approaches. He prescribed poems with "a noble and healthy outlook on life" [4] and advocated memorizing poetry whose themes center on the basic verities found in such poetry as Longfellow's. He himself had written therapeutic poetry that urges his readers and listeners to strive for the satisfaction and serenity to be found in "the balm of accomplishment and glad images from many happily worded, cheerful-toned songs." [5]

Dr. Smiley Blanton has written of the power of poetry to help his patients when they have felt overwhelmed, frustrated, defeated, depressed, angry, anxious or bereaved. He used poetry with individual patients as an ancillary therapy to buoy their flagging spirits through the use of direct encouragement, hopeful examples, and exhortation, and he urged his patients to memorize certain poems to help carry them through times of crisis. He recommended specific poems to counteract certain moods. For example, when you need courage he recommends Henley's "Invictus" or Joaquin Miller's "Columbus"; when you must leave someone dear, Shakespeare's "Parting is such sweet sorrow" or Byron's "When we two parted"; when you're anxious, Eliot's "Love Song of J. Alfred Prufrock."

Leedy [6] believes that the isoprinciple, which Dr. Ira M. Altshuler advocates in music therapy, can be used effectively in poetry therapy as well. The principle of selecting music to correspond with the patient's mood or mental tempo translates, in terms of poetry therapy, into selecting sad and gloomy poems for depressed patients.

Although I agree with Dr. Leedy that "the poem becomes symbolically an understanding someone with whom the patient can share his despair" [7] and that it is helpful if "depressed patients feel that they are not alone in their depression," I feel that the patient cannot be left in a morass of despondency that the poet gives no indication of his ability to extricate himself from. If the patient is to benefit by borrowing from the ego of the poet, he can borrow successfully only if the poet demonstrates that he himself is not emotionally bankrupt. The patient is more likely to respond constructively to a poem in which the poet reveals that he has suffered the same loss, despair, frustration, or loneliness as the patient, *but* in grappling with the problem has somehow managed to surmount the obstacles that seemed to be staring him in the face; somehow the poet has won through—or hopes to. By writing of the fact that he has experienced the same kind of suffering and has lived through the same purgatory that the patient is now experiencing, the poet is now qualified to serve as a counselor and to hook into the patient's private line of communication.

Having established some degree of communication, to what psychic level is the poet, abetted by the therapist, addressing himself? It is to the level of wish-fulfilling thought, extending into the realm of the primary process. It is to the need of the patient to be well, healthy, adequate, strong, accepted, loved. The poetry therapy session has become a crucible in which an elixir of attention, acceptance and affection is brewed. The poem provides the basic ingredients. The patients add many of their own. The therapist becomes associated with the empathic expression in the poem and is perceived to possess the same kind of understanding that is extended to the helpers in Alcoholics Anonymous or in Synanon, by those who have been "there" and returned.

At the Postgraduate Center for Mental Health, the poetry sessions are held in an atmosphere simulating that of a living room. At the beginning of the session, from 8 to 16 or 17 members may be present, and others may drift in later. Sometimes new members wander in uncertainly, but introductions are made usually at the beginning, sometimes at the end, of the session. One mimeographed sheet containing three or four poems is given to each person present. Occasionally, when it is impossible to get the mimeographing done on time, a therapy session may be held successfully by the therapist's reading the poem aloud twice clearly and slowly, supplemented by reading again certain lines of the poem that come under discussion. But the choice of poems under these circumstances becomes more critical; they must not be difficult to understand or else the therapist will find himself having to restate the poem in his own words, and too much of its effect will be lost thereby. Some verses by Robert Service were presented orally on two occasions and were successfully received and discussed, but there is little doubt that it is best to present each group member with a copy of the poems for ready reference as needed.

The poem should be read well, with proper attention given to creation of the appropriate mood. When you finish reading the poem, you are invariably met with an unknowable silence. Of course, you experience your own feelings and reactions, but you can't be sure how the others have responded. A good opening is to ask, "How do you like it?" or "How do you feel about it?" or "How does it make you feel?"—or some such question that gives the members a chance to blow about some of the surface foam that the poem may have churned up. You can almost do a round robin on this question; almost everyone will have some reaction, even if only "It leaves me cold." The technique of singling out someone to respond is to be used sparingly. At times, however, a response may be teased out through the silence by quietly joining glances with someone for whom you suspect the poem may have had some special meaning.

It has seemed rewarding to permit as many as wish to respond to the initial question. Having expressed whether they like the poem, they have made some kind of emotional deposit and are more likely to involve themselves in protecting their investment. After several sessions, the group catches onto the opening gambit, and subsequently, more often than not, the discussion is launched without the need of putting a question. Questions will be asked immediately about unfamiliar vocabularly, difficult syntax or ambiguities. Unfamiliar words should be quickly and simply explained; it is advisable to give readily understood synonyms as footnotes on the mimeographed sheet of poems. The therapist should bridge any syntactical obscurities by simply providing an easily comprehensible restatement. Our purpose is not to exercise the intellectual faculties or to improve vocabulary, nor are we bent on giving a course on "How to understand poetry." In the initial stage of the session, the therapist should be intent on zeroing in on the emotional theme of the poem. Of course he has a fairly good approximation of what this theme is, at least for himself. How it will unfold for each group member is at this juncture an open question—and must remain so till each one tips his hand.

Frequently the discussion of a poem will veer off in a direction that the therapist did not dream of when he selected the poem. Let it digress; others in the group may follow the vein, because meaningful associations have been aroused. Other patients, sensing the irrelevant digression, may become impatient and attempt to return to the poem's theme. I remark that we are more concerned here with the members' problems than the poem's, and this usually serves to encourage everyone to draw on extra reserves of indulgence to maintain the cohesiveness of the group.

It is the therapist's job to encourage the development of a nonjudgmental atmosphere. Criticism of others may develop in the initial stage because of varying interpretations of what the poem means. The therapist's approach here may be to point out that every reader recreates a poem in the light of his own storehouse of memories and experiences. "What does it mean for you?" and "Why can't it mean something different for him?" are questions that serve to encourage an accepting attitude.

Herein lies a significant difference between the English class and the poetry therapy session: the first objective of the English class is to determine the poem's meaning, of the poetry therapy session to seek the meaning that the poem has for the various members. There may be as many meanings as there are persons, and each meaning is valid in the context of the individual's peculiar experiences.

At times, when a multiplicity of feelings is being grappled with, when members tend to talk at each other instead of with one another and value judgments are expressed that may, unchecked, readily lead into personal attacks, it is apparent that we have moved into a stage where the basic dynamics of group interaction are about to operate. The potential for this development is always present, and the therapist should be prepared with some formulation whether the approach will be group-centered, i.e., functioning essentially as in group therapy; poem-centered, i.e., focusing on the content and meaning of the poem from the poet's point of view; or patient-poem centered, i.e., emphasizing the patient's exploration of his own feelings in the context of his past and current experiences as these feelings and experiences are made conscious by the stimuli of the poem. In the Living Room, the latter method has been fruitful. We do not countenance the use of one member by another as a target for hostile transference, although in other settings this reaction is an admissible development in the therapeutic process.

Whatever the clinical option of the therapist may be, the interaction of the patient, the poem, and the group has drawn the patient into the stream of human thought and feeling. The poem serves as a catalytic agent. Since the poet is the first to reveal the secret world of his own feelings at the beginning of the session, the awkward moments of hesitation frequently experienced at the beginning of the traditional group therapy session are readily circumvented. The poet's feelings function as a resonator in the patient's psyche, where corresponding fragments of memory and experience start to vibrate sympathetically, are shaken loose from their submerged moorings, and rise to the surface where they can be looked at in the daylight of reality. What previously seemed guilt-provoking or "sick" to the patient becomes less reprehensible or abnormal through the process of ventilation.

Just how poetry functions in the therapeutic process is a moot question. There are few research data to serve as a basis for a theory; we are at the stage of hypothesis and speculation. Recent research in dreams reported by Diamond [8] points to the therapeutic function that dreaming serves. Could not the effective therapeutic agent in poetry be similar to what exists in the dream process? Is the stuff that dreams are made on the same as that poetry is woven from? The poem and the dream both originate in the unconscious; both are created by "the spontaneous overflow of powerful feelings." Both rely on the "suspension of disbelief." Whether it be the *willing* suspension of disbelief, as in the hearer of the poem, or the *unwilling* suspension, as in the dreamer, in both instances the processes of reality-testing are either completely disregarded or kept waiting in the wings. The hearer and the dreamer, by suspending or short-circuiting reality, are able to make more immediate contact with their id wishes and their basic drives. In the dream, this is accomplished by paying little heed to the bonds of reality—time, space, and causality. In literature, long before our twentieth century surrealists, writers could not be contained by the so-called dramatic unities of time, place, and action. The Elizabethan dramatists gloried in violating them, and the poets, on a magic carpet of language, have been transported on surrealistic trips without benefit of LSD. As Emily Dickinson has put it,

> There is no Frigate like a Book
> To take us Lands away
> Nor any Coursers like a Page
> Of prancing Poetry—

Perhaps the most remarkable similarity between poetry and dreams is in the fusion mechanisms that both employ. The figures of speech of poetic diction—metaphor, metonymy (use of an associated attribute for the thing meant), and synecdoche ("the mention of a part when the whole is to be understood": Fowler's *Modern English Usage*)—and the processes of the dream world—condensation, displacement and symbolization—are so similar in their treatment of time, space, and the things of reality that one is obliged to consider whether they are not basically the same mental operations. In other words, the reality criteria of the secondary process—cause and effect, logic and reason, time and space—are circumvented through the use of poetic diction. The patient enters the world of primary process—of dreams and wishes, urges and drives, hates and loves, turmoil and fulfillment. But it is a *willing* suspension of reality testing. And he can explore this cave as deeply as he wishes; having entered willingly, he can return whenever he wishes. The rungs of reality are always within arm's reach, and he can readily scramble back through one ego-defense or another: "I disagree with the poet's point of view." "What he says doesn't hold water." "This poem has nothing to do with me."

On the other hand, the poem may touch off a series of psychic events that contribute to the patient's feeling of well-being in a way similar to what is experienced after having been involved in a creative act. In the creative process, the magnet of unconscious interest [9] scans the storehouse of memories and their associated affects, attracting the image experiences related to the conscious theme. The organizing ego so molds and shapes these into a communicable form that other egos that perceive reality in a somewhat similar fashion can sense the poet's ideation and affective messages. Thus it is the world of reality that provides the standard datum that serves as the common medium enabling the patient's unconscious to receive stimuli from the poet's unconscious. The poet's affective theme now serves as a magnet that performs a similar function in the patient's unconscious, bestirring early feelings related to the poet's theme. These feelings coalesce and rise to the surface facilitated by the group setting, sometimes taking the form of highly charged verbal productions, sometimes stopping just short at the preverbal level, where meaningful integrations can still be made.

Thus the patient has shared in a process of re-creation. The poet's affect-images have served as condensation nuclei to which the patient's vaporous and troubled feelings were drawn and given a form more acceptable, conscious, and functional. Perception has been expanded, doubt and uncertainty reduced, feelings validated, and guidelines underscored. A feeling of well-being usually pervades the atmosphere at the end of a poetry session because, I believe, each member feels that he has participated in a creative process. For a brief period he feels he has felt a human feeling that was his very own. For a while he was "with it," in and of the world of human feeling. He has reestablished a beachhead on the shore of a troubled sea and now has the hope of being able to fan out in many new directions.

The presentation of didactic poetry that undisguisedly urged a moral course of action on the reader almost invariably raised hostile reactions from a subgroup, which resented either *1.* the assumption of superiority, *2.* the arrogance of the poet, or *3.* the perceived attempt to impose a parent-child structure on the poet-reader relationship. The protests against the dictates of the poet-authorities had the quality of pained cries provoked by the poking into old wounds obtained in authority conflicts.

This type of poem served chiefly to arouse abreactions associated with the authority theme and to stimulate attempts to resolve this conflict. Invariably a poem of this type divided the group into two opposing camps, with each member loyally returning to the same standard he had previously defended. Though poems of the didactic type were significantly less successful in eliciting emotions from the deeper psychic levels—except in connection with the authority theme—I would still occasionally include one of them. They, too, seem to serve a therapeutic purpose. Some they seem to inspire; others they provoke; and still others seem to respond in a style resembling identification with the aggressor. All of these reactions are grist for the therapeutic mill. It is my impression that the following types of personalities are more likely to accept the precepts, dicta, and moralizings of didactic poems: *1.* dependent personalities who have not extricated themselves from old symbiotic ties, who form quick transferences to those who assume the mantle of authority, e.g., the unfaltering voice of the poet; *2.* people who think of themselves as highly moral, who harbor a deep conviction that good deeds will eventually be rewarded and evil punished by an Omnipotent One; *3.* immature personalities.

One of the poems that we worked with was by Louis Ginsberg. (I discontinued giving the name of the poet when I discovered that often some of the patients would seize on the poet's relation to the poem in order to resist their personal involvement.) It extols the pleasure derived from self-denial:

HUNGER AND THIRST [10]
Of all the fruits I ever pluck
To try to feed my fill,
The plum I leave upon the bough
Remains the sweetest still.
. . . . .
The sweetest kiss I ever had
Was one I did not take.
. . . . .
So, in the feast that I will set,
Before my life will sink,
Hunger will be the richest food;
And thirst, the sweetest drink!

Some of the reactions and interactions may give an idea of the process that takes place during a typical session. One patient remarks that she agrees with the poet that the contemplation of the ideal fantasy yields greater pleasure than the real satisfaction of the appetite. Most of the group, however, chose not to dwell on this theme. They respond more keenly to the undercurrents of self-denial, delay of gratification, and forbidden pleasure. Another one says, "This poem reminds me of nibbling around a prune Danish to delay eating the delectable center." Still another responds, "What happens if you take too long and the center goes rotten before you get there?" The first says: "It's like the pleasure you get in delaying the orgasm. You prolong the sexual act. It could be good, it could be bad, depending on the condition of your heart."

Another says: "In this poem you don't have the orgasm, you're just left at the dock as the ship goes by. You're just waving goodbye, and just standing there."

One of the patients bursts out: "Why, that's pure masochism!" Someone else quietly agrees: "It's like a sweet lie—it's a kind of tale we tell ourselves." Another is not entirely convinced by the attack on the poem. She says: "When I have a place to go to I sometimes linger on the way. Maybe I stretch out the time anticipating the pleasure to have more pleasure."

This last speaker is supported by a young woman who says: "I dread attaining my (PhD) degree." She is delaying the completion of her thesis, she says, because she is afraid its completion would leave a void in her life. Someone points out that she probably had plans to do something with her degree. Wouldn't those plans take up the slack?

One member says: "It's a sort of disallowed life. When the children are sent to bed when the grownups are having a party, they sneak down on the stairway and peek through the balustrade and they see the grownups having a party. It has something of that nature, especially when he says, 'Horizons are horizons when we view them from afar.'" At another point she says: "A woman's life consists of waiting. By nature she has to wait nine months for her children to be born; she waits for her children to come home; she waits for the clothes to dry on the line; she does a lot of waiting all the time. Waiting," she concludes, "is starved living."

No rigorous evaluation of the year's work was attempted. Nine or ten members attended almost every week throughout the entire year. Usually, at the end of the session, they would adjourn to a nearby cafeteria to prolong their enjoyment of each other's company and to continue the evening's discussion over a cup of coffee. Genuine expressions of appreciation were frequent for the opportunity to participate in the poetry sessions. One member credited them with overcoming her writing block. She had recommenced writing excellent poetry after many years of inactivity. Another discovered a talent for translating poems from the French; her translations served to trigger some of our most fulfilling sessions, although her appreciation of the poetry sessions alone would have been reward enough. Others often brought their original poems, which were always read and discussed, and they were invariably most rewarding. One disturbed young man was "hung up" on an unresolved relationship with his now deceased father. He would occasionally deflect the flow of the discussion by extraneous references to his special problem. The other members, sensing a special difficulty, at times attempted to help him by going along with his digressions; at other times, engrossed in their own themes, they would deal with him more abruptly. One gray-haired lady came religiously to every session, although she responded to only the most easily understood poems. Occasionally I would tell the members of the group that they need not understand everything in the poem, and I would try always to anticipate difficult lines that could be readily clarified.

One member, a 38-year-old bachelor who rarely missed a meeting, felt that the poetry session was "the high spot of the week," which, to him, was a series of days of otherwise unremitting dullness. Another member, a shy, sensitive, quiet young woman, wrote at the end of the year to say that she felt much better and that the poetry sessions had "helped me the most."

Whatever the therapeutic principle may be in the use of poetry in a group setting—the facilitation of catharsis, the sharing of common experiences in an accepting atmosphere, or the feeling of having participated in an act of re-creation with contributions from one's own "storehouse of memories and experience"—the comments and reactions of the patients and my observations point to the conclusion that the method helps to lift the cover to a deep well of feelings, which can then be discussed, dealt with, and integrated; that the patients can unburden themselves of these feelings in an accepting, nonjudgmental atmosphere; that they can express sad and joyous feelings without retribution; that, at a certain time each week, they can share, if they wish, some hitherto unexpressed feeling or look together through a new window.

REFERENCES

1. Butcher, S. H.: Aristotle's Theory of Poetry and Fine Art, New York, Dover, 1951, p. 255.
2. Smith, L. H., and Twyeffort, L. H.: Psychoneuroses: Their origin and treatment, *in* Piersol, G. M., and Bortz, E. L., eds.: The Cyclopedia of Medicine, Surgery and Specialties, XII, Philadelphia, Davis, 1945.
3. Poetry and Medicine, *in* MD: Med Newsmagazine 8:144 (#7, July) 1964.
4. Greifer, E.: Principles of Poetry Therapy, New York, Poetry Therapy Center, 1963, p. 16.
5. *Ibid.*, p. 17.
6. Leedy, J. J.: Poetry Therapy, A New Ancillary Therapy in Psychiatry, New York, Poetry Therapy Center, 1966, p. 7.
7. ———: Unpublished paper, 1966, p. 1.
8. Diamond, Edwin: The Science of Dreams, New York, Macfadden-Bartell, 1963, pp. 113 ff.
9. Sharpe, E. F.: Dream Analysis, London, Hogarth Press, 1961, pp. 42 ff.
10. Ginsberg, L.: *in* Lieberman, E., ed.: Poems for Enjoyment, New York, McGraw-Hill, 1931, p. 101, with permission.

CHAPTER 4

The Universal Language of Rhythm

JOOST A. M. MEERLOO, MD
*Associate Professor of Psychiatry, New York School
of Psychiatry, New York*

*Once we have command of the rhythm
We have command of the world.*
NOVALIS

DURING THE SECOND WORLD WAR, I had a personal encounter with the healing powers of a kind of poetry therapy. It was during one of the most trying times of my life. I remember how three prisoners lay crowded across the one dirty cot in the cell, on a thin layer of straw where fleas and bed bugs held their nightly feast. We were from different lands and understood only a few words of each other's tongues. To make matters more uncomfortable, we had no idea whether the morning would bring death or liberation.

The humid summer night was devoid of sleep. After a while, one of us made a feeble attempt to hum, and then began to intone some lyrics in his own language. Gradually, we took over in turn each other's chanting of intimate thoughts in measured cadences. That was how we managed to soothe ourselves with a kind of verbal hypnosis, which took the place of sleep. We were lucky to have discovered something ecstatic in our playful rhythmization of words.

No great poetry was spoken that night, or on many another similar occasion. But it was my repeated experience in those stressful years that people in extreme anxiety, frozen by the enemy into complete passivity while awaiting their fate, would suddenly find a rhythmic voice inside themselves—a voice that spoke for their essential "me." It is a pity that more of this war poetry by non-poets has not been gathered. Almost written in blood, these verses were smuggled out of prison or concentration camp, while the authors waited for an echo in their silent isolation. With the liberation, the emergency poets stopped writing their verses. But they had found the secret of communion through rhythm and poetry, a form of communication usually used by more creative talents.

On the assumption that there is a universal rhythmic communication with complex biological and psychological aspects—as I described more elaborately in my studies on *Mental Contagion* [11,13] —I will limit myself here to some clinical features of rhythmic interaction. In some people, such communication will break out into dance, in others into music and singing, in still others into poetry. Indeed, we find that rhythm is back of all great creative cultural achievements.

Therapeutically, all forms of communication may be used to expand the usual means of interaction and mutual relationship between patient and therapist. It may be too pretentious here to use the terms music therapy, dance therapy, or even poetry therapy. They are adjuncts to the totality of interactions and transactions in every human contact.

Rhythmic interaction is of great importance in any form of human communication. The moment there is rhythm, something is shared by the participants. The young child reacts more to the cadences of poetry than to the words: he claps his hands in time, mouths and recites the music of the words. At the other end of the life span, when many functions of the mind have broken down, senile patients repeat rhythmic whisperings of the music of words. When verbalization of the message is no longer possible, the meter remains.

Biologic Rhythms

At this moment, the investigation of a variety of rhythmic functions is in full swing. The ancient Greek physicians were already keenly interested in the manifold rhythms of man: "The body," said Hippocrates, "consumes time by its functions." Life is a conglomeration of many rhythmic events, known and unknown. Today's scientists are becoming more and more aware of man's built-in biologic clock.

Among animals, various instances are observed of actual and accurate instinctual measuring of cosmic time without benefit of outer clocks. Fish in an aquarium rise to the surface to await their dinner at exactly fixed times. Certain worms of the seashore dig themselves into the sand shortly before the beginning of floodtide. Many butterflies change their coloring with the coming of day and night. The rhythm of not only sunrise and sunset but also the moon awakens analogous phenomena in many animals. There are worms that come out of the beach sand only at full moon. And many's the woman whose passions rise to full height with the coming of the full moon.

Darwin reasoned that man, having come forth from the sea, must still have in him a tidal rhythm, and he felt that we must accept some interrelation between the lunar phase and the menstrual hormonal process, even though the direct links are unknown.[6,14] Moreover, the term lunacy for mental disturbances belongs to the realm of explorable concepts of continuous geophysical action on man.[10] Psychiatrists are quite familiar with the cyclic psychoses and neuroses dependent on the season of the year as well as the tides. Usually, we human beings are not aware consciously of being subjected to various cosmic and biologic rhythms. Only when a too fast jet flight changes our adaptation to the day and night cycle do we recognize our adaptational troubles.

Periodic events in man are under the control of the autonomic nervous system. Yet the moment we start to measure bodily functions, for instance temperature, we become aware of a cosmic rhythm. We observe hormonal rhythms, to which the menstrual cycle belongs. We recognize the variation in moods related to the seasons, and we find, for example, the periodic seasonal appearance of stomach ulcer.[19]

Pathologists tend to relate certain periodic diseases to unknown rhythms of life—cyclic neutropenia, periodic arthralgia, periodic paralysis. With the use of the electrocardiogram, the electroencephalogram, and the electrodermatogram, normal and pathologic rhythms can be detected. Breathing, of course, has its distinct rhythms, as do the intestines, the heart and the muscles, the molecules and even the intra-atomic particles.

Embryonic Rhythmic Behavior

From the eighth intrauterine week, the organism lives in an envelope of rhythm; rhythmic reactive and protective movements are noted. The fetus reacts to sounds from the outside world; it lives in a floating rhythmic sound world (the word *rhythm*, incidentally, is derived from *rheein*—to flow) filled with auditive impressions. There is the sound of the maternal heartbeat and vessels, with a mean frequency of 70, and superimposed upon this the different rhythm of the fetal heart, with a mean frequency of 140.

Observation of fetal movements as reaction to sounds, combined with the knowledge that amniotic fluid is a better sound conductor than air, makes the existence of a prenatal syncopated rhythmic sound world more than likely. We can imitate the whole physical uterine plant and reproduce the various sounds in this experimental setting by holding our head under water and hearing the prebirth world. This experiment makes it easier for us to understand why there is in later life such a strong universal spontaneous reaction to syncopated music. The fact is that an old mnemonic pattern has been invoked with all its unconscious associations with previous nirvanic joys.

Some of the nonsense verses recapture for us the archaic syncopated rhythm:

> The water it soon came in, it did,
> The water it soon came in;
> So to keep them dry they wrapped their feet
> In a purky paper all folded neat,
> And they fastened it down with a pin. [9]

"Rhythm," says Sister Paul Gabriel,[4] "has the earliest appeal and is likely the most lasting." She quotes the following poem for a child:

> 'Tis all the way to Toe-Town
> Beyond the knee-high Hill
> That Baby has to travel down,
> To watch the soldiers drill.
>
> One, two, three, four, five
> A row; a captain and his men
> And on the other side, you see
> Are six, seven, eight, nine, ten.

The pleasure of rhyme and rhythm comes long before baby knows that the poem deals with his toes.

Rhythmic rocking, dancing, and floating in the amniotic fluid belong to normal intrauterine movements.[15] The child in the womb yawns (intrauterine drinking), scratches, cringes and stretches in response to outer stimulation. From patients in psychotherapy we have learned that the ecstasy of jazz music, not to mention rock and roll, is brought on by various reminiscent feelings of a lost long ago and far away happiness.

Postnatal Rhythmic Interaction

In cultures not so mechanized and civilized as our own, we can observe a rhythmic motoric interaction between mothers and newborn babies. This interaction develops when the child is brought to the breast immediately after birth. Baby's tiny hands open and close in rhythm, pawing at the breast (the milk reflex so clearly visible in cats when they are stroked); baby's head moves back and forth from one nipple to the other, and both mother and child move to and fro in a tender swaying—a "milk dance"[12] reminiscent of the rhythm of coitus. This is as if the basic acts in the service of the continuity of life were governed by the same rhythmic interaction. At the same time, it tells us why these same rhythmic interactions are so often suppressed in a puritanical hospital setting: I have known obstetrical nurses to scold the new mothers for going through such "childish" paces.

The rhythmic interaction between mother and infant is probably phylogenetically derived from an adaptive nipple-seeking behavior seen in higher animals. The newborn lamb is rejected by mother and flock and has to die if it cannot reach the nipple within a specific time span. For by its weakness it would expose the waiting flock to dangerous predators.

Mothers who breast-feed their children, especially among so-called primitive people, unwittingly use the same rhythmic movements every time they give the baby the breast. Even the infant's suckling occurs in rhythmic design, like thumbsucking at a later age. Usually these rhythmic interactions disappear when the period of breast feeding is delayed (frustrated) from four to six hours after birth. In our technological age, many hospitals delay the first feeding and libidinal encounter between mother and baby for 24 hours.[18]

Abnormal Rhythmic Expressions

The study of intrauterine movements and early infantile adaptational responses is important for pathology. The early repressed rhythmic reflexes return in neurotic and psychotic children in whom, according to psychoanalytic experience, oral deprivation and the lack of motoric pleasure become overwhelming trauma. Also, we repeatedly observe in therapy that even in older patients, either in deep hypnosis or in deep regression, early infantile motoric interaction patterns return spontaneously. Various adults complain about these rhythmic contractions of legs and body in half sleep shortly before falling asleep. The uncontrollable movements wake them fully again.

The startle reaction in infants also shows a pattern of rhythmic defense movements slowly petering out. Such a startle can also break out into rhythmic jumping in either frightened or extremely happy older persons. A film of Hitler, made after the surrender of France was signed at Versailles, shows him making just such stamping movements.

Spontaneous rocking, jumping, bouncing, headbanging are often also seen in well-cared-for infants. Mittelman[16] calls them autoerotic movements. They usually appear in the first year of life and are residuals of the repressed early adaptational rhythms. These returning repressed movements can persist and be used as a masochistic self-hurting reaction to some frustrating experience.

Incessant scratching, headbanging,[3] genital rubbing, early masturbation and rhythmic rocking may all be interpreted as manifestations of displaced appropriate innate rhythmic adaptational reflexes in the service of primary gratification.[11] Many children use headbanging as a means of exhausting themselves and putting themselves to sleep. Even when it hurts, it gives sweet rhythmic catharsis. Frightened mothers who dread this can be taught to recite nursery rhymes and folk songs to their children as a substitute for the potentially harmful headbanging.

> I'm a lean dog, a keen dog, a wild dog and lone;
> I'm a rough dog, a tough dog, hunting on my own;
> I'm a bad dog, a mad dog, teasing silly sheep;
> I love to sit and bay at the moon, to keep fat souls from sleep.[4]

Autistic children show a return of early adaptational rhythms, chiefly to and fro rocking. They can sit a whole day long in a chair and do nothing else. The pawing, milking movement is often used towards those whom they want to touch, or they direct the same movement towards their own genitals. Compulsive masturbation is often a displaced milk reflex.

Headbanging is more frequently seen in autistic than in neurotic children. Often they get head wounds as a result of these wild orgiastic movements and develop, besides, as a reaction to any outside frightening stimulus, a wild dancing stamping step, which often resembles the uterine dance. In a camp for schizophrenic children, I was able to observe these rhythmic movements at close hand. One boy who loved to float for hours on a diving board in the swimming pool showed all these rhythmic movements, interrupted from time to time by agitated masturbation. It is not yet widely known that we can make use of these rhythmic signals to break through the autism of the child and build up a rhythmic sign language through sound or touch or movement.

These rhythmic manifestations call for more thorough clinical investigation. This writer intends if possible to study the whole gamut of rhythms in a total rhythmic profile. Such movements may also be seen in neurotics during therapeutic sessions. Many bizarre motions can be explained as a return of early frustrated adaptations. Especially in deep regression, while producing early infantile memories, patients on the couch are apt to reenact various rhythmic movements, particularly of the feet. The same is true for patients in hypnosis. The frequency of such movements and signals is usually slower than the heart rate and depends on subjective experiences relating to very early reminiscences.

The Communicative Function of Rhythm

Most mothers know by instinct that rhythmic movements soothe and relax the baby. Maternal and infantile pulsations covibrate. Rocking the cradle, singing lullabies, carrying and cuddling the child, holding it "under her heart" (in the double sense), rhythmic stroking of the back—these serve to supply and guarantee feelings of security and protection. Masserman [10] explains this dependency on rhythm as one of the magic *ur* defenses of man, the miraculous transformation of chaos into pleasurable order. The outside rhythm is incorporated into a personal beat and order of time. As we noted previously, the rhyme and rhythm of poetry often have a much more compelling force than the actual meaning of the words. Through rhythm, old phylogenetic memories are aroused, and rhythm helps us memorize what formerly seemed chaotic.

Our cooscillation with biological rhythms and the rhythms of the outside world brings us back to the Never-never land of our youth. The rhythm of the waves of the sea has a lulling, sleep-inviting action. It is when people cannot live and move in unison with this rhythm that they become sick—seasick. The whole world is experienced then as one vast cauldron of danger.

At birth, the rhythm of maternal schedules begins to intrude upon the biologic rhythms of the infant, the measured meter of solemnity and duty. The first clock the infant hears is the maternal heartbeat as it lies at mother's left breast. Waiting for feeding in hungry expectancy creates the first mnemonic impression of boredom and empty time—feelings that play central roles in dreams of frustrated people.

Monkeys as well as human babies behave more quietly when resting near the maternal heart. An artificial reproduction of the same beat often has a quieting influence. Those familiar with the training of pets know that a yelping anxious puppy can be soothed by a ticking clock wrapped in a blanket. Above all, rhythm gives a sense of familiarity. Hypnosis starts with a rhythmic soothing of the subject, and the lulling of lullabies is as old as mankind.

Sometimes the intrusion of artificial schedules may lead to an educational eurhythmia, or a clash—a dysrhythmia. Here the child pits his own rhythm against someone else's. The manic-depressive vacillation of moods is often explained as such an early acquired dysrhythmia. Social schedules are the huge synchronizers intruding into biologic rhythms. Psychosomatic diseases often start as defense against the intrusion by outside schedules upon biologic patterns. In attempting to control the unpleasant routine, the counterroutine begins to control the young protester.

The Language of Rhythm

At this moment, we are not able to give an exact analysis of the complex symphony of rhythms in our organism. Clinically, we are aware that every individual has a personal profile of rhythms. Future analysts of these profiles will be better able to predict the interference and cooscillation between outward rhythmic profiles, such as music or poetry, and inward rhythmic profiles. Rigid habits are often broken down by more primordial rhythms; they can even free repressed primitive impulses. It was impressive to find a silent catatonic patient starting to talk again after dancing.

This subject of rhythmic communication has become more and more significant since we have become aware that rhythm in one person can be transferred directly to another. Rhythm represents the collective memory of mankind; there exists a compulsion to imitate and cooscillate. The unobtrusive rhythm that I tap out on a desk while giving a lecture is unwittingly taken up by some of the people in my audience. This inadvertent interplay and interaction can often be observed among children, the dance of one provoking a dance in the playmate.

> It's hopperty, skipperty, high and low
> Summer's the time for fun. [4]

All of us experience this compulsive reverberation and co-

The Universal Language of Rhythm

oscillation in the group. Few can resist the seductive pull of the marchers in a parade. We all succumb to this magic effect of rhythm. A group that chants collectively "we are not afraid" mesmerizes itself into being brave. Most of the primitive rituals and revivals that make a solid deindividualized mass of the group do it by incessant and insistent rhythmic movements. The rhythmic taking over of sound and motion in dance and chant is token contact and facilitates mutual identification.

Such rhythm may serve as the vitalizing impulse that changes accumulated violence into creative discharge. Order suppresses crude instinct. But we members of the technologic era are unwittingly subjected to various contaminating rhythms. Public opinion engineers use jingles and rhythmic slogans to make their suggestions penetrate more readily into our minds, no matter how resistant we try to be. Television and movies resort to a variety of rhythms and tunes so that we may become that much more involved with the suggestive actions on the screen.

Political propaganda uses rhythmic slogans, such as the Nazi "Sieg Heil, Sieg Heil" or the Fascist "Duce, Duce," to sweep the masses into receptive and submissive identification with the leader. Certain tricky beats and tunes catch us. We repeat them and go over them in our minds time and again:

> "Beware the Jabberwock, my son!
> The jaws that bite, the claws that catch!
> Beware the Jubjub bird, and shun
> The frumious Bandersnatch!" [2]

Our need to cheer and sing, to scan and rhyme words is partly a conquest of the mechanical beats pounding in us, partly the need to covibrate and cooscillate with others and feel at home in a group. Our word *emotion* means moving away or moving together in cooscillation and com-motion with another being. Such rhythmic com-motion in the group may be observed when taking home movies in various family settings. If the films are flashed on the screen at a faster than normal speed, we can detect a continual rhythmic moving to and fro in the conversational circle. Similarly, the interaction in group psychotherapy is always combined with subliminal contagious movements.

Rhythm and Mental Contagion

Mental contagion is by definition the subtle transmission of feelings, thoughts and attitudes from one person to another. This form of psychic contamination may usually be traced to a common regression, to infantile physiologic responses.[11] Rhythm provokes rhythm; laughter provokes laughter; fright provokes fright. The distress call by one induces feelings of distress in the other. Scratching in one brings on itching in another. These phenomena are all subject to the common rule of mental infection: *The more an expression evokes infantile archaic responses of the organism—the innate biologic signal code—the more infectious it is.*

Archaic communication may be described as a rudimentary remnant of biologic signals, originally used as a warning to fellow creatures to flee or hide. The important implication of this rule of mental contamination is that it is so much easier to transmit regressive forms of communication, such as chaos, fury, panic and revolt, than to infect people with good examples and restraint. In Northern Italy, collective singing of spontaneous poetry, the ristornelli, is used as a token duel between groups.

One group of youngsters going through the gyrations of the last phase of rock and roll induces another group to regress to the same form of rhythmic interaction. In the meantime, the energy output increases. I have witnessed positive rock and roll furies. In dancing, one surrenders to the rhythm of the music, a major surrender to the greater rhythmic occurrences in the world.[8] There are tribes that use their magic dances to bring on and promote the rhythmic contractions of the mother's womb while she is in the throes of giving birth. Others beat the tribal drums and dance to stimulate the temporary pugnacity of war.

Poetry makes use of an archaic rhythmic language through which the symphony of vocal rhythms is often more expressive than the semantic overtones of the words. A national anthem stirs up in every breast the patriotic yearning to belong to the group. There is a deep resonance in people when they hear or see archaic sign behavior. The inner resonance unwittingly fills them with phylogenetic and ontogenetic nostalgia. The Bushmen dance on and on to keep the moon alive. The shared regressive fantasy and experience lead to mutual imitation. Alas, regression is much more contagious than progression!

Future study will have to direct greater attention to the analysis of these phenomena. We will have to ask ourselves which rhythm does what? The compulsive patient, for instance, cannot step out of his own rhythms and obsessive repetitions without developing enormous anxiety. Psychodynamically, it is known that the compulsion to repeat rhythmically is often used as a defense against the shock of new adaptation.

In some cases, mental contamination is merely the result of an induction of the same rhythm. In others, certain rhythms may interfere with existing defensive rhythms and thereby open new roads of communication and new adaptations. Finally, all this wherewithal of rhythmic communication will have to be clinically measured and tested.

In music, the transfer of emotions is much more complicated, but it follows the same principles, the same rules of mental induction and cooscillation. There are soothing rhythms, exciting rhythms and ambivalence-provoking counterpoints.

In poetry, inner ambivalence is also expressed in a harmonizing rhythm, sadness and joy, assertion and submission, acceptance of fate alongside rebellion—as in Francis Thompson's

THE KINGDOM OF GOD
"*In no Strange Land*"
O world invisible, we view thee;
    O world intangible, we touch thee;
O world unknowable, we know thee;
    Inapprehensible, we clutch thee!

Yea, in the night, my Soul, my daughter,
    Cry,—clinging heaven by the hems:
And lo, Christ walking on the water,
    Not of Gennesareth, but Thames!

In general, rhythm means recognition and responding to something familiar. Such preoccupation with familiar messages can be used as a defense against feelings of pain. In olden days, quacks pulled teeth under the soothing rhythm of drum beats, and today some dentists still resort to music with a lively beat.

Last but not least, there is the rhythmic gestural language of wooing. In Oriental lands, the rhythm and cadence of breathing is used to ignite erotic feelings in the mate. Every flirtation makes spontaneous use of this intuitive knowledge of the effect of rapid breathing. A lover can tell from the inhaling rhythm at the other end of the telephone whether his distant beloved accepts him or not. In the Orient, rhythm and chanting are used to bring a group of believers into a collective hypnosis. All this, of course, can be explained by well-known physiological and chemical processes.

Catharsis and the Language of Rhythm

All through history we encounter dance epidemics in which the masses tried to reduce tension and anxiety in frenzied movements. Music and dance, the rhythmic intercommunication of man, were once the first forms of magic medicine. Indeed, the common regression to a cluster of interacted movements gives delight and catharsis and revitalizes us. However, the same human beings may also be seduced by rhythm into giving up their integrity and self-awareness completely.

On the other hand, there are some people who, on the basis of early infantile rhythmic frustration, are unable to join in any dance movements and thus cannot experience this common joy that is as old as mankind. Some are not touched by poetry either. They are motorically frustrated and do not understand gestures and pantomime. A cold logic has taken over the vital rhythms of life. No matter how intelligent they may be, they are excluded from a vast field of human intercommunication.

Rhythm, in short, is life itself. The tune is the mind. Music reflects to us the symphony and total profile of rhythms that we ourselves comprise. In the rhythm and repetition of themes in music and poetry, emotional abreaction takes place. The handling of counterpoint by composers evokes in listeners their own contrasting feelings, and this new harmony of contrasts temporarily frees them from inner tension and ambivalence. Rhythm can completely revolutionize our body system. Poet or composer may first inhibit us and provoke frustration, but then, suddenly, with new rhythms, liberate us.

Rhythm is an energy-saving device. The girl may not feel like walking, but be sure she can dance. A moment ago she felt she could not move anymore, but now she speaks her own gestural language in the musical trance of rhythm. By the same token, a swift game of tennis, which is a dance in itself, refreshes the players, and systematic exercise redoubles the individual's energy.

Rhythm in any form expresses many feelings that were repressed formerly. It ties the unawareness of hidden things together so as not to cause confusion by too much sophistication and by what Burrow [1] calls the smugness of formulation. Rhythm is the integration of chaotic inner and outer events into one's own "musical" experience.

In each of us dwells a need to repeat old patterns of behavior. We imitate not only others but also ourselves. It is sometimes a great struggle in psychotherapy to liberate a patient from such compulsive self-imitations and repetitions; and without a therapeutic regression to the origin of his ancient language of rhythms, the patient will fail in his attempt at self-recollection. For this reason poetry, as a well-chosen form of communication, is a welcome adjunct to psychotherapy.

REFERENCES

1. Burrow, T.: Preconscious Foundations of Human Experience, New York, Basic, 1964.
2. Carroll, L.: The Hunting of the Snark; and other Nonsense Verse, New York, Peter Pauper Press, 1955.
3. FitzHerbert, J.: Some further observations on headbanging and allied behavior, J Ment Sci 98:330, 1952.
4. Gabriel, Sister P.: Poetry—the child's heritage, Child and Family 5:29, 1966.
5. Hooker, D.: The Prenatal Origin of Behavior, Lawrence (Kans.), Univ Kansas Press, 1952.
6. Inman, W. S.: The moon, the seasons, and man, Brit J Med Psychol 24:267, 1951.
7. Klages, L.: Vom Wesen des Rhytmus, Kampen auf Sylt, Kampman Verlag, 1934.
8. Langer, S. K.: Feeling and Form, New York, Scribner's, 1953.
9. Lear, E.: The Complete Nonsense Verse, New York, Dover, 1951.
10. Masserman, J. H.: Say id isn't so—with music, *in* Science and Psychoanalysis, New York, Grune, 1958.

11. Meerloo, J. A. M.: Archaic behavior and the communicative act, Psychiat Quart 29:60, 1955.
12. ———: The Dance—from Ritual to Rock and Roll, New York, Chilton, 1960.
13. ———: Mental contagion, Amer J Psychother 13:66, 1959.
14. ———: The time sense in psychiatry, in The Voices of Time, New York, Braziller, 1966.
15. Minkowski, M.: Neurobiologischen Studien am Menschlichen Foetus, Handbuch Biol Arbeitsmethoden, vol. 5, Berlin, Springer, 1928.
16. Mittelman, B.: Intrauterine and early infantile motility, Psychoanal Study Child 15:104, 1960.
17. Read, Herbert: Education Through Art, New York, Pantheon, 1945.
18. ———: Poetic Consciousness and Creative Experience, Zurich, Eranos Yearbook, 1956.
19. Reiman, H. A.: Periodic disease, JAMA 166:141, 1951.
20. Solberger, A.: Biological Rhythm Research, New York, Elsevier, 1965.
21. Van Der Post, L.: The Creative Pattern in Primitive Africa, Zurich, Eranos Yearbook, 1956.

CHAPTER 5

Principles of Poetry Therapy

JACK J. LEEDY, MD
Director, Poetry Therapy Center, New York

As POETRY THERAPY CONTINUES to be explored and its values demonstrated, one hopes that this newest (and oldest?) of the ancillary therapies in psychiatry and psychotherapy will become an established part of the total treatment of the emotionally ill. For poetry therapy can play its adjunctive role in mental hygiene clinics, or in hospitals, or in private practice, with one patient or groups of patients. The principles that follow are based on my experience over the past ten years as psychiatric consultant to the poetry therapy groups of the Mental Hygiene Clinic of Cumberland Hospital and Project Teen Aid, OEO, in Brooklyn, conferences with other psychotherapists who utilize poetry in treating their patients, and many hours with my friend and associate, the late Eli Greifer.

1. The Isoprinciple

The isoprinciple, effective in music therapy, has proved important in the choice of poems for use in poetry therapy. As music that has the same feeling as the mood or mental tempo of the patient has proved a valuable tool, so poems that are close in feeling to the mood of the patient have been found helpful. Depressed patients, for example, are helped by poems sad and gloomy in tone yet having lines or stanzas that reflect hope and optimism, especially toward their conclusion. By reading, studying, memorizing, reciting or creating this kind of poem, depressed patients come to feel that they are not alone in their depressions, that others are also depressed, that others have been depressed and recovered from their depressions, and that no disgrace attaches to victims of extreme alterations of mood. For them, crying precipitated by a poem is often therapeutically helpful: the poem becomes symbolically an understanding someone with whom they can share their despair.

Because of the dangers of suicide and suicidal trends, gestures and ideas in the depressed, the therapist should not choose poems that *a*. offer no hope or that might increase the depth of the depression by implying that life has no meaning; *b*. increase guilt feelings; *c*. imply that God, father figures or mother figures forsake people, seek vengeance, and cannot be relied on in times of crisis; *d*. encourage, glorify, or even mention suicide; *e*. are confused, defeatist, homicidal, vulgar or debasing—Dryden [1] long ago remarked this sort of poetry:

> O gracious God! How far have we
> Profan'd thy Heav'nly Gift of Poesy?
> Made prostitute and profligate the Muse,
> Debas'd to each obscene and impious use,
> Whose Harmony was first ordain'd *Above*
> For Tongues of *Angels*, and for *Hymns* of *Love*?

—*f*. encourage silence and discourage vocalization, particularly of feelings of hostility; and *g*. are persistently pessimistic with self-destructive love and a fearful hatred of life, like, for example, some of the poems of Robinson Jeffers.

For depressed patients, poems like the following are suggested: Thomas Carlyle, "Today"; William Cowper, "Light Shining Out of Darkness"; Holmes, "The Chambered Nautilus"; Walter Savage Landor, "You Spoke, You Spoke, and I Believed"; Longfellow, "The Day is Done," "The Rainy Day"; Milton "On His Blindness"; Shelley, "Ode to the West Wind"; Robert Louis Stevenson, "The Celestial Surgeon"; Francis Thompson, "In No Strange Land"; Psalm 23: "The Lord is my Shepherd" (*Dominus regit me*); Whittier, "My Soul and I," "The Light that is Felt," and "The Eternal Goodness."

2. The Poetry Therapist

In the future—the near future, one hopes—poetry therapists will be registered in accordance with standards to be established by a yet unorganized National Association for Poetry Therapy, not unlike the registered occupational therapists or the music therapists. Professors K. F. Edgar and Richard Hazley, of the Indiana University of Pennsylvania, have proposed a curriculum for the training of poetry therapists, and trained therapists should increase in numbers and competence. Presently, psychotherapists, poets, teachers and social workers are assuming the roles of poetry therapists. Those occupational therapists who are interested and informed in poetry would greatly help as poetry therapists, also, because of the acute shortage of them.

Poetry therapists act as cotherapists in a poetry therapy group. They work with the psychotherapist in selecting the poems for the patients, in teaching them to read aloud and to cultivate their ability to listen to poetry, and in discussing in the group both the lives of the poets, where helpful, and the poetry itself. Reading poetry aloud enables the patients to respond more directly to its rhythms and patterns, and listening to it has a healing effect upon them.

At the beginning of a session, the members of a poetry therapy group may be stimulated and engaged by five minutes or so of group singing, usually led by the therapist. For this, the following songs have proved helpful: "Count Your Blessings," "Que Sera, Sera," "America," "God Bless America," "White Christmas," "Always," "Pal of My Cradle Days," "Silver Threads Among the Gold," "Sleepy Time Gal." As far back as the Elizabethan days, the poet often not only composed his own words, but wrote the music for them and played his compositions on the lute. The magic of verse is in its combination of thought, feeling and music.

3. Therapeutic Implications

Poetry therapy has guided patients to constructive adjustment after every approach known has been tried and failed. It helps some patients make their emotional disorders easier to bear, assists the process towards their recovery, and helps them to develop a philosophy of life that abets their adjustment to their misfortunes. Memorizing poems, enhanced by giving awards or prizes to those who memorize poems or even stanzas, has great value for the patients and should be encouraged. After memorizing a poem, the patients gain a feeling of mastery and think better of themselves.

Poetry encourages patients to explore their feelings, to feel more deeply, to extend their emotional range yet to discover patterns, also, of control and fulfillment. As Frost has written:

Theme alone can steady us down. Just as the first mystery was how a poem could have a tune in such a straightness as meter, so the second mystery is how a poem can have wildness and at the same time a subject that shall be fulfilled.

It should be the pleasure of a poem itself to tell how it can. The figure a poem makes. It begins in delight and ends in wisdom. The figure is the same as for love. No one can really hold that the ecstasy should be static and stand still in one place. It begins in delight, it inclines to the impulse, it assumes direction with the first line laid down, it runs a course of lucky events, and ends in a clarification of life—not necessarily a great clarification, such as sects and cults are founded on, but in a momentary stay against confusion.[2]

Poetry therapy helps patients to become more spontaneous and creative. Poetry is one of man's deepest expressions, and emotions are thereby released. A poem has been described as the shortest emotional distance between two points, the points representing the writer and the reader. This may explain why communication through poetry is established so readily, and why patients themselves are moved so frequently to attempt their own composition of poems. Psychotherapists are becoming increasingly aware that poetry can help their patients. For over forty years, Dr. Smiley Blanton used poetry in his practice as a psychiatrist. He writes, in *The Healing Power of Poetry*, that poetry can be of help with patients who need courage or feel overwhelmed; who suffer from insomnia; who are in love and must at times leave someone they love; who are angry or frustrated; who are depressed, anxious, or bereaved; and who are growing old.[3]

Certain poems, such as Coleridge's "Kubla Khan" and "The Ancient Mariner," Keats' "La Belle Dame Sans Merci," Longfellow's "Evangeline," Poe's "Annabel Lee" and Byron's "Indian Serenade" have spellweaving, hypnoidal, or hypnotic effects on some patients. The decision to use these poems in a poetry therapy group should be made by the psychotherapist.

4. The Poetry Therapy Group

Members of the poetry therapy group are usually enthusiastic about group reading. It is pleasurable for them to read together. Group reciting of poems helps to increase ego strength, decreases the duration and intensity of anxieties, and decreases also tendencies toward introversion and paralyzing inhibitions. The diction of the members is often improved. In the poetry therapy group, all references to unconscious material, dreams, fantasies, and motivations as related to the poetry, or to the associations stimulated by the poetry, are to be discussed at the discretion of the psychotherapist.

Poetry therapy groups may be structured with patients having the same diagnoses, like that for schizophrenics at Dixmont State Hospital, Pittsburgh, and that for mental defectives at the Staten Island Aid for Retarded Children, Inc. Or poetry therapy groups may include patients of different diagnoses.

Patients are encouraged to write their own poems. It has been noted that during periods of crisis, or when patterns of behavior or feelings are changing or have been recently changed, or when new insights are discovered, the patients often write poems, often in great quantity, and sometimes of considerable quality. The two poems that follow were written by patients in the poetry therapy group at Slippery Rock State College in Pennsylvania.

SNOWDRIFT

To walk the virgin snow alone.
To look back at your own footsteps
In the hissing stream of a ventilator
Swirling with fury into nothingness.
I feel guilty,
Destroying the perfect layer of white.
A thoughtless tramp destroyed beauty.
The ugliness of single tracks
not mated with another.
And no one to notice them.

NEW LOVE

She has new leaves
After her dead flowers,
Like the little almond tree
Which the frost hurt.

5. Therapeutic Poets and Poetry

With some patients, poems that are more regular in their rhythmic scheme have proved more helpful than poems with less conventional patterns. Poems with regular rhythms, those that most nearly approximate the beat of the human heart, affect many patients deeply. This is to say that some masterpieces of poetry may not be therapeutic, whereas mediocre poems, never included in anthologies, may be extremely helpful or right for a patient, and may be his bridge to reality.

Before listing poets and their poems useful in poetry therapy, one needs to say a word about standards. A psychotherapist will choose verse that is useful to psychotherapy, however fine or poor it may appear to critics old or new. Some of it may be of the most inferior, some of the most superior order of poetry: for poetry therapy, the standard is not whether it is good or great poetry, but whether it will help heal the ill. For this purpose, Longfellow may be better than Shakespeare, Herrick than Milton, Greifer than Donne, or Holmes than Sophocles. And a happy meeting of "the time, the place and the loved one all together" may work a miracle.

THE DAY IS DONE [4]

Come, read to me some poem,
   Some simple and heartfelt lay,
That shall soothe this restless
   feeling,
   And banish the thoughts of day.

Not from the grand old masters,
   Not from the bards sublime,
Whose distant footsteps echo
   Through the corridors of Time.

Read from some humbler poet,
   Whose songs gushed from his heart,
As showers from the clouds of summer,
   Or tears from the eyelids start;

Such songs have power to quiet
   The restless pulse of care,
And come like the benediction
   That follows after prayer.

Then read from the treasured volume
   The poem of thy choice,
And lend to the rhyme of the poet
   The beauty of thy voice.

The poems given in the chapters of this book as used successfully may suggest a wider range of poetic than of therapeutic values, wide enough, in any case. So be it. As poetry therapy develops, as it is developing rapidly, and its practitioners learn more of our great English poetry, one can find no reason why the greatest poets may not prove of the greatest worth in psychotherapy, as they are in literature.

In addition to the poems earlier suggested for the depressed, the following poems have been useful in poetry therapy groups: Shakespeare's sonnets, especially 29 and 30, and "The Uses of Adversity" from *As You Like It*; Alfred Tennyson's "Sweet and Low"; Emily Bronte's "Last Lines"; Walt Whitman's "Song of Myself"; Arthur Hugh Clough's "Say Not the Struggle Naught Availeth"; Robert Frost's "Stopping by Woods on a Snowy Evening"; John Masefields's "Tomorrow"; Gerard Manley Hopkins' "God's Grandeur"; and William Ernest Henley's "Invictus."

Patients, particularly those who are in mental institutions, are encouraged when they learn that great poems have been written by poets who themselves were patients in mental hospitals. John Clare wrote "I Am" while in the Northampton County Asylum. Christopher Smart, who was also confined to an asylum, scratched "A Song to David" [5] with a key upon the wall of his room because he was not permitted the use of pen and paper. These verses are from his long, magnificent poem:

> O thou, that sit'st upon a throne,
> With harp of high majestic tone,
>   To praise the King of kings;
> And voice of heav'n-ascending swell,
> Which, while its deeper notes excell,
>   Clear, as a clarion, rings:
>
> To bless each valley, grove and coast,
> And charm the cherubs to the post
>   Of gratitude in throngs;
> To keep the days on Zion's mount,
> And send the year to his account,
>   With dances and with songs:
>
> O Servant of God's holiest charge,
> The minister of praise at large,
>   Which thou may'st now receive;
> From thy blest mansion hail and hear,
> From topmost eminence appear
>   To this the wreath I weave.

REFERENCES

1. Dryden, John: To the Pious Memory of the Accomplisht Young Lady Mrs. Ann Killigrew. Excellent in the Two Sister-Arts of Poesie, and Painting. An Ode, *in* Crane, Ronald S., ed.: A Collection of English Poems 1660–1800, New York, Harper, 1932.
2. Frost, Robert: The Figure a Poem Makes, *in* Complete Poems of Robert Frost, New York, Holt, 1939. With permission.
3. Blanton, Smiley: The Healing Power of Poetry, New York, Crowell, 1960.
4. Longfellow, Henry Wadsworth: The Complete Poetical Works of Longfellow, Boston, Houghton, 1922. Five stanzas only.
5. Smart, Christopher: A Song to David, *in* Crane, R. S., ed.: A Collection of English Poems 1660–1800, New York, Harpers, 1932.

CHAPTER 6

Poetry as Therapy—and Therapy as Poetry

MILTON M. BERGER, MD
Fellow, American Psychiatric Association, Past President, American Group Psychotherapy Association, Association for Group Psychoanalysis and Process

BELIEVING THAT IT IS hardly sufficient in itself for the emotionally ill, I do not practice poetry therapy per se. But I have used it for nearly 20 years. For a psychoanalytically oriented psychotherapy to be an artistic as well as a scientific process, it must find its authentic form and texture in a living, creative manner, as therapist and patient(s) relate and communicate. Practicing a psychotherapy in which a continuous diagnostic assessment is integrated with an ongoing working-through of obstructive psychopathologic forces, I have found that poetry brought creatively into the therapeutic situation benefits patients.

Experience has taught me that poetry, created or used during the psychotherapeutic encounter, can often help a patient to reach levels of emotional insight more adequately than conventional dialogue. It enriches the encounter by allowing the patient to identify with other human beings, who have experienced similar conflicts, anxieties, and feelings, and who have been able to state, for all humanity, a universal theme or dilemma.

Therapy is a process akin to life for exposing, exploring, experiencing, mixing, uniting, or integrating the

conscious and the unconscious
concrete and the abstract
feeling and the thought
specific and the general
past and the present
individual and the universal
earthbound and the space-probing
personal and the impersonal
everyday and the unusual
rational and the irrational,
and
what is not yet considered rational
or irrational, although it is
perceivable, being, becoming.

All of these processes are also components of the poetic process. The naked and refined imagery, symbols, rhythm, rhyme and flow in poetry may be therapeutic in life * or in psychotherapy, when the poetic statement clarifies for emotional and/or intellectual understanding and integration a universal experience in a manner comprehensible to the patient-person in one or several levels of his being.

As an aspect of the total psychotherapeutic spectrum, poetry may help to create order where chaos existed, whether the chaos is in the patient himself or in his relationship with others, including the therapist.

> *If I am not for myself, who is for me?*
> *And being only for my own self, what am I?*
> *And if not now, when?*
> THE TALMUD

These questions, attributed to Rabbi Hillel,[1] I often share in therapy—with a new patient, perhaps, to say who I am, that is, to give my attitudes, beliefs, values. I imply, and often state openly, that my patient has the choice to remain and work in psychotherapy with one who tries to live by and with such values, or to leave and find another therapist with different values. Patients frequently ask: "How will I know? How can I learn when you should be for yourself and when for others? I am confused." They are asking for a pat answer to obtain structure from me, the authority figure, concerning what is one of the most difficult dilemmas in the existence of every man—that is, each and every man with sensitivity and feeling for others and not for just himself. All this in a world in which John Donne, the Dean of St. Paul's, has admonished us:

---

* "Fortunately, psychoanalysis is not the only way to resolve inner conflicts. Life itself remains a very effective therapy." Karen Horney: *Our Inner Conflicts*, New York, Norton, 1945.

Any man's death diminishes me, because I am involved in mankind, and therefore never send to know for whom the bell tolls; it tolls for thee.[2]

Classically, psychotherapy was considered the "talking cure." Spoken words bring to the listener not only the impact of the meaning of and "free associations" to the words themselves, but also the impact of sound, pitch, rhythm, timbre, accent, aliveness or deadness, feelingness or flatness, and other qualities that affect the listener and the relationship between the speaker and the listener. To bring to the psychotherapeutic encounter symbolic communications other than those inherent in the traditional talking cure serves, then, to enhance the probability of a successful outcome in psychotherapy. Such augmentation can occur:

a. through the patient's writing and reciting his own poetry, or poems written by others, or poetry that has stirred him emotionally or intellectually;

b. through the therapist's sharing a poetic line or couplet that comes to him during a psychotherapeutic session with a patient or group, or by the therapist's acknowledging his appreciation of a poetic utterance by the patient or himself;

c. by bringing into the individual or group session a passage of a poet's writings. A poem that is appropriate and in context to the process and content of the psychotherapeutic hour can be shared. If the therapist is able to trust his patient with himself, he can even use his own poetry.

Another possibility, which I stumbled on recently in working with a 72-year-old presenile patient who had not prepared himself for his declining years, was to write poetry during our session. I encouraged him to write a poem to his wife for their 50th wedding anniversary while I wrote one to my wife, not for our 50th wedding anniversary. He required stimulation, guidance and support en route, as well as repeated assurance that his creative production was in fact worth receiving as an expression of sentiment from him.

Poetry as Therapy

A capacity for appropriateness in timing is a *sine qua non* for successful living and for successful psychotherapy. Timing for some persons is more natural, easy and accurate than it is for others; and often based on intuitive awareness and integration of "what? and how? here and now," is going on intrapsychically and interpersonally and how this relates to past events and people.

During the course of individual or group psychotherapy, situations arise between my patients and me, or in the lives of one or more patients, that suddenly bring to mind the statement of Ecclesiastes. And then I recommend to my patient that he look up Ecclesiastes [3] on his own, or go to my bookshelf for the Bible:

> For everything there is a season, and a time for every matter under heaven:
> a time to be born, and a time to die;
> a time to plant, and a time to pluck up what is planted;
> a time to kill, and a time to heal;
> a time to break down, and a time to build up;
> a time to weep, and a time to laugh;
> a time to mourn, and a time to dance;
> a time to cast away stones, and a time to gather stones together;
> a time to embrace, and a time to refrain from embracing;
> a time to seek, and a time to lose;
> a time to keep, and a time to cast away;
> a time to rend, and a time to sew;
> a time to keep silence, and a time to speak;
> a time to love, and a time to hate;
> a time for war, and a time for peace.

Kahlil Gibran's lines regarding time are helpful for those who overemphasize either the past or the future.

> Yet the timeless in you is aware of life's timelessness,
> And knows that yesterday is but today's memory and tomorrow is today's dream.[4]

> But if in your thought you must measure time into seasons, let each season encircle all the other seasons,
> And let today embrace the past with remembrance and the future with longing.[4]

For patients who are unable to sense that a present opportunity is perhaps crucial in their lives, and that this exact moment is one in which they may be the right person in the right place to risk constructively moving their own and others' growing edge forward, I turn to Shakespeare's lines from *Julius Caesar* (IV, 3):

> There is a tide in the affairs of men
> Which, taken at the flood, leads on to fortune;
> Omitted, all the voyage of their life
> Is bound in shallows and in miseries.

In working with individuals—married couples particularly—and families, I often turn to my bookshelves for T. S. Eliot's *The Cocktail Party*.[5] Having just experienced a moment in which a patient, a couple, or a family have been expressing their frustrations due to the nonfulfillment of the neurotic claims that they make on others and on life, i.e., expecting what they have a right only to hope for, I read them the following passage, its essence spoken in the play by Sir Harcourt-Reilly, the "priest psychiatrist":

> *Celia:* But what, or whom I loved,
> Or what in me was loving, I do not know.
> And if that is all meaningless, I want to be cured
> Of a craving for something I cannot find
> And of the shame of never finding it.
> Can you cure me?
> *Reilly:*   The condition is curable.
> But the form of treatment must be your own choice:
> I cannot choose for you. If that is what you wish,
> I can reconcile you to the human condition,
> The condition to which some who have gone as far as you
> Have succeeded in returning. They may remember
> The vision they have had, but they cease to regret it,
> Maintain themselves by the common routine,
> Learn to avoid excessive expectation,
> Become tolerant of themselves and others,
> Giving and taking, in the usual actions
> What there is to give and take. They do not repine;
> Are contented with the morning that separates
> And with the evening that brings together
> For casual talk before the fire
> Two people who know they do not understand each other,
> Breeding children whom they do not understand
> And who will never understand them.
> *Celia:*   Is that the best life?
> *Reilly:* It is a good life. Though you will not know how good

Till you come to the end. But you will want nothing else,
And the other life will be only like a book
You have read once, and lost. In a world of lunacy,
Violence, stupidity, greed . . . it is a good life.

Though this passage may initially be experienced as cynical, resigned or hopeless, repeated experiencing of its meaning may lead one to appreciate its reality-oriented validity. Mature family life requires us to appreciate that perfect fulfillment of our wishes and wants by others is not the common experience of earth-bound creatures.

A colleague [6] informs me that he often shares Dostoevski's phrase, "Hell is the condition of those who cannot love," [7] and often brings into therapy sessions Hamlet's soliloquy, "To be or not to be. . . ." Sometimes he uses that alone; at others he finds it is appropriate to continue with more: "Whether it is nobler in the mind to suffer/The slings and arrows of outrageous fortune,/ Or to take arms against a sea of troubles,/And by opposing end them (III, 1)."

And he confronts his alcoholic patients with their need to blur out reality rather than to face it by quoting Housman,[8]

"Terence, this is stupid stuff:
Look into the pewter pot
To see the world as the world's not."

In family group therapy, when parental overprotectiveness and domination are a key theme, I sometimes turn to Gibran's *The Prophet* [9] and read his "Children," simple to comprehend even by patients without a college education or special capacities for abstract thinking:

Your children are not your children.
They are the sons and daughters of Life's longing
for itself.
They come through you but not from you,
And though they are with you yet they belong not
to you.

You may give them your love but not your thoughts,
For they have their own thoughts.
You may house their bodies but not their souls,

> For their souls dwell in the house of tomorrow,
> which you cannot visit, not even in your dreams.
> You may strive to be like them, but seek not to
> make them like you.
> For life goes not backward nor tarries with yesterday.

In psychotherapeutic sessions with couples or groups of couples, I often refer to Gibran "On Marriage" [10]:

> But let there be spaces in your togetherness,
> And let the winds of the heavens dance between you.
>
> Love one another, but make not a bond of love:
> Let it rather be a moving sea between the shores of your souls.
> Fill each other's cup but drink not from one cup.
> Give one another of your bread but eat not from the same loaf.
> Sing and dance together and be joyous, but let each one of you be alone,
> Even as the strings of a lute are alone though they quiver with the same music.
>
> Give your hearts, but not into each other's keeping.
> For only the hand of Life can contain your hearts.
> And stand together yet not too near together:
> For the pillars of the temple stand apart,
> And the oak tree and the cypress grow not in each other's shadow.

Gibran has an unusual gift for so communicating the paradoxes of life that clarity arises from confusion, separateness and togetherness can abide in the same house, and self-interest and others' interest can coexist.

Therapy as Poetry

A number of people, I have found, can't stand happiness. The minute that something wonderful happens in their lives, they neurotically "louse it up." A sensitive, robust, intelligent man in his thirties, whose "bull in a china shop" manner frequently denied to himself and others appreciation of sensitive delightful moments in everyday living, brought this poem into his psychotherapeutic session one day. Experiencing and writing it attested to his constructive growth in psychotherapy.

> ON A NOTE OF DELICIOUSNESS
> Did you ever shiveringly tingle?
> Oh, wonder, wonder and more wonder
> Close your eyes and feel the catch in your throat
> Let it spread and engulf you
> Sighing makes it go away too soon
> Sometimes I can't stand the bubbling
> I swallow hard and shorten my breath
> I change the swirling into gas, into a contracted sob
> I can't deeply fool myself for long
> My inside smile cannot be kept a stranger
> My eyes are betrayed by their own gaze
> My memory laughs and coughs up the contagion
> It is useless to restrain my own happiness
> I'll live without the everpresent proof
> Without the confirmation of the mystery
> There is no enchantment in the detective
> I will not kill my own wonder this time

Implicit is his awareness that past destruction of his moments of happiness had often been accomplished through a compulsive overintellectualization, a scientific, objective need to know "why?" and to have visible proof before acknowledging his simple feelings to himself. This poem reflects his growing capacity and willingness to be open to finding his total authentic self through uncertainty, exploration, self-discovery and acceptance.

Cases

In the middle of an individual psychotherapeutic session, a 44-year-old guilt-ridden, marginally depressed bachelor professor of economics, who is often paralyzed with anxieties and self-flagellation, asked: "What is my need to torture myself and feel so guilty that I am not perfect when I am confronted with evidence of my real or fancied inadequacies?" This man—the son of an ineffectual, middle-class father and a guilt-provoking, dominating, overprotective mother—has been driven with high motivation for achievement in life in order to fulfill his mother in ways that his father did not, in order to receive his mother's pat on the head for being "such a good boy." In answer to his question, I said, "Because of your mother in you." He immediately burst into the familiar song: "My mother and me,/And baby makes three,/In my blue heaven" —and then laughed a gallows laugh.

Another example of therapy as poetry occurred when a 19-year-old sensitive, gifted, introspective, brilliant high-school dropout temporarily terminated her therapy to resume her education in her home town, located some distance from New York. She sent a letter to her group, in which she shared her feelings and reflections about its various members. Her words moved us deeply:

> What is it to care
>   And to make that caring into life?
> I have hidden from that part of myself for so long
>   That it hurts to break the bars that hold me.
> I get cut in my own shattering glass.
>   But it is all right if I don't bleed to death.
> Now the most painful thing is that I can't
>   Call up the voice and tone of my own thoughts.
> Only some images slide by,
>   In faint colors and fade in dark ones.
> I would give you these colors
>   If I could catch and hold them.
> But it is not easy to give
>   That kind of love
> That occurs from
>   Only a thing called living.

However, in that and later group meetings, none of her words touched us so much as "Loneliness is just not being friends with oneself."

Another incident of therapy as poetry occurred in a psychotherapy group when a 38-year-old divorced, self-effacing mother of three children, who had been trapped within the immaturity perpetuated in her by her mother, shrieked to her group: "If only my mother would stop looking at me with old eyes." This poetic reference to being looked at or looking at others with *old eyes* was later used frequently by members of her group and myself. It says much that's deeply felt, in few words, literally and figuratively.

While this same patient was functioning as a help-rejecting complainer, she remarked defensively of her "weekend blues": "But I get so very waterlogged on weekends." About two years later, having made a fair amount of progress from passive-dependent defensiveness to a healthier state of satisfying self-assertiveness, she stated in a demanding fashion to her peer group member Sam, "So start unzipping yourself and open up." This remark followed a period in which Sam had been busy talking, in his own help-rejecting fashion, about his difficulties in sharing a dream that he had the night before.

I have emphasized elsewhere [11]:

> The bringing into the group of one's artistic creation, whether a painting or a poem, may be experienced as a gift to the therapist or group or may indicate increasing trust in others; decrease in fear of criticism or needs to be perfect; a desire to bring out what has been taboo as an expression of increasing feeling of self; or a patient may feel his back against the wall and be driven to force himself at least to open up this way.

During the period between Thanksgiving and Christmas of 1955, a patient, Harold R., a 33-year-old schizoid mathematician, compulsively intellectual and socially inept, brought to his psychotherapy group three poems that he had recently composed, one entitled "I Dance." Through the imagery of his poetry, he was able to communicate what his compulsive intellectualization and defensiveness had blocked. It had a profound effect on the whole group and, more specifically, his peer interrelationships. All of them felt much closer to him, were more understanding, and were able to accept him and know him better after the reading than they ever had during the two years they had been together.

One group member cried—Esther, a 42-year-old Brooklyn housewife, who had belabored the group for some time with problems concerning her passive-aggressive husband and her overprotected, rebellious daughter—and shared with the group her interest in poetry, which went back 25 years, and particularly the effect on her of the poetry of John Keats. She had never been able to share this interest in poetry with any adult she respected. The group became aware of the presence of a compartmentalized, refined sensitivity in her, whereas they had experienced her primarily as egocentric and impervious to the deep inner feelings of her husband and daughter.

Another group member, Joan, brought to tears, said that experiencing Harold's poetry produced in her a "startle reaction" that triggered a new warmth towards him. Another group member, Mollie, stated, "I don't understand poetry, so my mind wandered." After a pause she continued, "I do not feel very much—*just* that I had more of a feeling for Harold." Mollie's difficulties in acknowledging "what is," both in herself and others, led her to belittle and only begrudgingly to express positive feelings. Sam spoke of how pleased he was at how receptive the whole group had been to Harold's first attempt at poetry, and he felt that he could now risk bringing to the group the following week some of his photography. He did so; and with the group's continued encouragement of his developing and heretofore secret new direction for his creativity, he eventually gave up his work as Executive Secretary for a Foundation and developed his photographic skills so that today his work receives acclaim both artistic and financial.

Conclusion

Years ago, while looking in *Bartlett's Quotations* for the particular Shakespearean line, "All the world's a stage . . . ," I mistakenly looked in the index under the phrase, "Life is a stage." I experienced serendipity.* Suddenly, in this moment of failure to find the correct line, I had stumbled on the making of a prose-poem of my own. I simply utilized the material in the index, which begins "Life is . . . ," and through some alterations and some additions of my own, created a "poem":

LIFE IS

> This is—is what life is—
> Life is a battle
>   a blunder and a shame
>   a bubble
>   a copycat
>   a dance
>   a disease

* The gift of finding valuable or agreeable things not sought for.

    a dream in the night
    a flower
    a foreign language
    a good thing
    a highway
    a jest
    a ladder infinite stepped
    a lie
    a loom and a game of pool

—and on for nearly 100 more lines.

I have used this "poem" with patients during individual and group psychotherapeutic encounters to demonstrate an experience of a creative process, and to share this impression of what *life is*—which is *all and everything*.

Engle and Carrier [12] claim all and everything as the material of poetry:

> Modern poetry is full of things which many readers never saw in verse before: a brickyard, the evening compared to a patient etherized upon a table, politics, rats on a city dump, the terms of psychology. To the modern poet there is nothing in the world which cannot be put into poetry as long as it can move the reader. For the purpose of poetry is not to provide a soft bed for the tired reader to rest in when he hasn't the strength to do anything more energetic. The purpose of poetry is to expand and intensify your sense of life by giving you examples of one man's look at the intensities of his own life as the intelligence in his head has ordered them into the shape of the poem.

Poems and poetic expressions, created during psychotherapy or brought in from the territoriality of others, can be valuable therapeutic ancillaries. They can express movement, change and growth in intellectual or emotional illiterates, can allow for the evolution of fantasy and imagery towards expansion of one's growing edge, and can sustain and support an individual moving towards a clearer definition of himself, his potentials, and his road towards self-fulfillment.

REFERENCES

1. Rabbi Hillel: The Talmud, Ethics of the Fathers, chap. 1, par. 14.
2. Donne, J.: Meditation xvii, Devotions Upon Emergent Occasions, London, 1624.

3. Ecclesiastes, S. A. II: New York, Simon & Schuster, 1957, p. 758.
4. Gibran, K.: The Prophet, New York, Knopf, 1952, pp. 70-71.
5. Eliot, T. S.: The Cocktail Party, act 2, New York, Harcourt, 1950, pp. 139-140.
6. Kronmeyer, Robert, EdD: Personal communication.
7. Dostoevski, F. M.: Brothers Karamazov.
8. A Shopshire Lad, 62.
9. Gibran, K.: *op. cit.*, pp. 21-22.
10. *Ibid.*, pp. 19-20.
11. Berger, M.: Nonverbal communication in group psychotherapy, Int J Group Psychother 8:161-178, 1958.
12. Reading Modern Poetry, Glenville (Ill.), Scott, Foresman and Company, 1955.

Poetry Therapy with Disturbed Adolescents
Bright Arrows on a Dark River

MORRIS ROBERT MORRISON, MA
Department of English, College of the City of New York

> *Because the literary experience tends to involve both intellectual and emotional facets of the personality in a manner that parallels life itself, the insights attained through literature may be assimilated to the matrix of attitudes and ideas which constitutes character and governs behavior.*
> DR. LOUISE ROSENBLATT [1]

THE EFFECTIVENESS OF POETRY THERAPY is rooted in the power that all literature possesses to assist the individual in his search for self-understanding and emotional liberation. Poetry is especially useful because of its unique qualities: A poem can initiate an intellectual and emotional experience with exceptional immediacy. It is the poet's special gift to involve one with his first lines.

The reader may enter as a guest into the private world of the poet, yet he soon recognizes familiar landmarks. He quickly finds that he is no outsider. Though the poet speaks for himself, the reader discovers his own psyche, his own thoughts and feelings, being expressed. He is not so alone as he had imagined himself. He finds his identity disclosed in the world of a fellow human being. The very pulse of poetry and the pattern of its rhythms appeal to something basic and atavistic in our nature. Poetry, drama, and religion have all evolved from a common ritual whose purpose it was to annul the participant's consciousness of separate personality, exalting him to union with his group and its God.

The secrets of the dance have been traced to our physiology; dance rhythms correspond to those latent in the human system and are capable of evoking them. This, too, is a faculty of poetry. T. S. Eliot has said: "The human soul, in intense emotion, strives to express itself in verse. It is not for me but for neurologists to discover why this is so." The appeal of poetry is to the mind on both its conscious and unconscious levels. Poetry releases one from the world of the particular into the healing ambience of the universal. To one suffering from a sense of alienation, the awareness that another's steps have preceded him on the same lonesome road is comforting for its reassurance. Poets expressing their deepest fears, insecurities, and anxieties give voice to what we feel deepest within ourselves. This helps us find our way back to the mainstream of society.

For the practice of poetry therapy, no special equipment is necessary. All one needs is a room with a fair amount of privacy. Everything else is left to the resources of the imagination. In New York City, recently, "An Evening with Frost" enjoyed a highly successful run. It was presented on a bare stage (no backdrop) with a minimum of props (a table, two chairs, and a lectern), yet all New England came alive to the audience. One saw pastures and woods, farm houses and their interiors, and a west-running brook flowing before one's eyes. It is this very reliance on the role of imagination and the implicit participation that it elicits that account for so much of the therapeutic value of poetry.

Lorene

The first view I had of Lorene was of a girl of sixteen, carelessly dressed and smelling of alcohol, who kept her head averted so that her hair spilled about her face, masking most of it. What she couldn't hide of her skin showed itself covered with eczema. Because of this skin ailment, I was assigned to instruct her at home, a place she never left; she neither paid nor received visits. Her mother, employed as a domestic, was gone most of the day. Her sole companion, her grandmother, 75, appeared just as withdrawn as my pupil.

Though in the early part of the term she had come to accept my presence as her teacher, she made no attempt to improve her appearance. Although she gave up resorting to liquor, she still seemed to wish only to hide behind her hair, behind a book, or, as quickly as possible after I left, in any one of the rooms of the railroad flat in Bedford Stuyvesant. One could only guess at the extent of the agony experienced by this adolescent girl. Along with the emotional debasement caused by her disfigurement, there was the accompanying physical pain of her constantly itching skin. During our lessons she would claw savagely at her face. Still, she would not go when the clinic referred her to a hospital where a series of tests might suggest a cure.

It was Lorene's ambition to graduate from high school with a commercial diploma and to secure employment some day as an office secretary. Her typing was neat and careful. She was orderly in her bookkeeping, and she applied herself diligently to her lessons in stenography. Her reaction to literature, however, while dutiful, was uninspired.

In the course of our work in English we came upon a poem by Emily Dickinson [*]:

> I'm Nobody! Who are you?
> Are you—Nobody—too?

I studied Lorene's face. For the first time she was not pretending interest. She brightened at:

> Then there's a pair of us!
> Dont tell! they'd banish us—you know!
>
> How dreary—to be—Somebody!
> How public—like a Frog—
>
> To tell your name—the livelong June—
> To an admiring Bog!

Something remarkable followed. Lorene asked me for information.

[*] *The Poems of Emily Dickinson*, ed. Thomas H. Johnson, Cambridge (Mass.), The Belknap Press of Harvard University Press, 1958. Pages 206–207. With permission.

She wanted to learn something of the poet's life. I told her the story of Emily Dickinson—of her idiosyncracies, her isolation, her unhappiness, of the posthumous discovery of her poems and her brilliant position today in world literature. She was fascinated. She seemed to have found a rapport with Miss Dickinson.

Not all of Emily Dickinson's poems were so easy to understand as the first we studied, but Lorene's enthusiasm for the poet, whose life story she reread several times, helped her, with my assistance, to overcome the special difficulties in the writing. This eagerness to learn about poetry and poets' lives was carried through to an interest in Edna St. Vincent Millay and others.

One day when I came to see her, she had brushed her hair away from her face and had bound it together with a ribbon. Apparently she no longer needed to hide from anyone. She began to go to church. During the summer, treatment at the hospital improved the condition of her skin. That fall she returned to regular classes at her high school. I heard from her later: she was doing nicely both socially and scholastically. When I saw her recently, the eczema had disappeared.

It is clear that Lorene's problem was emotional as well as medical. The lines of communication between her and the outside world needed mending before anything could be done for her at the hospital. The line, "I'm nobody," must have moved her strongly, reflecting as it probably did her own opinion of herself. Additional defenses fell with the question, "Are you nobody, too?" Lorene was also undoubtedly gratified to be included in the admonition "Don't tell—They'd banish us you know." Emily Dickinson had reached her, and Lorene in turn reached toward the poet. In Emily Dickinson she could identify with someone as lonely and as "odd" as herself. This was apparent in her eagerness to memorize as many of Dickinson's poems as possible. Pretty clearly she sought to incorporate some part of the poet into her being. After this discovery of kinship with a celebrated writer, she could accept her own self. When Lorene brushed the hair away from her face and permitted the world to look at her, she had traveled an incalculable distance.

Barbara

I was on my way to John Jay High School when an attractive girl suddenly opened the door of a parked car and rushed towards me, greeting me warmly. She had heart-warming news. She was doing well at school and had recently won a scholarship to art school. It was Barbara, radiating vitality and charm. In appearance and manner, she was incredibly transformed from the hostile withdrawn fifteen-year-old, dressed in sloppy jeans, who had been one of my home-bound pupils.

When I first visited her at her home, two years prior to this encounter, I found her drawn into her chair as into a corner. She seemed prepared to defend herself against any intruder and from the beginning was not only openly hostile to her mother but critical of everything and everyone in her environment. When I attempted to interest her in the term's work, she yawned in my face. She soon let me know that she had little use for me or my teaching and couldn't wait for me to leave. Her attitude seemed to scream out, "Leave me alone!"

From her school records, I learned that Barbara had been an excellent student in English. During one of our lessons, I asked her what writers she liked best. In her estimation, none of those she had studied in school were any good. Her current idols were Jack Kerouac and Allen Ginsberg. When I said that I greatly admired Ginsberg's *Kaddish*, she seemed surprised that a square like me could see anything worthwhile in the beat writers. For my master's thesis, I had made an extensive study of the Symbolist poets, Rimbaud and Mallarmé, predecessors of today's *avant garde*. When Barbara heard this she seemed slightly impressed. When I compared Rimbaud to Ginsberg, she listened. I suggested to her, later, that in place of the conventional home work she write a poem. She could select any subject and write in any way she chose. At the following session, when I inquired about the assignment, she said she hadn't done it. Later she did bring out, almost reluctantly, six lines she had written. I praised them highly, though I took exception to the phrasing of one of them. Subsequently she wrote another poem and, as the term progressed, went on to produce an impressive series of highly creditable writings.

The following poem reveals Barbara's talent and illustrates the beginning of a new insight into herself.

>Perhaps if I tried to communicate
>To someone I don't know
>Who wouldn't care
>And wouldn't think of me
>And would carry nothing of me away—
>Or to something not committed to listen
>Some object, some state of being
>That couldn't feel . . .
>
>I've only negative expressions
>Emptiness
>You would be listening only to the sound of no sound
>
>In "you" or "I" there is nothing real
>What is there in front of my eyes
>Besides objects?

She continued to write poems of unexpected merit into which she poured her tortured feelings. "What is Next?" is worthy of inclusion in any anthology.

What is next?
This is the time I pose the question
When there is no wash hanging out in the black night on the line
When little drops of water are falling from the faucet
And the poison food isn't doing much good killing that hungry fat mouse
I look around the room
      And say out loud
Because there isn't anybody around to hear me
      What is next?
All my fingernails are in my stomach
And I want something more than this can of Hawaiian Punch
      Which is too cold and is
      Hurting the back of my front teeth
How would it be if I just went out the door and tried to be friends
      With the few people on the street
Ignoring the quietness of the night
And yell to them
      What is next?
And then run in and slam the door and stand on the kitchen chair
      And raise my arms and feel how the heat is rising
Uncertain, with no answer,
Ashamed, for the embarrassment

So now my teeth are brushed and the involuntary muscles are putting
    Me under the kitchen table
Humming and singing quietly to myself
As the sun comes and night begins again—comes rolling out from in back
    Of my tongue   What is next?

Shortly after the composition of this poem, we passed a significant little milestone. At the conclusion of a lesson, I said as usual before leaving, "Good-bye, Barbara. Have a good day." For the first time she responded, "You too, Mr. Morrison." She began to take more care of her appearance and pursued her studies with greater interest. She seemed particularly intrigued with solving problems in geometry, and responded with a kind of hunger to its coherence and structure. Her homework assignments, from this point on, were done conscientiously.

Old friendships that had been cut off were renewed. She talked about these friends with me. Much of the original tension in our relationship disappeared. There was no doubt that by this time Barbara had reestablished real communication with the world and that there were other things in front of her eyes "besides objects." She did well that June in her Regents examinations and, on the recommendation of the psychotherapist who had worked with her during this period, returned to John Jay High School in September.

Setting into order words that dramatized her cowering posture and her dissatisfaction with the outside world helped her to see herself more clearly in her relationship with that world. She learned to externalize her emotions and become more objective about them. Questioning her ability to communicate helped her to realize that she wanted to communicate. Seeing herself huddled under the table helped her to understand that her real wish was to be out in the open. Even though these poems may prove to be forerunners of distinguished work to come, what is most meaningful at this point is that their creation assisted importantly in redirecting Barbara to a rewarding rapport with life.

Francisco

It was in the orthopedic ward at King's Hospital that Francisco, a sixteen-year-old boy of Puerto Rican origin, first came to my attention. The following poem, done as a class assignment, was written with his left hand, because his right was badly mangled, and it tells of the events that led to his hospitalization.

Bad dreams
What do they mean?
That's what I'm going to explain
There were two dreams
Similar to my accident.

In the first
I charged at some one
Or at myself
I was trying to kill some one
Or some thing
But in that some one
I saw myself.

That was my first nightmare
With the feeling of fear and death
Right upon me.

I remember seeing myself
Going around in a continuous circle
And in that circle there were two people
One of them was me.
And the other seemed to be me, also.
That's what I could not believe.

I awoke in my bed
Half-scared to death
Then my mother came into my room
And asked in Spanish,
"Que te pasa?"

And I said,
"Nada pasa, Mamma."
Then she said,
"O. K. Good night," and left.

I was afraid to go back to sleep

So prayed till morning came.
I began to believe the nightmare wasn't coming back
But it did come back in the same way
In a second dream
So right there, I knew
Those two dreams meant something.
I knew the fear would be back
But I did not know when it would be coming back.

It did come back
On September 23
I did everything normally.
I ate
And went to school.
But as evening came
I started getting nervous
And cold.
Then something hit me
It spoke to me
"Get a knife!"
And I went straight out
To find my destiny.

I got my knife.
As I walked, feeling jittery and strange
I got more nervous
Then, I thought
I should get high
To do what I must do.
I bought booze and was high.

I caught guts
And went to face it out
The face in the dream—my friend
I was scared
But I showed heart
Only too much

With my blade
I charged at him
To cut him open.
But with a wire
He had the best of me.
Did he disgrace me, Man.
I knew it
As soon as the aerial slashed my face.

It was anger and fear
That hit me that night.
Anger began piling up on me
As I kept fighting.
He was my friend
But I knew right there
That I must fight with him
When I stabbed him
I knew it was going to be the beginning
Of a long nightmare.
As soon as the aerial touched my face
The pain was like in a dream
But this was for real.
I couldn't believe it was right there.
It was like the nightmare falling upon me
I acted like an animal.
I wanted to kill my friend.
I charged, but as I charged him
He slashed me.

I fell to my knees
He kept on slashing
I was in great pain
Then another friend
Saw what was happening.
He picked up a garbage can
And chased him off
I got up from the ground and touched my face.
I felt the cut and blood
It was unbelievable.

I ran to South 9th street to the Center
Because I did not know
Where else to go.

All my friends saw my face, and asked,
"What happened?"
I started going crazy.
I kicked and hit at everyone in sight
My friends held me so that I could cool down.
One of the counselors took me to the basement
To wash the blood off.

When I took the water in my hands
I began to think
How I had disgraced myself.
I couldn't show myself to my parents.
Then my madness got to me.
I didn't care
About myself or the world anymore.
I turned around.
The first thing I saw
Was a window.
I hit at it.

As my hand pushed through the glass
I felt funny and tired.
I did not know what was happening
I cursed like any thing.

Even God!
When I stopped cursing
I looked down and saw my hand hanging.
I panicked like a woman

And bled like a dog.
Just then the counselor came in
And grabbed my hand
I yelled
I felt so weak
Like when a bunch of guys are on top of you
And when they finish
You try to get up

I begged the counselor
"Kill me, please.
Please kill me.
I don't want to face life anymore."
He put my hand in the sink
And kept it there.
I thought he put water on it
But it was the blood that was pouring out
Then he told me to cool it
Or I'd bleed to death.
I played it smart and cooled down.

He yelled for help
Someone came down.

It was another counselor
He pulled off my shirt
And tied it to my triceps
To stop the blood
Then the Priest came
And confessed me.
I was afraid to die
So prayed to Him up there.

After a while the cops came
That's when I stopped praying.
They asked me what happened to my hand

So I told them
Then they asked about my face.
I said I fell down.
They didn't believe me.
They called me a liar.
The ambulance came
And took me to Greenpoint Hospital.
That's when I really felt bad

When all these people saw me
I knew what those people thought about me.
They said in their minds
"Look at that hoodlum
With the scar on his face."
I could tell by their eyes.
When they took me to Emergency

I heard one of the doctors say
"This boy needs surgery."
Man,
I never thought I'd be operated on.
I once saw a picture
But me? That's something new.
When they had me in O.R. they said to me
"Sorry, son, but that hand has got to come off."
I couldn't talk so I began to cry.
Then the doctor told my mother
What was going to happen.
My mother said, "No"
She asked to transfer me to another hospital.
They took me to Kings County Hospital.
There they saved me and my hand.

Here I am in the hospital
Still waiting.
The doctors told me I am very lucky
I didn't lose hand or life.
They are trying to fix my hand
But they told me
That my hand won't be like it used to be
But God! I hope I have learned my lesson

The night of September 23, 1965	Thank God.
I almost knew what death meant.	I've ruined my hand for life.
I was a fool	Please God, give me the power to get used to it
But I am glad I haven't come to my end.	I only pray for that!

In our city slum areas, as the the young come into conflict with the cultural patterns of their elders, scorning them for their inadequacies and shrugging off their authority, a new family comes into being. This is The Street, which tramples on gentleness and sensitivity. Here the boys develop loyalties to the street gang and to its leader—frequently a psychopathic adolescent lionized for his ruthlessness. The "turf" is the testing ground of their manhood. For the boys virility is symbolized in the switchblade. In a hail of broken bottles, bricks, stones and other missiles, they battle a foe from another block, and in this "rumble" establish their masculine role.

They adopt a smooth vocabulary: "man," "cool," "turf," living up to the gang ideal. Under cover of bravado they conceal from each other their secret fears, their anxieties and insecurities. It is cool to be conspicuously dressed in tight pants with slash pockets and to wear boots with Cuban heels or sharply pointed shoes. Their girl friends help to romanticize this way of life.

With a kind of swagger, Francisco carried this street style into the hospital ward. He affected a Van Dyke beard. He addressed me as "Teach," and asked me to call him by his gang name, "Frenchy." Exceedingly cavalier about his lessons, he proved clever at devising excuses for failing to perform his scheduled assignments. I permitted him to "outsmart" me and, since he enjoyed telling me about his gang activities, these stories became the focal point for some of our lessons. As his stories of certain skirmishes reminded me of the legends of the *Iliad*, I took the occasion to retell several adventures from this epic poem. He was fascinated. This was my cue to borrow a copy of Homer's poetry from the library and lend it to him.

The hospital nurses told me that he stayed awake all night reading. They couldn't imagine his being interested in anything but comic books. Francisco, however, was insatiable in his eagerness to know all the stories in the *Iliad* and to memorize the names of the heroes. Achilles, Hector, Diomed rolled off his lips as though he had been raised on them. I had him retell their adventures in writing. He caught the rhythms and language of the text so amazingly well that I could scarcely believe he had not plagiarized. I checked; he had not copied. The astonishing thing was that only a short time before this he seemed unable to spell the simplest words and appeared to know nothing of the structure of a sentence. Yet, describing the death of Patroclus, he wrote: "Achilles heard and saw the Trojans coming upon the Greek camp and Hector slaying many Greeks but only the mighty Diomed still showed courage." I could not praise him sufficiently, and he accepted my commendations as though they were food and drink. Recognizing his hunger for praise, I found many opportunities to tell him how well I thought of him. Since he had spoken of his accident, I asked him to write about it. He did. I was moved by the emotional pitch of his writing. Francisco was proud to hear me refer to his talent. Shortly afterwards, he shaved his beard, surrendered his swagger, and began to comport himself with dignity about the ward. He spoke to me about his future, of his new faith in education, and of his desire to marry and become a family man. After he left the hospital, I received word from the psychiatric social worker assigned to his school that she was impressed with Francisco's changed attitude. A plan for vocational rehabilitation was being prepared with his full cooperation.

It would appear that somewhere in the Homeric skirmishes he had dropped the false values of the gang along with his haunted sense of fear and anger. He was able to accept his true role, that of Francisco, a young man with a future. Gone was "Frenchy," cocky but scared; gone also the theatrical routine that led nowhere.

Katina

Her hometown newspaper predicted a glorious career for Katina as, full of romantic hopes and dreams, she prepared to embark from Greece to study in the United States. Her married sister, now a resident in obstetrics at a Brooklyn hospital, had preceded her. They shared an apartment and Katina was about to enter the second half of her senior year at Prospect Heights High School when she developed glomerulonephritis, necessitating home instruction after five weeks of hospitalization.

Lethargic and depressed, she emanated defeat and hopelessness. She had experienced a crushing sense of failure at school. Eager for popularity among her classmates, she felt that they, and some teachers as well, had ridiculed her because of her awkwardness in English. She felt that both academically and socially her adjustment had been disappointing. New acute physical pain brought on by a renal infection added to her despondency.

Aloof at first, she later asked me to address her as Tina. Her notebooks were replete with doodles. When subsequently she permitted me to examine them, I found among the drawings an impressive representation of Christ, portraying His agony as he dragged the cross to Calvary. The exhausted look in Katina's eyes showed that she knew only too well the crushing weight that she dramatized with this great realism. Her other drawings were of coffins and their tenants, of weeping figures and skeletons—all indications of her preoccupation with death and loss. Obviously, Tina possessed extraordinary sensitivity and the talent to express her emotions in artistic terms. I was not surprised to discover later that she could respond to the poetry of Keats and Shelley with an instinctive appreciation of their intent. Having noted her absorption in Keat's "Ode to a Nightingale," I related the mood of the poem to the poet's state of mind and asked her to describe her own emotions in verse form for her next assignment. Her deep-seated unhappiness was visible at once in her first poem.

AUTUMN
My dreams
Yellow leaves, lifeless, dead.
My life
Skies gray, dark, filled with rain.
My hope
Pale, cowardly, scared.

The autobiographical reference is too explicit to be missed. I was understandably lavish in my praise and encouragement of her talent. A succession of gifted verses followed this first effort, all alike, sad and heartbreaking.

CONTRAST

Creation adorns the earth with flowers.
I feel the beating of swallows' wings.
The white mountain gets younger.
But dawn has not arrived in my heart.
Only affliction nests there

WINTER

In my heart
Where cold winter reigns
Are the icicle tears
Of two nightingales
Who died, singing together
Of their golden love.

Shortly afterwards, writing of fate as a woman, she referred to the sterility of her life:

MY DESTINY

She reminded me that eyes were made for tears
She instructed me to respect darkness
My destiny stands over me like a strange lover.

Here she projects the terror that haunted her previous doodling.

Give me your little hand,
The only treasure of my life.
And don't leave me alone.
And don't withdraw from my side.
Now that there appears at the turn of the street
The elevation on which they have set up my cross.

Disillusion is brilliantly described in

EXPERIENCE

Remember
The bright sunsets in the bamboo of your youth
When you sang
Against the shouting of the wind?
Then you were a hollow reed
Easily broken,
Now that you've become a tree
Filled with substance,
You understand so well
The beauty of the sunset
But you don't sing anymore.

The first school day after Easter, I arrived at Tina's apartment for the morning lesson. There was no response to my ring. I was about to leave when Tina's sister opened the door. She had been sleeping and had no idea where my pupil might be. We were both beginning to feel alarmed when I heard some one running up the stairs. It was Tina, out of breath, her face radiant, her eyes sparkling. She had left the house at six o'clock that morning to observe the sunrise in a nearby park. Then to commemorate the event, she had composed a poem, which she gladly showed me. It provided unmistakable evidence of her return to psychic health.

DAWN

The sun has arrived in the sky
Saying "Goodby" to the dark daughter of time.
Life begins with the kiss of the sun.
The sun is a young boy looking at me, lustful,
With his large beautiful eyes.
I am so pretty when his rays caress
These velvet petals of mine that
Barely touch my delicate green trunk.
Everything is so peaceful, so still,
That I can almost hear the heart beat of this radiant blond boy.
It is a pity that I cannot sing the beauty of the dawn,
But God made me a flower,
Reflecting the miracle of this lovely morning.

The imagery of her later poetry continued to bear the imprint of that radiant morning.

LOVE

Your embraces were created to hold me
And my dreams.
Your eyes to incise my figure,
To let me exist.
Your hands to take the colors
Of my sorrow,
And hang smiles everywhere.

In June, after graduation, she was to return to her family in Greece for a visit. Before she boarded the plane, she confided to me, "I'm happy. I'm so happy." So by unburdening herself of an obsessive despair through the medium of words, she had successfully reintegrated a personality previously damaged by maladjustment at school and the deleterious effects of a protracted illness. I believe that she has also produced some truly memorable verse.

The metaphors of Tina's tribute to poetry reveal the therapeutic magic it has held for her.

TO POETRY

You shine on my bitter days
Like a sky full of stars
Like the sun that breaks his arrows
On a dark river,
My beloved poetry
Folds my soul into blue elements
So that I can be water,
Tempest, or flame.

REFERENCES

1. Rosenblatt, Louise: Literature as Exploration, New York, D. Appleton-Century, 1938.
2. Drew, Elizabeth: Discovering Poetry, New York, Norton, 1933.

CHAPTER 8

Thoughts on the Poets' Corner

KENNETH BURKE, LITT D

Poet, Novelist, Critic

Prior to form, the earth was "void, and darkness was upon the face of the deep." The linkage of form to creativity has rendered it a central concern for the artist, the philosopher, the psychologist. It is in these merging roles that Kenneth Burke has for many years conducted his major excursions into the province of form. His earlier references to art forms as "equipment for living" remind us of Frost's statement that "where there is doubt there is form for us to go on with. Anyone who has achieved the least form to be sure of it is lost to tht larger excruciations. The artist, the poet, might be expected to be most aware of such assurance, but it is really everybody's sanity to feel it and live by it."[1]

In his essay here, Burke grants that "expressing the repressed is intrinsically therapeutic." Once before, in "Literature as Equipment for Living,"[2] *he had illustrated how works of art might be considered as "strategies" for "purification, propitiation and desanctification, consolation, admonition and exhortation." In the psychodynamics of form are discoverable "equipments for living." Yet in considering the "demonology" of the creative process, we are admonished that there do exist certain "complicating factors that threaten the result." He brings to the fore such psychoanalytic concepts as incomplete repression, overdetermination and the judgmental vs the nonjudgmental aspects of language and form.* MRM

LET'S START WITH A MINIMAL PROPOSITION of this sort: All other things being equal, there's relief in expressing the repressed. Obviously, the situation can readily become altered. For instance, though the expression may give *immediate* relief, it may be of a sort that threatens to involve *subsequent* discomfort. Here's an example by analogy, involving not poetic but alcoholic expression:

104

> That night he told off his boss,
> It all seemed so simple at the time.
> What a load was lifted from his mind,
> But the next day, oof! [3]

The most exacting conditions of this sort are to be found in the case of works that bring the writer into conflict with powerful and repressive political authorities. Recall how Aristophanes, when under pressure from the politicians, aimed his comic barbs instead at Socrates and Euripides, who were safer victims of his poetic enterprise.

Insofar as Aristophanes was first of all a comic poet, attached to his trade as such rather than to any particular quarrel, even a self-censored choice of comic victims may have provided "expression enough," though a sufficiently expert analysis of his text might show how it also served as a *deflected* expression of his attacks on those same political authorities to whom not only he but even the butts of his jokes (Socrates and Euripides) were essentially opposed.

In any case, our point is: Whereas we begin with the (quite probably) sound assumption that the expression of the repressed is intrinsically therapeutic, there can be complicating factors that threaten this result. Let's consider a somewhat random list offered purely as illustrations:

The poet may become "conspiratorial," in planning to hide his identity behind a pseudonym.

He may fear lest his notes fall into the wrong hands, or lest they be stolen by a rival.

He may become involved in painful aesthetic conflicts that are even irrelevant to the repressions for which his expression was artistic medicine.

Insofar as he modifies his message for protective purposes, he may feel guilty.

Since imagery is ambiguous, he may become expert in an imagistic style of expression whereby confession and secrecy become interchangeable terms. Such deflective kind of expression allows the poet to confront his situation with an accuracy that is astounding (once you know how to decode it); yet he himself may be blind to the ultimate extrapoetic implications of the very motives he has thus deflectively encoded.

Presumably much the same motives that are conceivable in cases of explicit censorship also operate in the sheerly moralistic ("conscientious") censoring of the imagination, except that in such cases the strands that we have here isolated can be telescoped into a simultaneity. I mean, whereas in an explicit case of political censorship an author might first clearly conceive of a vigorous attack on an opponent, and then deliberately ask himself how much he should tone things down in order to be discreetly self-protective, the poet can enact a more "radical" kind of self-censorship whereby his project originally occurs to him in terms that already embody the "spontaneous" (and "unconscious") censoring of the problematical motive. (For instance, the poet's censorable and censored erotic hankerings after his mother might be symbolically both expressed and disguised *at the start* by the "spontaneous" emergence of plans for a story about a sick inventor who fell in love with his nurse.) And, when such integration of expression is implicit in the imaginative project itself, the various other strands I have mentioned could also be implicitly part of the expression's motivational background.

Add, now, a further likelihood. No expression emerges simply out of repressions. It is also transforming all sorts of nonsymbolic things into symbols—and many of such expressions did not arise out of the morally repressed; they were simply hard to express, as it's not clear just what one is seeing at a distance, whether or not the thing one is trying to see is something that one does not really want to see. A poem, like a dream, must find analogies for much more than the repressed. (Another way of saying so is to say that a given expression is "overdetermined.")

Indeed, is it not likely that a large part of any poetic act derives simply from implications of the given symbol-system (as one language suggests a pun that other languages don't)? Hence, some kinds of expression are attempts simply to solve problems, or exploit possibilities, local to the given system.

Furthermore (if we may at this point introduce a phenomenological observation), there is a kind of "technical guiltiness" intrinsic to the nature of communication as such. Even before beginning his poem, the poet is "indebted" to his audience, however vague the conception of his audience may be. True, he may be talking only to an idealized portion of himself (for "internal dialogue" is intrinsic to the nature of language-using).

Thus, as regards the purely *formal* considerations I am now trying to deal with, his audience may exist but "in principle." Yet there are obligations of form implicit in the norms or "proprieties" of expression as such (since the expression can't depart far from the limits imposed by the rules of its particular symbol-system). That is, there are self-judgments inherent in the nature of the medium one is using, though different poets employing the same idiom will necessarily differ as to exactly what such "proprieties" are—hence their poems will incorporate correspondingly different self-judgments. Similar considerations apply to the use of poetic forms. (For instance, even if a contemporary poet were deliberately to attempt writing a tragedy exactly as Greek tragedy was written at the time of Sophocles, the use of such formal "proprieties," with their corresponding "self-judgments," would involve an attitude of "indebtedness" to his contemporary audience quite different from the indebtedness of an ancient poet using those same forms at the height of their traditional vitality and expectation.)

The very success of one work already rebukes its author with the uneasy question, "But how about next time? Is this the end of you?" And the question is particularly apt inasmuch as a work can attain its formal ideal only by truly being the *culmination* of something. But though this kind of "technical guiltiness" can in itself be a cause of incessant unrest, it also provides a notable "humane" incentive. For there is a sense in which the poet is forced, by the sheer necessities of form, to attempt *revising even himself*. He cannot be content with the mere spontaneous expression of any personal problem in its immediacy. He must seek modes of artistic *appeal* (the "debt" theme again).

Simplest example: Though in its nonformal, purely personal motivation, his work may have been rooted in nothing better than spite against a rival, in the writing of it he must resort to many inventions that are not related to mere personal spite. And, most humanely of all, lo! he can do the best job only if he can somehow humanize the ideal portrait of his rival. So we need not be surprised if there even comes a point at which the spite is wholly transformed, if only for a flash. Such are the paradoxes of *formal* indebtedness, at least in principle. And since the poet is formally guilty insofar as he is not a man of formal principles, even slovenly form presses towards the ideal outcome.

Form, as so conceived, also has the humane advantage of presenting the problematically censorable under controlled conditions which, by the very nature of the case, permit of much expression that could otherwise but remain underground or wholly criminal. The logic of expression seeks ever to set up institutionally a place where, without fear of punishment, one can go and curse the king. And though the aim is on its face troublesome, also obviously it helps by perennially scheming to move things in the direction of freedom.

In any case, much of the exhilaration in the so-called "creativity" of expression must reside in the fact that the given symbolic act somehow encompasses a great complexity of motives (many of which can never be explicitly differentiated in the sense that psychoanalysis aims to isolate some "primal scene" as a motivating factor, or in the sense that imagery of food or violence can serve as surrogates for erotic impulses). Also, there is the possibility that the profoundest works of art embody a "primal scene" not in the sense of some past situation enigmatically rediscovered, but rather in the sense that "in principle" it symbolically and "medicinally" sums up some notable aspect of our existence. "Priority" in this sense is not temporal at all, but more like the kind of priority that metaphysics aims at, if you will agree with my notion that the metaphysician is saying in effect: "Existence as I understand it is the kind of situation that would result if it were grounded in such-and-such an ultimate situation beyond the immediately empirical."

A few attendant considerations suggest themselves.

Art would probably be most therapeutic if it were never identified with any particular artist. "Mine" is one devil of a word. Maybe the nearest an *ego* can come to total "cure" is by suicide, and that isn't much of a solution. In any case, the communicative aspect of art is our best step by way of a substitute. Commercialism raises trouble insofar as it asks that the artist turn spontaneity into a business. Yet it helps provide a forum for the expression of the problems that it raises—and the mere existence of a forum can call forth goods that would not otherwise have arisen. (From forum to form?)

Where speculations on these matters are concerned, I would propose one admonitory rule of thumb. Since, in past eras, many of the world's keenest minds treated central problems of human motivation in theological terms, I devoutly join forces with those who believe that one should always ask, at least experimentally, whether any theological account of motives can be shown to have a secular analogue. In the case of our present quandaries, I'd naturally think of the problematical relationship between churchmen's theories of "demonology" and contemporary concerns with "creativity."

Thus, at least for heuristic purposes, we should ask whether one possible embarrassing analogue should always be kept in mind. Even if one's dream has been an ecstatic vision of Christ or Mary, the churchmen admonished that it might be a delusion imposed upon the dreamer by the Prince of Darkness. And similarly, should we not be on guard lest "creativity" escape proper quizzical inspection? I mean: Creativity should not bear the mask of purely and simply a "good" word.

Rather, keeping in mind possible secular analogues of the demonological, should we not always be on the look-out for systematic ways of distinguishing between "creativity" that heals and "creativity" that endangers (including further twists whereby a poorly paid and poor-paying artist might, through the creative sacrificing of himself, contribute to the comfort of trivial people for whom his dedicated sufferings provide a conversation-piece at cocktail hour)? There is much here still to be puzzled over.

I shall never forget an incident among some young dancers who were sportively improvising. It came one particular fellow's turn. He started to dance—and all of a sudden something electric and almost terrifying happened. This was something else. No fun here: this was for keeps. The dance instructor, the old pro, confided to me that he was worried. Somehow or other, that poor kid was bringing more of himself to market than a dancer safely could. It's as with the, until now unsung, adolescent football hero who split his heart, when almost winning the game for Siwash High.

P.S. These notes might not help prove that it's easy to *cure* a poet. But they might help indicate why it's hard to *kill* one.

REFERENCES

1. Frost, R.: *in* Thompson, Lawrence: Robert Frost: The Early Years, New York, Holt, 1966, pp. 22–23.
2. Burke, K.: Literature as equipment for living, *in* Philosophy of Literary Form, Baton Rouge, Louisiana State Univ Press, 1941 (Vintage Books, 1957), Second unabridged edition, Baton Rouge, Louisiana State Univ Press, 1967.
3. Burke, K.: Alky, Me Love, *in* Collected Poems 1915-1967, Berkeley (Cal), Univ Calif Press, 1968.

CHAPTER 9

Validation of Poetry Therapy as a Group Therapy Technique

KENNETH F. EDGAR, PhD   RICHARD HAZLEY, MA
Indiana State University of Pennsylvania

> *When power narrows the areas of man's concern, poetry reminds him of the richness and diversity of his existence. When power corrupts, poetry cleanses. For art establishes the basic human truth which must serve as the touchstone of our judgment.*
> JOHN F. KENNEDY

ALTHOUGH MOST COLLEGES AND UNIVERSITIES offer some form of individual counseling to students with personal problems, few appear to offer group therapy within the campus clinic. Nor is it difficult to understand why. Students are reluctant to be "open" in the presence of peers who might recoil from revealed dependency, impoverished personality, sexual inversion and the like. Yet this openness may be the crucial variable, as Mowrer states [18]:

Would it be too arbitrary an assumption to propose that people become clients because they do not disclose themselves in some optimal degree to the people in their life? I have come to believe that it is not communication per se which is fouled up in the mentally ill. Rather it is a foul-up in the process of knowing others, and in becoming known to others.

Considering group therapy at Slippery Rock State College, we became interested in poetry therapy, a technique in group psychotherapy being pioneered at Cumberland Hospital in Brooklyn by Jack Leedy, MD, psychiatrist, and Eli Greifer, poet therapist. It seemed possible that group discussion through poetry might provide a means by which members could know and become known by others. It was felt that by using a poem as a starting point and as an objectification of known but inarticulate feelings, the members of a group might be provided with the means to open themselves through the interpretation of poetry, however obliquely at first, that conventional group therapy did not offer.

The choice of poetic material, according to Leedy,[18] should be guided by the isoprinciple developed in music therapy: the material should express the same mood or emotional state that the patient is experiencing. Leedy suggests that depressed patients are helped by poems that are sad and gloomy; through them, they recognize that they are not alone in their depression. Eli Greifer[4] stresses memorization as cogent in the therapeutic process: "We have here no less than a psychograft-by-memorization in the inmost reaches of the brain, where the soul can allow the soul-stuff of stalwart poet-prophets to 'take' and to become one with the spirit of the patient." Greifer's thesis[5] on poetry therapy finds support from Reik,[20] who writes of the therapeutic potential of poetry.

The greatest actors do not enter into the personality of a tragic hero, but they become Hamlet, so to speak. They do not imitate his experience, they actually experience his destiny, with the help of the same psychical possibilities within themselves, and of memory-traces within their own experience. Poetry has touched upon a fragment of buried life, has stirred the actor's own hidden possibilities.

Observing the enthusiasm of patients at Cumberland Hospital's Mental Hygiene Clinic, the authors attempted an experiment to evaluate the effectiveness of poetry therapy as a group technique in the college counseling clinic.

Procedure

Sixteen students who had applied for individual counseling at the college clinic and had taken a battery of projective tests were asked whether they would be willing to participate in an experiment involving poetry as a tool in group psychotherapy. It was explained to the students that they had been invited to participate because they shared some common problems with each other. No further details were offered. All of the students, eight males and eight females, accepted. On the basis of a psychiatric interview and the evidence from the projective battery, it was believed that the common problem experienced by the group was inadequate psychosexual identification and failure to become weaned from the "family of orientation." All 16 were either juniors or seniors at the college; the IQ range was 108–135, the mean 120. By sex, the mean IQ was 127 for the girls and 113 for the boys. The group was then divided by sex and each of the members was asked to draw numbers, either one or two, from a hat. The eight boys and girls who had drawn the number one were assigned to the control group, and control group members were informed that, should they wish, they could be admitted into treatment or seek treatment outside the college at any time, and at the beginning of the second semester they could be admitted into the experimental group.

PRETEST

The pretest battery, administered in September, 1964, consisted of:

a. An MMPI profile [3, 8]
b. The Draw-A-Person test [7, 15]
c. Cards 6BM and 7BM of the TAT
d. Card #1 of the Rorschach

The MMPI, the DAP, and the TAT were evaluated as measures of dependency. Card #1 of the Rorschach was interpreted, as Ledwith's text [12] suggests, as "being indicative of either the parental figure with whom the child experiences the greatest conflict, the relationship of the child to his parents, and/or a condensed self-image."

METHOD

The experimental group met every Thursday, from 4:00 to about 6:00 PM, in a comfortable room designated for group therapy. Sessions were always informal. The participants sat around a large table; coffee was served and, on occasion, cakes or cookies. The only structuring was that of a simulated family setting with the cotherapists placed at opposite ends of the table. It was hoped that this setting would encourage transference and that the presence of two males would not preclude the feeling of family which the cotherapists desired to create. As Clark [2] has pointed out, a "patient may think of a male analyst as both a father and a mother figure, at once, for the therapist's anima is in the situation as well as his ego." Or, as described by Lundlin and Aronov [14]:

. . . a simulated family setting is created by the presence of two authority figures. . . . The physical characteristics of the therapists become less important than subtle psychological differences. . . . One therapist will be seen as more aggressive and masculine the other as more protective and feminine.

Poems were selected that expressed feelings thought to be troubling members of the group. Menninger's [16] statement was considered an axiom: "Psychiatrists realize from clinical experience what poets have proclaimed in inspired verse, that to retreat permanently into the loneliness of one's own soul is to surrender one's claim upon life." Copies of poems that the therapists thought appropriate were made and distributed to group members, and the poems were read and discussed. Members were then encouraged to describe any feelings made manifest by the readings of the poems. A search was made for what Stekel [22] in dream analysis termed the "personification of the parapathy." Members were frequently encouraged to write additional stanzas of their own and read them to the group. These discussions were not concerned with the student's ability as a poet, but rather with the feelings being expressed. Jung's [10] evaluation of poetry and the poet was thought to be significant: "When a form of 'art' is primarily personal it deserves to be treated as if it were a neurosis."

The concern in the student's writing, therefore, was with the expression of his "parapathy" as found in the central theme of his poetry, or in his reactions to the poetry of others. This is what Gutheil [6] would call his "symbolic parallelism." For example, a poem expressing the despair of not having a "self" would be read. Individuals would react with their own feelings as a result of hearing the poem. Then, several at least, would try to add a stanza or even two. These stanzas would be analyzed somewhat as Bonime [1] would approach a patient's dream:

The action of the dream . . . symbolizes part of the total living process of the patient. Although only fragments of a dream may be preserved, or although the dream may be no more than a flash, a tableau, a sensation, a sound, a word or a pain, process is implied.

The philosophy of this chapter is concerned with the belief that "process is implied," also, in the production of a poem or in the individual reaction to a poem. Reik [20] claims that it "is with the antennae of our own unconscious that we feel what is the essence of the thoughts and emotions of our patients, not with the tools of reasoning and logic." The purpose of the experiment with poetry therapy was to encourage each individual to respond with his feelings as he heard the reading of "inspired verse," or read what was, perhaps, not so inspired, his own verse. It was recognized, of course, that, as Reik [20] states, "to get hold of an unconscious thought or emotion is only one part of the analytical process. To follow it, to observe its consequences, reverberations and repercussions in the unconscious life of the person is the other part." A part of the group process in this experiment was to observe and react to the unconscious emotions manifested by various individuals as they responded to their own poetry and the poetry of others.

POSTTEST RESULTS

In January, 1965, the same projective tests that were administered earlier as the pretest were given for the purpose of comparison. The posttest interview involved an effort to determine whether the student had improved as a result of 26 hours of poetry therapy. The tests were administered to the eight original subjects designated as the experimental group. The control group had ceased to exist, since four of the eight subjects requested treatment before the 12th hour of the experiment had been completed.

There are two significant limitations to any attempt to generalize on the data gathered by this study. First, the failure to obtain data for a control group makes it difficult to answer the usual question regarding whether the members of this group might have changed over the period of four months due to factors other than poetry therapy. Second, eight subjects do not constitute a sufficient sample. The authors report their results, therefore, as interesting data that suggest that poetry therapy may be a profitable area for continued research.

The results of the projective tests were submitted to three psychologists, who served as an evaluation team. They were instructed to evaluate the data and to conclude simply on the basis of a dichotomy: improved or not improved. The unanimous conclusion was that seven subjects were improved and one was not improved as determined by a blind comparison of pre- and posttest responses to the four projective devices. This was with one exception consistent with the results of the posttest interview conducted by the psychologist member of the poetry therapy team. In addition, the seven students judged to be improved indicated that they believed that they had profited from poetry therapy. The student judged not improved stated that he had found the treatment "interesting but of little real value to him." In summary, then, seven of the eight students participating in 26 hours of poetry therapy were "improved" as determined by a psychiatric interview, a self analysis, and an evaluation of projective data by a team of psychologists. A sample of the data is reported below for student AJ, female, aged 20, IQ 128.

Discussion

The evaluation of the pre- and posttest data indicated that the female members of the group profited more than the males. This greater change in the females might be attributed to the higher mean IQ level, which would indicate that the type of poetry used in this experiment (geared to the college-level student) requires a certain level of intellectual functioning before it can exercise a therapeutic effect. For noncollege groups, then, less difficult poetry, even doggerel, might be advisable. It is also possible that, both therapists being male, the females were able to effect greater sex-linked transfer. The authors concluded, in agreement with Mintz,[17] that the study might have been improved by using male and female cotherapists to stimulate more concretely the "reproduction of the original family situation."

In reference to the conjecture that a certain level of intellectual functioning is required to make this method meaningful, it is necessary to report that the one individual whose tests failed to indicate change had the second highest IQ recorded for the group. But there were other factors. The student was an English major obsessed with the idea of being a poet. And although he did, in fact,

MMPI T SCORE

Pretest		Posttest	Difference
Scale 2 (Depression)	80	71	−9
6 (Paranoia)	71	59	−12
7 (Psychasthenia)	75	64	−11
8 (Schizophrenia)	73	68	−5
10 (Social)	81	81	0

TAT

6BM

Pretest themata
Life is bitter, hopeless, unalterably lonely.

Posttest themata
One must make an effort not to be bitter in life, even if it means staying away from mother.

Difference
She feels not quite so hopeless.

7BM

Individuals can become so frightened in life that they lose confidence and beg for help.

One must make an effort to solve one's own problems.

Increased responsibility for herself.

DRAW-A-PERSON

Pretest
A bent, old man about 70 years of age (3 inches on the page). Heavy black lines, much shading. She broke her pencil under excessive pressure while making the drawing. Comments while drawing included: "He sure looks like he's carrying the world on his back, doesn't he?" "Poor old man. He looks like he ought to just go home and die."

Posttest
A sturdy college boy (7 inches on the page) with a feminine face. She was relaxed while making the drawing. Comments while drawing included: "I can't make boys look like boys." "Oh, he's almost too pretty to be a boy." "He looks like my brother."

Difference
Evidence manifest that she is abandoning the internalized father for whom she attempted to be a "boy" and is beginning the transition toward female identification.

RORSCHACH CARD #1

Pretest
A girl being swallowed up somehow by an angry old woman, a sort of witchy old woman; it just sort of seems like she's being absorbed into the woman.

Posttest
I see a girl tied to a stake. She's spread-eagled sort of and it looks like she's gotten one leg free and she's struggling to get loose.

Difference
She is in the process of breaking away from the bondage imposed by her disapproving and hostile mother

make a greater contribution of his own poetry than any other member of the group, it appeared to the cotherapists that writing, for him, was part of what Horney [9] has called the idealized image. In this case, the individual appeared to be concerned primarily with securing an admiring audience for his poetry. He was frequently condescending when other poems, by either recognized authors or members of the group, were read. During the reading of poetry written by other members of the group, he pretended to be pained and attempted to exchange "knowing" glances with the cotherapists. He was not interested in any discussion of latent meaning or "symbolic parallelism." It is suggested, therefore, that in forming a poetry therapy group, the psychologist might be wise to exclude that type of individual with literary ambitions cathected to the idealized image. Poetry therapy in this case would possibly increase the protecting arrogance and magnify the discrepancy between actual and idealized self.

A further observation in the technique of poetry therapy as it developed in this experiment concerns the importance of what Reik [20] has called the "psychological moment." After approximately 12 hours of treatment, one of the major goals of the experiment had been reached: the group had become cohesive; it was evident that the members had come to know and care for each other and were willing, via their interpretations of poems, to be relatively "open" with each other. From this point on, it became increasingly apparent to the cotherapists and to the members of the group that when one individual reacted very strongly to a particular poem, the time had come for the entire group to focus on that person and sometimes to spend the entire hour discussing just a few lines of poetry as they related to that individual. It became increasingly clear to the cotherapists that these times constituted the precise moment "to communicate the repressed meaning of a series of symptoms or the hidden sense of some attitude of mind...." The following example will illustrate.

During the 14th meeting, a poem was read that expressed the effort of the author to come to terms with his real self. The author expressed acceptance of the real self in terms of his effort to be satisfied with the house he had built. Though imperfect, out of plumb, out of joint, he had built it, and he would live in it. A particular student reacted with considerable distaste, stating that he did not "like that poem at all." The recorded dialogue is self-explanatory:

> Therapist: What would you say if I told you that I feel like that?
> Student: You mean like that house?
> Therapist: Yes. What would you say if I told you that I feel that way sometimes? Out of joint. Imperfect.
> Student: I wouldn't believe you.
> Therapist: But if it was true?
> Student: Then I would feel sorry for you, very sorry for you.

Although this student had the lowest IQ in the group (108), he affected an attitude of superiority and a marginal tolerance of the other members of the group. He was openly contemptuous, for example, of several students who claimed to prefer modern jazz to classical music; he protested that he could not find anyone at the college able to challenge him at chess; he stated that he did not go home between semesters because his mind had "outdistanced" his parents and that efforts at conversation were overwhelming chores. In reacting to the poem, he was in fact reacting to the threat to the idealized image employed in the service of protecting him from anxiety, from feelings of meaninglessness. His overreactions to the poem prompted the cotherapists to ask him to read the poem aloud, which he did, disdainfully. Then he suddenly snapped his fingers and stated: "Hey, I just remembered a dream I had last night. It just popped right into my mind." He reported the dream:

> I enter an elevator and press the button and it starts up. Pretty soon I realize that I'm really up too high and that I'm actually just on a platform. The sides of the elevator have disappeared. I'm frightened because I realize I've gone higher than is safe but I don't know how to stop the elevator.

He reacted to the request to simplify the dream with the statement: "Well, I'm in danger because I've gone too high and there's a real threat I might fall off the platform." To the request that he describe the affect in the dream, he said: "A feeling of absolute loneliness." No dream analysis was attempted. It was felt that too much probing into the meaning of the dream would take the student beyond his capacity to adjust at that time.

The poet therapist and his psychology colleague are encouraged to be aware of this "psychological moment," for it may come and go almost unnoticed.

Finally, the authors found that some of the members of the treatment group responded in a sequence that appeared consistent with Jung's [11] concept of emerging archetypes from the collective unconscious.

> The first manifestation of the *"child"* is, as a rule, a totally unconscious phenomenon. Here the patient identifies himself with his personal infantilism. Then, under the influence of therapy, we get a more or less gradual separation from and objectification of the "child," that is, the identity breaks down and is accompanied by an intensification . . . of fantasy, with the result that archaic or mythological features become increasingly apparent. Further transformations run to the hero-myth. The theme of "mighty feats" is generally absent, but on the other hand the mythical dangers play all the greater part. At this stage, there is usually another identification, this time with the *hero*, whose role is attractive for a variety of reasons. The identification is often extremely stubborn and dangerous to the psychic equilibrium. If it can be broken down and if consciousness can be reduced to human proportions, the figure of the hero can gradually be differentiated into a symbol of the *self*. (Italics added.)

Two students in particular serve as good examples of psychological growth as observed in emerging archetypes. One of these, male, submitted a poem entitled "Mom and Dad." It dealt quite frankly with the desire to hold on to them. A later poem, written for the 13th session, was a fantasy dealing with the heroics of a soldier in WW II. The poem he presented during the last week of treatment was called "Wherever I Go, I Go." It described a preoccupation with the search for job, love, home, children. It was not childlike, not heroic, but rather a simple expression of his emerging concern for the developmental tasks ahead, in proper sequence and phenomenologically sound.

A second student, female, wrote an early poem that she entitled "Asleep at my Mother's Breast." A later poem (15th session) was frankly sexual:

> . . . the arching goddess,
> a silken lure,
> behold the hero
> entwined
> at the Gates of Eden.

Her final poem, presented during the last week of treatment and titled "Sad Ann," described the feelings of a girl who realized that she was not at all a goddess, that she was too skinny, but that hopefully her "lover" would see through to her soul which was "beauty enough for the rest of her." Again, it appeared that the student had projected the child, had, in short, objectified the child, then the hero (goddess), and was beginning, at the conclusion of the semester, to objectify and to attempt a differentiation of the goddess into a symbol of the self. The authors concluded:

Poetry therapy may offer the individual the opportunity to project the child, hero, and self through the medium of verse, each archetype in its natural sequence, and that therapy will of necessity be of at least four months duration to allow time for the objectification of the archetypes. A caution is presented here, specifically that the therapist, watching for the epiphany of the hero, be aware that failure to attenuate the inflation of identification at this point may result in the entrenchment of the idealized image with its corresponding impoverishment of real self.

It is conjectured that this is perhaps what happened with the student in this experiment who did not appear to change from pre- to post-test.

Summary

1. For treatment using a group technique called poetry therapy, eight students were accepted on the basis of data obtained from: 1. a psychiatric interview; 2. MMPI; 3. Draw-A-Person; 4. Card 6BM and Card 7BM of the TAT; and 5. Card #1 of the Rorschach. The students were all junior or senior rank in college, four were male, four female, and the range in IQ 108 to 135. By sex, the mean IQ was female 127, male 113.

2. The group met every Thursday from 4:00 to 6:00 PM in a large room with two cotherapists, one a psychologist and the other a poet and professor of English. In principle, the method of treatment consisted of the selection and reading of poems thought to convey symbolically feelings and attitudes being repressed by the members of the group. The students were encouraged to associate freely to the poem and to write their own poems. These free associations and the themata of poems were then subject to a conventional type of analysis employed in most group therapy.

3. After the completion of 26 hours of treatment over a four month period, a second psychiatric interview and the same projective battery

was administered as the post-test. A panel of three clinical psychologists was asked to evaluate the data and to conclude simply whether, in their opinion, improvement had occurred. They agreed unanimously that seven students had "improved" and that one apparently had "not improved."

4. A discussion of the data called attention to four specific phenomena:

a. The females improved more significantly than the males. The relevance of IQ was not determined to be significant in this study, but it may offer an avenue of fruitful research for another study, i.e. Does the individual with a high IQ tend to profit more from poetry therapy than the average or subaverage individual? Or would a different type of verse be equally profitable with a group with fewer cultural advantages?

b. "An individual with an idealized image feeding upon his competence as poet or writer may not be a suitable candidate for this form of therapy inasmuch as the sessions may enhance the image at the expense of the already deflated real self."

c. "The therapists should watch for the emergence of the 'psychological moment' in individual patients, that moment of special readiness to accept change sometimes signaled by an original poem or an especially strong reaction to the poem of another."

d. "There appears to be some tendency for the original poems of individuals in group therapy to resemble the projections of Jungian archetypes, the child, the hero, the self."

5. The experiment did not involve a control group and it is difficult to generalize upon data employing a small number. It is recommended, therefore, that the experiment be repeated and an attempt be made to employ a control group.

REFERENCES

1. Bonime, Walter: The Clinical Use of Dreams, New York, Basic, 1962.
2. Clark, Robert A.: Six Talks on Jung's Psychology, Pittsburgh, Boxwood Press, 1953.
3. Dahlstrom, W. G., and Welsh, G. S.: An MMPI Handbook, Minneapolis, Univ Minnesota Press, 1960.
4. Greifer, Eli: Poetry therapy, The Brooklyn Psychologist, September, 1964.
5. ———: Principles of Poetry Therapy, New York, Poetry Therapy Center, 1963.
6. Gutheil, Emil A.: The Handbook of Dream Analysis, New York, Grove Press, 1951.
7. Hammer, Emanuel F.: The Clinical Application of Projective Drawings, Springfield (Ill), Thomas, 1958.
8. Hathaway, S., and Meehl, P.: An Atlas For the Clinical Use of the MMPI, Minneapolis, Univ Minnesota Press, 1951.

9. Horney, Karen: Our Inner Conflicts, New York, Norton, 1945.
10. Jung, C. G.: Modern Man In Search of a Soul, New York, Harcourt, 1933.
11. ———: Psyche & Symbol, New York, Doubleday, 1953.
12. Ledwith, Nettie H.: A Rorschach Study of Child Development, Pittsburgh, Univ Pittsburgh Press, 1960.
13. Leedy, J. J.: Poetry and medicine, MD Med Newsmagazine, 3, 1964.
14. Lundlin, W. H., and Aronov, B. M.: Use of co-therapists in group psychotherapy, J Consult Psychol 16:60–76, 1952.
15. Machover, Karen: Personality Projection, Springfield (Ill), Thomas, 1949.
16. Menninger, Karl: Love Against Hate, New York, Harcourt, 1942.
17. Mintz, Elizabeth E.: Transference in co-therapy groups, J Consult Psychol 27:34–39, 1963.
18. Mowrer, O. Hobart: The loss and recovery of personal identity as clinical problems, unpublished manuscript, Univ of Illinois, 1963.
19. Murray, H. A.: Thematic Apperception Test, Cambridge (Mass), Harvard Univ, 1943.
20. Reik, Theodor: Listening With The Third Ear, New York, Grove Press, 1948.
21. Rorschach, Hermann: Psychodiagnostics. ed. 5, New York, Grune, 1921.
22. Stekel, Wilhelm: The Interpretation of Dreams, New York, Grosset & Dunlap, 1943.

Poetry, a Way to Fuller Awareness:
Added Dimension in Treating Addicts

W. Douglas Hitchings, MB, BCh, BAO
*Fellow in Child Psychiatry,
Postgraduate Center for Mental Health, New York*

For the Quaker, of great value and meaning is the Psalmist's admonition, "Be still and know that I am God."[1] In the stillness, the outer objective mind quiescent, one waits for the gift of the Inner Light, known by many names—*the sea, God in every man,* an *opening,* the *mysterium coniunctionis*. It might be defined as a state of being peculiar to one's self, yet shared by all who turn themselves inward to the depth of their beings. In this state, there is peace and rest and healing. Throughout the ages, physicians have known that they were partners only in the healing process, that although they might set the stage and prepare the grounds, the healing itself comes from another source. This knowledge seems equally true for today's physician of the mind.

Gerhard Adler has written [2]:

> Man is beset by doubt about the meaning of life, chaos threatens, and the ten thousand things have revealed their questionable character. The problem of the relationship of subject and object has been posed, and where a constructive answer is attempted, as in art, more and more it is sought and found within, in man's relationship to the inner object, to the "thing in itself," which has to be abstracted and distilled from the chaotic multiplicity of the external world. . . .

> This struggle for an inner point of vantage, for knowledge of an inner reality in which fragmentation of the outer reality can find synthesis and a new meaning, comes to expression in some of the leading artists of this century. Thus Paul Klee, in his diary, wrote of the need for an "orientation towards the Beyond." Such an orienta-

tion, which leads "beyond" the conflict between man and world, subject and object, is an orientation inward, a turning toward the psychic center and universal ground of all reality. Another pioneer of modern art, Kandinsky, expressed this as the "Greater Reality," and Franz Marc spoke of his "yearning" for indivisible being, of his search for the "inner mystical construction," and said that his aim was to "disclose an unearthly being that dwells behind all things."

Poetry may be utilized in reflecting the inner turbulent mental state experienced by the patient. Thus the inner becomes the outer, or the conscious, making it tangible and workable. We would suggest that poetry may also quiet the outer so that the inner, greater reality may be experienced. When one finds oneself in touch with the inner reality, poetry may be the vehicle of expression to make known to the outer consciousness, the peace, joy, happiness and pain of the inward state.

Through poetry, we may share with others a variety of emotions and thereby establish a bond of relationship. It has been said that all poetry is a prayer and an adoration. Early Quaker poets, such as John Greenleaf Whittier, and some of those of the present day, such as Winifred Rawlins, are aware of the healing power of poetry. Through their work, they provide a way of simplicity, sincerity, and moderation whereby the inward may be reached and expressed outwardly. Thus Whittier:

> THE ETERNAL GOODNESS
> And so beside the silent sea
> I wait the muffled oar;
> No harm from him can come to me
> On ocean or on shore.
>
> I know not where His islands lift
> Their fronded palms in air;
> I only know I cannot drift
> Beyond His love and care.

As a therapist, I have felt often that to be able to give a more accurate picture of what was being attempted in therapy would be of help. Treatment of a 38-year-old patient had been difficult. She repeatedly expressed the idea of being stupid, worthless, a complete idiot. She did, however, have a strongly developed artistic side to her personality, and in our work, we agreed to try using poetry from time to time. We used a selection from Kahlil Gibran's *The Prophet* to attempt to define the work before us; it was concerned with self-knowledge.[3]

> And a man said, Speak to us of Self-Knowlege.
> And he answered, saying:
> Your hearts know in silence the secrets of the days and the nights.
> But your ears thirst for the sound of your heart's knowledge.
> You would know in words that which you have always known in thought.
> You would touch with your fingers the naked body of your dreams.
>
> And it is well you should.
> The hidden well-spring of your soul must needs rise and run murmuring to the sea;
> And the treasure of your infinite depths would be revealed to your eyes.
> But let there be no scales to weigh your unknown treasure;
> And seek not the depths of your knowledge with staff of sounding line.
> For self is a sea boundless and measureless.
>
> Say not, "I have found the truth," but rather, "I have found a truth."
> Say not, "I have found the path of the soul." Say rather, "I have met the soul walking upon my path."
> For the soul walks upon all paths.
> The soul walks not upon a line, neither does it grow like a reed.
> The soul unfolds itself, like a lotus of countless petals.

The patient felt that these lines spoke to her condition; she said that they were beautiful. Patient and therapist both sensed an inner response that at this time this was the right thing. Weeks went by. The patient hung on to her original feeling of knowing. Doubts were expressed that she was equal to the task. Questions were raised concerning how we might better go about the task. At this new time, we attempted to sense the simplicity, but complete commitment was required to carry out the task. We turned once more to poetry.

> I salute you: There is nothing I can give you which you have not got; but there is much, very much, that, while I cannot give it, you can take.
>
> No Heaven can come to us unless our hearts find rest in today. Take Heaven! No peace lies in the future which is not hidden in this present little instant. Take peace!
>
> The gloom of the world is but a shadow. Behind it, yet within our reach, is joy. There is radiance and glory in the darkness could we but see, and to see, we have only to look. I beseech you to look.
>
> And so, at this time, I greet you. Not quite as the world sends greetings, but with profound esteem and with prayer that for you now and forever the day breaks, and the shadows flee away.[4]

The patient again felt that these lines expressed something that she had previously sensed. We felt that a bridgehead of reality had been established in a sea of dimly felt sensations and shadowy, possible truths. A few weeks later she brought, these lines, written at a time of turbulence between herself and her husband.

> Hope—Haven for children and innocents
> Mystical panacea for their ills
> Unreal place
> Who trods your ethereal plains?
> Only those who believe in you.

Again we discussed her doubt about her ability to deal with the darkness that she felt. She stated that she felt able to cry, which was a new development in her life. A poem that proved helpful at this time dealt with the subject of pain.[5]

> And a woman spoke, saying, Tell us of Pain.
> And he said:
> Your pain is the breaking of the shell that encloses your understanding.
> Even as the stone of the fruit must break, that its heart may stand in the sun, so must you know pain.

And could you keep your heart in wonder at the daily miracles of your life, your pain would not seem less wondrous than your joy;

And you would accept the seasons of your heart, even as you have always accepted the seasons that pass over your fields.

And you would watch with serenity through the winters of your grief.

Much of your pain is self-chosen.

It is the bitter position by which the physician within you heals your sick self.

Therefore trust the physician, and drink his remedy in silence and tranquillity:

For his hand, though heavy and hard, is guided by the tender hand of the Unseen,

And the cup he brings, though it burn your lips, has been fashioned of the clay which the Potter has moistened with His own sacred tears.[5]

At this stage in her therapy, the patient undertook volunteer work on a ward in a hospital that cared for chronically ill patients. She expressed the idea that she found great meaning in caring for those who had no one to care for and love them. She was also more confident of herself as a person: she was able to take trips alone, whereas before she had always to be accompanied by another person. While the patient continues to have many problems, poetry has been a useful therapeutic aid, and has helped us to reach insights not available previously.

I believe that therapists should always be open to speak with meaning and understanding in very difficult situations if possible. To me, the rewards of this attitude have been surprising. During my training, I spent some time on the detoxification wards for male addicts. These patients came often from slum areas, had been addicted to one or several drugs for considerable periods of time, and had had run-ins with the police and consequent imprisonment. They were "kicking the habit," and, in addition to experiencing periods of physical discomfort, were tense, often depressed and openly hostile to any ideas that reflected the way of life among "the squares." After I had known them for a time, I decided to read poetry, expecting to be hooted down in derision or coldly ignored. To my surprise, neither happened. While a couple sat on the floor of the hospital corridor, I started to read. Another drifted in to the group, then another and another, until at the end of the hour we formed a group of about a dozen. I felt that it might be helpful to find something that would convey the feelings stirred in the addict as he lives his life on the outside: feelings of death, crime and punishment are ever-present companions. We read of the farewell and the preparation of the trip away from life which is poignantly related by *The Prophet*.

> And his soul cried out to them, and he said:
> Sons of my ancient mother, your riders of the tides,
> How often have you sailed in my dreams. And now you come in my awakening, which is my deeper dream.
>
> A seeker of silences am I, and what treasure have I found in silence that I may dispense with confidence?
> If this is my day of harvest, in what fields have I sowed the seed, and in what unremembered seasons?
> If this indeed be the hour in which I lift up my lantern, it is not my flame that shall burn therein.
> Empty and dark shall I raise my lantern,
> And the guardian of the night shall fill it with oil and he shall light it also.
>
> These things he said in words. But much in his heart remained unsaid. For he himself could not speak his deeper secret.[6]

Most of these addicts had been arrested at one time or another. This area of their lives was one of hostility, pain, and bewilderment. In our attempt to lessen the difficulties here, we read of crime and punishment.[7]

> Then one of the judges of the city stood forth and said, Speak to us of Crime and Punishment.
> And he answered, saying:
> It is when your spirit goes wandering upon the wind,
> That you, alone and unguarded, commit a wrong unto others and therefore unto yourself.
>
> Oftentimes have I heard you speak of one who com-

mits a wrong as though he were not one of you, but a stranger unto you and an intruder upon your world.

But I say that even as the holy and the righteous cannot rise beyond the highest which is in each one of you,

So the wicked and the weak cannot fall lower than the lowest which is in you also.

You cannot separate the just from the unjust and the good from the wicked;

For they stand together before the face of the sun even as the black thread and the white are woven together.

And when the black thread breaks, the weaver shall look into the whole cloth, and he shall examine the loom also.

And how shall you punish those whose remorse is already greater than their misdeeds?

Is not remorse the justice which is administered by that very law which you would fain serve?

Yet you cannot lay remorse upon the innocent nor lift it from the heart of the guilty.

Unbidden shall it call in the night, that men may wake and gaze upon themselves.

And you who would understand justice, how shall you unless you look upon all deeds in the fullness of light?

Only then shall you know that the erect and the fallen are but one man standing in twilight between the night of his pigmy-self and the day of his god-self,

And that the corner-stone of the temple is not higher than the lowest stone in its foundation.[7]

After the readings, awkwardly, one by one, the patients approached me. They were eager to borrow the book from which the readings were taken. On following days, still others inquired when they would have their turn at reading. They commented about the meaning of certain lines. They stated that they had heard these ideas expressed in ethnic groups in which they had grown up.

Of course, no therapist would be sufficiently naive to think that he had accomplished a great deal of work. However, to establish one meaningful relationship with a drug addict, where two minds may meet for however brief a period, is a thing not to be dismissed lightly. Before one can walk, he must learn to take the initial step. And who is to say for certain that poetry does not release the energy for this first outreach to a more meaningful way of life?

In attempting reconstructive therapy, I have often been impressed with the similarity to death and birth—death of the old, the hated, the dirty, and the unacceptable; birth of the new, the something not yet evident. The process, seemingly, is always one of pain, darkness, and tribulation. A 40-year-old father, who felt entirely unequipped for his task and saw himself as a continuous failure, found comfort in the following lines [8]:

> Whisper of running streams, and winter lightning.
> The wild thyme unseen and the wild strawberry,
> The laughter in the garden, echoed ecstasy
> Not lost, but requiring, pointing to the agony
> Of death and birth.
>
>   You say I am repeating
> Something I have said before. I shall say it again.
> Shall I say it again? In order to arrive there,
> To arrive where you are, to get from where you are not,
>   You must go by a way wherein there is no ecstasy.
> In order to arrive at what you do not know
>   You must go by a way which is the way of ignorance.
> In order to possess what you do not possess
>   You must go by the way of dispossession.
> In order to arrive at what you are not
>   You must go through the way in which you are not.
> And what you do not know is the only thing you know
> And what you own is what you do not own
> And where you are is where you are not.[8]

There may, indeed, be only one "Royal Road" to the Unconscious, but many of us may have to travel the lesser known highways "in order to arrive there, to arrive where you are to get from where you are not." Poetry is one of these highways—one that has not been too heavily traveled yet. It may be that for some it will provide a safer, more meaningful journey, because for them the signposts are written in language that they can read and understand.

REFERENCES

1. Psalms 46:10.
2. Adler, Gerhard: On the Question of Meaning in Psychotherapy, New York, The Analytical Psychology Club of New York, Inc., Spring, 1962, pp. 7–8.
3. Gibran, Kahlil: The Prophet, New York, Knopf, 1952, pp. 62–63.
4. Fra Giovanni: 1513 AD.
5. Gibran, Kahlil: *Op. cit.*, pp. 60–61.
6. *Ibid.:* pp. 9, 11–12.
7. *Ibid.:* pp. 45–46, 48–50.
8. Eliot, T. S.: Four Quartets, *in* Collected Poems 1909–1962, part 3, New York, Harcourt, 1934, pp. 186–187.

CHAPTER 11

The Psalms as Psychological and Allegorical Poems

Therapeutic Applications in a Clinical Setting

JOSEPH H. GELBERMAN, DD
*Rabbi, The Little Synagogue,
Director, Mid-Way Counseling
Center, New York*

DOROTHY KOBAK, MSW
*Psychiatric Social Worker, Bureau of
Child Guidance, Board of Education,
New York, and Associate Director,
Mid-Way Counseling Center*

THE PSALM IS A SONG, "a Song of the Soul." As a song of the soul, it became necessary to render the emotional impact of the message through a creative vehicle—poetry rather than prose. For even in poetic construction, the implied aim of the author was subtly interwoven, since the Psalm is distinctive in language and rhythm from the prose of the Scriptures and historical books. The purpose therefore would seem to indicate that the Psalm was devised to express truth and experience on a *feeling* rather than an *intellectual level*. Much as Jesus used the parable to illustrate spiritual ideas in familiar reference to environment, the psalmist used poems in a specific meter and style to stimulate and evoke emotional reactions to the confronting perplexities of life.

The poetic form of the Psalm, therefore, had the function of acting as an "attention getting" mechanism, to emphasize and insist that the message of the Psalm be understood. It was no accident that three means of poetic structure were used as an important aid in grasping the meaning of the text, whereby a word in one line would explain an obscure word in another, and the clue be extended to the entire clause. For example:

1. The same thought expressed in different words (XI, 1):

> In the Lord put I my trust:
> how say ye to my soul, Flee as a bird to your mountain?

2. The thought reinforced by the method of contrast (I, 6):

> For the Lord knoweth the way of the righteous:
> but the way of the ungodly shall perish.

3. The thought continuing from line to line to build a cumulative effect (I, 1):

> Blessed is the man that
>   walketh not in the counsel of the ungodly,
>   nor standeth in the way of sinners,
>   nor sitteth at the seat of the scornful.

A meaningful conclusion, merely by examining the artistic form, is that the urgency of the message was the author's prime goal, and the therapeutic effort of the message could be rendered only by poetry. This alone could evoke an emotional involvement, as distinguished from the authoritative prose of the Talmud, which sought as the body of Jewish law and thought to establish a more sober guide to everyday conduct.

Although David probably originated a new style of Hebrew lyrical poetry in the Psalms, it is more important to their therapeutic value that he became a model for poets in later generations, since he drew on his personal experiences for the themes of his poems, and so did his successors who continued to add to the Psalms. As a result, Psalms, originally dated from around 600 BC, continued to become a wonderful collection of poems, lyrical, dramatic, and elegiac, that contained something to fit almost every mood and to understand every need. Herein lies their therapeutic significance—that the authors, because of their personal involvement, identified with the people, and the seeker, equally within the Judaic or Christian concept, could feel himself understood and explained in the Psalms.

The psychological impact of the Psalms, from the perspective of mental health, induces some interesting necessity to examine the classification of their subject matter also. In rabbinical literature, the Psalms are referred to as "the Book of Praises," or "verses of praise," by Talmudical authorities. Yet an examination of the Psalms illustrates that content also includes "elegy" and "ethics."

Spiritually, however, praise indeed is the outstanding tone in which God is hailed for His goodness, for His vindication of the righteous, His Fatherhood over all mankind, and His power as the Creator and ruler of the Universe. The elegy in numerous Psalms tells of the sufferings of individuals, adding the possibility that "sin" was a cause, and therefore confesses guilt with a plea for pardon, while supplicating for relief of pain. And in terms of ethics, several Psalms offer direction for a right way of living, declaiming vices and proclaiming the joy that is attainable for faithfulness to God's wishes.

As such, the Psalms are thoroughly human documents, reflecting the difficulties of existence, the struggle to remain faithful to ideals, the overcoming of doubt, the fight for victory of the better self, and the conquest of despair. These reflections are with certainty the same yearnings as those of people today, whether the battle is waged alone with the self or in dialogue with the therapist or clergyman. Concretely, the psalmist asks in essence, when singing of God and man: "Who am I?" or what is the meaning of life. Then further: "What is Good and Evil?" or how can I undersand suffering. And lastly: "What is my purpose?" or how can I fulfill myself. In searching for answers, the psalmist generally raised more questions, but only after he had first started out on a "positive" note. He proceeded on to search for a catharsis, so that the middle of the Psalm often contained the sadness, the misery, the depression, the doubt, perhaps even the "temper tantrum." But almost always the keynote towards the end of the Psalm was victory.

It was no idle routine that the positive note came first, for the awareness of God was an intimate experience with the psalmists. They felt that they were *always* in His presence. But being thoroughly human characters under the strain of adversity, they often felt that He had "hidden His face." Yet they were ultimately saved from despair, since never did they bring themselves to think that He was indifferent to what was happening, otherwise life would have geen stripped of meaning.

Although the psalmist in his poem taught that inner security related to his acknowledged dependency on a God who cared about him, his allusions to the *power* of God were less frequent than his allusions to God in terms of His *attributes*, such as love, mercy, and justice. It is the "nature" of God that colors the Psalms, not as abstract doctrine but as the *inspiration* of man's living. It is here that the applicability to healing emotional difficulties is pertinent.

This faith in life, or "will to meaning," relates therapeutically in the clinical situation. In the need to establish a goal for the emotionally distraught patient, a goal based first on an existential truth that life has meaning, the *"how"* to mental health is determined only after the *"why I must persist"* is established. In attempting to ascertain this, a consideration of the paradox of man becomes an inevitability. It is not only the paradox of the individual client in his own search for identity, but the contemplation of the ultimate meaning of man. For every man who finds his identity adds to the total significance of man in a cosmic sense. But the converse can be equally valid: man's understanding of his metaphysical position, in the vast universal sense, enables him to approach his individual goal in emotional healing with a zest or "inspiration" that implements the will and begets assurance in the therapeutic ongoing.

The Psalms can be utilized very pertinently in this context as they speculate on the majesty of God, in juxtaposition to the infinitesimal nature of man. Yet everywhere they define man by proclaiming him as a divine creative work, endowed with the godly spirit. They then outline the supreme purpose in very definite and specific terms, mandating that man's powers and opportunities should be translated into daily activities, or "works," in order to glorify life. In a song of cause and effect, the Psalms suggest that only by this means can true happiness or mental wholeness be attained. It is for this basic contention that the doctrine of immortality was not stressed in the Psalms, since these poems advocated again and again that man's concern is with his life on earth, and how to express it valiantly.

The emotionally disturbed person, however, cannot express life valiantly. He depresses life, for he is unliberated when bound by his illness. In recognizing this, the psalmists concerned themselves with man's environment and man's frailties or, more pointedly, good and evil, specifically as it related to man's choice and com-

Psychological and Allegorical Poems 137

mitment. This concept becomes therapeutically valid with clients who suffer the guilts and resentments of their own or other's "wickedness." The Psalm frequently refers to the destruction of the wicked: its motive was not malicious joy over the penalties to evildoers but relief in the demonstration that faith in life had been justified. The "penalties" in the therapeutic sense, when defined allegorically, relate to the ensuing neurosis, thereby illustrating by the resultant disability that life had to be lived a new way, with therapy as the tool for relearning, or "destroying the wickedness," and reaffirming wholeness.

This applicability was tested in therapy sessions, with various clients, in individual and group situations. The therapy conducted was housed in a religiopsychiatric clinic in a synagogue, was available on a nonsectarian basis, and included all races. Clients are not necessarily part of the religious program, and some are highly spiritually oriented while others are frankly agnostic.

In terms of selectivity of clients for use of the Psalms, initial testing out was with a warmly receptive elderly woman—a paranoid schizophrenic with whom a supportive therapy was being done to maintain her. In her case, since the therapist was also the rabbi to whom she clung tenaciously for safety and solace, his reading of the Psalm was a spiritual encounter with deep emotional significance. Since her paranoid frame of reference kept her fraught with fear at her imaginery dangers, the same portions of Psalm 34 (verses 6 and 21) were read and repeated at each session:

> This poor man cried, and the Lord heard *him*, and saved him out of all his troubles.

> Evil shall slay the wicked: and they that hate the righteous shall be desolate.

The first verse assured her that she was not abandoned, and that rescue was a certainty. The second verse assured her that her "enemies" would be cut down, thereby decreasing her fear of them. All this was to be done by a power greater than herself, whose identity was in truth particularized in her rabbi-therapist. She wept copiously at her release at each reading and left each session assured, saying: "It will be good." Naturally, in view of her illness, there were no depth changes, but the goals were to sustain and maintain, and the use of the Psalm accomplished its goal.

In a more complicated situation, portions of Psalm 91 were used with a brilliant, highly intellectual young man, whose problem centered around his inability to relate or express feelings. Buried in this defense of an aloof exterior was a fear that the world might treat him hostilely and he must protect himself against hurt by emotional restraint, lest he be vulnerable to attack. Basically desirous of a dependency relationship, he fought it by assuming a detached independence and often critical intolerance. Yet therapy revealed a yearning for closeness and a hidden warmth, which was imprisoned while waiting impatiently to be liberated.

The therapist, who was female, introduced the use of the Psalm, suggesting experimentation as to emotional impact, but concentrated on the allegorical interpretation at the outset in order not to depart too radically from his dominant intellectual frame of reference. Verses 5 and 13 of Psalm 91 were used initially:

> Thou shalt not be afraid for the terror by night;
> *nor* for the arrow *that* flieth by day;
> Thou shalt tread upon the lion and adder: the young lion and the dragon shalt thou trample under feet.

These two verses were selected as examples to illustrate psychological implications in content. Based on the allegorical interpretation by Dr. Emmet Fox, the "terror by night" is likened to the subconscious problems or terrors of the "mental night," those whose roots are out of sight and buried in the unconscious. In contrast, the "arrow that flieth by day" refers to difficulties of which the conscious mind is aware, a "daytime problem."

The second verse draws a further contrast between the subconscious and the consciously realized difficulty. The lion was allegorically interpreted as any intimidating difficulty about which we are informed and that stands in our path. In a word, the lion (problem) is no hider; he charges in the open. But the attack of the adder or snake is hidden (in the unconscious), and the poem elaborates that the adder develops into a dragon—or formidable neurosis with highly destructive power.

Psychological and Allegorical Poems

The client reacted to this very positively and enjoyed the mental exercise. He had "accepted" the Psalms. In venturing further, the therapist selected more blatantly charged emotional material (verses 11-12).

> For he shall give his angels charge over thee, to keep thee in all thy ways.
> They shall bear thee up in *their* hands, lest thou dash thy foot against a stone.

The client reacted to this with a guarded sense of hope, which struggled with excitement to remain kindled. Clearly the emotional reaction, over and beyond the allegorical interpretation of angels as higher thoughts, took precedence over his usual critical analysis of a concept. He wished for the promise to be true and *allowed* himself to be warmed by the possibility.

The goal in using the Psalm was to breed some familiarity, acceptance, and comfort in an emotional climate, the experience thereby enabling him to translate this comfort in relating more feelingly to others in future situations. Since his mode of reacting and thinking was to move only in a known, safe, intellectual sphere, we used the verses also in order to suggest some courage in venturing out into new "less safe" unproved ideas—ideas that might have to be taken on faith. This gave him an opportunity to test out traveling from the known to the unknown in his thought world and to seek new definitions of old ideas, which were not based purely on rational examination.

Another use of the Psalm was in a group therapy session with four members, in the third year of existence. It was conducted by the Rabbi and a female therapist. Verses 5 to 7 of Psalm 91 were used:

> Thou shalt not be afraid for the terror by night;
> *nor* for the arrow *that* flieth by day;
> *Nor* for the pestilence *that* walketh in darkness;
> *nor* for the destruction *that wasteth* at noonday.
> A thousand shall fall at thy side, and ten thousand at thy right hand; *but* it shall not come nigh thee.

The initial reactions expressed were superficial, conforming, and generalized. "It could make you feel better if depressed, or it might give you greater inner security." However, when confronted with an appraisal of the immediate emotional impact at the reading of the Psalm, the more subtle implications of their stresses were revealed. One member exposed a whole new area of reaction hitherto not discussed. He evidenced extreme discomfort, saying that he found that particular portion of the Psalms morbid and depressing because he actually took the passage literally. He was afraid of it. He "saw" the arrows flying towards him, he was repelled by the word "pestilence." He told more of his actual terror by night when anxieties kept him sleepless and fearful. He liked the Psalms and had often read them, but for him Psalms of "thanksgiving" were more appropriate and he preferred them. This member's defense mechanism consisted of humor, irresponsibility, and escapism. The Psalm had obviously touched off an ability to express and understand his overt behavior more significantly in the light of his "on the spot" reaction.

A second member, extremely repressed and "proper," said that she was skeptical about the Psalm in that it could not apply to people who "miss the mark" and didn't deserve it. With support by therapist and group members, she was finally able to liberate her fear of being "evil" and to confess certain jealousies that she had been harboring.

In both cases, considerable interaction with the other group members was promulgated, opening a new area of interrelationships within the group. In view of the fact that the cotherapists were male and female, a "mother-father" role had been a prevalent function. The spiritual nature of the Psalms, added to by the presence of the rabbi and the "family" characteristics of the group, operated as an enabling process to release material heretofore repressed. Interpretations were freely given on a spiritual, allegorical, and psychological level. The session emerged as highly dynamic with the Psalms as the springboard from which the members advanced towards greater self-awareness.

The Psalm then is a versatile ancillary to therapy. It has applicability in the clinical healing process 1. when used to create an emotional climate divorced from prior or later intellectual insights, 2. when an identification on a personal and cosmic level with individual and universal suffering can be captured with a similar catharsis reexperienced vicariously, and 3. when the inspirational impact on striving towards the goal of "victory" has been stimulated by the attraction towards the positive assurance that initiates and completes the Psalm.

Perhaps a paradoxical conclusion suggested by the Psalm as a therapeutic poem is the message that unless one can "rejoice" with his problems, he cannot rejoice in his joys! It has been said that we need the poetry of life to sustain the prose. Perhaps the client needs poetry in therapy to sustain him in the arduous task of rebirth. The Psalm, as a Song of the Soul, is a "rod and a staff" to support him.

REFERENCES

1. King, E. G.: Early Religious Poetry of the Hebrews, New York, Cambridge Univ Press, 1940.
2. Friedlander, M.: The Jewish Religion, Anglo-Jewish Scholar, 1943.
3. Davison, A.: The Psalms, Christian Hebraist, 1942.
4. Cohen, D. A.: The Psalms, Soncino Press, Ltd., 1945.
5. Prothero, R. E.: The Psalms in Human Life, 1943.
6. Frankl, Viktor: Man's Search for Meaning, Boston, Beacon, 1963.
7. Fox, Emmet: The Secret Place, New York, Harper, 1941.

CHAPTER 12

Poetry as Communication in Psychotherapy

HAROLD GREENWALD, PhD
Director, Group Therapy, Center for Creative Living, Faculty, Metropolitan Institute for Psychoanalytic Studies and Community Guidance Service, Private practice, New York

FOR MANY YEARS, my patients have been writing poems—concerning their sessions and their feelings about themselves and others—and bringing them to me. At first, I did not realize what significant communications they were. I believe that most patients can tell their therapist how to treat them if he will listen carefully. But only recently did I see the value of their poems and begin to use them therapeutically. I have encouraged them to use poetry as communication, and have asked some of them to write a poem between every session.

Poetry is of value in group therapy, for some patients, although they find the group emotionally involving, find expressing themselves in it difficult. It is of value because many of its functions are the functions of therapy. Both "increase our awareness of one's own inner reactions," [2] make a portion of the unconscious conscious, lead to "an expanded understanding of the nature of other people's behavior and of the messages they send, and also greater awareness of one's own behavior and of the impact this has on other people." [2] As T. S. Eliot has written [1]:

Beyond any specific intention which poetry may have, there is always the communication of some new experience, or some fresh understanding of the familiar, or the expression of something we have experienced but have no words for, which enlarges our consciousness or refines our sensibility.

Communication in Psychotherapy

A patient has achieved emotional insight when his behavior changes.[3] Actually to do something oneself makes it possible to experience it more fully and therefore more nearly to integrate it into one's behavior. Poetry brings emotional insight more readily because it requires the patient's doing rather than reading or being told. More striking than any report of mine of the value of poetry for therapy are examples of poems written by three of my patients.

Sybil

Sybil came for therapy because she was unhappy about her marriage and unable to work constructively. Very able, she yet limited herself to part-time clerical jobs because she would not discipline herself to work steadily towards a career. She had a long history of homosexuality. After earlier therapy, she had made a heterosexual adaptation and married a passive and ineffectual young man, who did not consider supporting her and their child one of his duties. At about the time she wrote this poem, she was considering leaving her husband, and she was attracted by a young woman whom she had met.

WE WHO ARE AFRAID OF NIGHT

Like the child waiting in the night
For warm hands and arms to wrap
Themselves around his loneliness—
To spend himself in tears of sudden safety
And of love,
We too, in the dark aloneness of a self unloved,
Unanchored, abandoned and denied,
Still summon with silent child cries
The ancient hope—
The old sure magic of sweet wantedness.

The child still lives in us
With that eager hurt of innocence bewildered—and betrayed
Ah, painful paradox.
To sense the rescue
And know there is none.
But driven by old dreams, pale and powerful
Remembrances of the soft dear touch of love
We wait.

> One waits. One always waits.
> It is forgotten that nameless need
> The years have beaten from our tired hearts.
> But like some unshaped, primeval force, it beckons
> Crowds out reality, blunts stiff reason
> And we are grotesque with helpless wanting
> Turning our minds inwards—backwards
> Dull too, is pain with young memories,
> That weaken and defy
> Submit and die.
> We do not live who wait in such unhope.

Here she expresses her reaction to her husband's imminent departure, the betrayal she experienced in his interest in another woman, and the regression to a longing for a mother's warmth. "Like the child waiting in the night/ For warm hands and arms to wrap/ Themselves around his loneliness." It is no accident that she became interested in a woman, as she had always regarded homosexual sex as a mother-daughter relationship, although she played mother oftener than daughter. This is no unusual paradox: the neurotic often takes the part that she would like someone to assume to her. Although she was desperately searching for a mother to relieve her pain, loneliness, desertion and sorrow, she yet gave someone what she herself could not find. Prose limps after the poignancy of Sybil's poetry.

Eventually, she broke up with this woman, with whom she lived after divorcing her husband, and became involved with another woman. I pointed out that because the second woman was a companion much better suited to her, the danger and pain might be worse than before. She denied it, and wrote the poem that follows.

> To mine own executioner
> Be true.
> Lie still in trembled ecstasy,
> (Oh, ardent pain,
> Fear-pleasured, wish-wondered over
> In passion's sweet disguise)
> Throat-naked to the knife's caress.
>
> Beguiling destroyer,
> Unwitting abettor
> In this long preserved conspiracy,
> Take me with your kiss.

> Warm my chilled and frightened heart
> With woolen words of love.
> Comfort me with appetites,
> Taste of this tenderized spirit-flesh
> (Spiced with artful self-deceit)
> Explode my reason
> With deft confusion
> Rip away the muscled logic
> Slow crush the contentious bones of survival.
> Madness is numbing
> If it is total
> and death by loving
> Is a skillful way to die.
> (A most desirable consequence
> for natural prey)
>
> Your lips, your words, your needs
> Of the moment
> Are welded into a terrible truth.
> But they are only the instruments.
> I die by my own hand.

How clearly she sees the pain that awaits her—her need for the woman, the excitement she brought, the destruction. Many authors have pointed out the essential masochism of the homosexual relationship. "And death by loving/ Is a skillful way to die." These two poems may tell us more about the mechanics and dynamics of female homosexuality than many learned papers. The wish to return to the arms of a comforting mother, the search for pain and the suspension of reason, these are in them.

Lewis

Lewis is a brilliant scientist, who came for therapy because he felt unable to proceed in his professional life. He suffered from depression, despite his ability to mask it usually with a glittering sense of humor. The first poem here gives his presenting symptoms better than an entire battery of projective tests could.

> GRAVE BIRD/INERTIA'S LAMENT
> Of wounded times the grave bird wails
> Reveling in secret pockets of pride
> That he does nothing.

Over the lost horizon, Shangri-la
Beckons with shiny burdens of delight
But he does nothing.

In the vacant morning of his brain
Enters the perverse imp of his despair
And he does nothing.

Downbeating shafts of pain disturb
The dusty surface of his softened nerve
Yet he does nothing.

Whittling the bark of hours
From the tragic tree of time
He does nothing. He weeps
As he does nothing. He dreams
As he does nothing. He mourns
As he does nothing.
Nothing.

As Lewis' first poem gives his presenting problem, so his second presents his life history.

EVOCATION

How came such poisoned pap from so excellent an udder?
The infinite promise and sweet grace of all the
   many rounded shapes of childhood,
Charming, long-ago time when, without conscience or wit,
But with much pleasure,
I followed the song of myself.

And later, in the way it went—
The great Boy time:
Oatmeal and airplanes and skin-the-cat
And mumblety-peg and territory
And double-dutch when the fat-legged girls were by.

And rainy days. Inside at last
With chins on window seats, atop no warming hearth
But great steamy iron beasts fastened to the floor
That sputtered and spat and covered the
   icy windows with vapor
That saw fine use to write my own name in.

> I write my name today with no such pride,
>   nor recognize the boy who did it once.
> Memory is a conjurer,
> Preparing tricks alien to nature and
>   confounding simple truth;
> The boy is not the man, nor ever was, but only this:
> That once there was a boy.
>
> Whence his sweet nature came, like new corn on
>   a slender stalk,
> Mulling the wine of life with gentle spice,
>   tasted out the earth—
> That herb is lost.
> Tall, rapid man, raised from a broken spell, am I;
> The boy is gone.

It shows forth one of the problems that many suffer from who use an intellectual defense. "Tall, rapid man, raised from a broken spell, am I;/ The boy is gone." Among many others, Eric Berne [4] has pointed out that the child should be retained within the adult; it is the child remaining within us who makes possible the joy and creativity of living. The adult within us is too busy coping with the world's reality; to make creativity possible, we need the imaginative qualities of the child. By eliminating the child from his life, Lewis eliminated the pleasure from his work, and it is no wonder that having done so, he was depressed.

And the third poem of Lewis' given here depicts his transference, on many levels.

MY ANALYST

> Short sleek and witty sits this gravid owl
> And with Boswellian calm
> Surveys the shavings in an empty glass.
>
> The pieces wend, blend, mend—
> the shards are curried, combed and glued
> and burnished to a lustrous milk.
>
> The eunuch turns in grim, beseeching grief
> To Jupiter and Moses, his right hand
> to set the bone that hid the stars away.

And tells the story of his life, the bitter truth
In words of cool deception, Mother-fed;
To synthesize the Ego from the Dead.

As love whose purple tongue denies the flame
Of passion and defiles its name
Gives up its ghost, recruited to the game
And anger stalks the country hungrily.

Into this night the great scythe cuts its swath
In furrows deep with light. In its cold train
A cicatrix of crystal hue
Burns like a fire in a dismal rain.

And lo! The satyrs weight of wine and nymphs
Bursts like a sack of hair and rusted nails
Gorged with Himself—Narcissus pallid sun—
Spills in the ditch as from a running sore.

Something to fill the blasted, feral void—
Something of value, redolent of life;
A day of striving, loving without pain,
Rutting with Pan's delight, scorning the Devil's wife.

Puckish he sits and pulls the tightening string
Hovering the puppet higher from his ground
Testing his wings in new, sweet-scented air
Dry-eyed he laughs—and cries—and turns his chair.

One of this patient's problems was his dependency needs; in the second stanza, he writes of material "burnished to a lustrous milk." The feeling of impotence, of inability to do anything, causes him to transform himself into a "eunuch." In the transference, one must expect a reliving of some major problems of the individual. This makes it possible for the analyst to work through or deal with the problems, because the patient presents them in relationships with the analyst as he has with people significant in his past. Notice that the "eunuch turns in grim, beseeching grief/ To Jupiter and Moses" and, in the next stanza, "And tells the story of his life, the bitter truth/ In words of cool deception, Mother-fed." The relationship between the search to have his dependency needs met by the analyst and the fostering of dependency by the mother is made poetically if not explicitly. As in all dependent people, behind the dependency is great anger, and so—"And anger stalks the country hungrily."

Lewis was essentially passive-aggressive, and such a man has as his outstanding characteristic the wish to be dependent but the refusal to be controlled. This dependency he expressed in the earlier references to milk and the grim beseeching grief. The refusal to be controlled and the anger at experiencing control by the analyst he expressed by allusion, "Puckish he sits and pulls the tightening string/ Hovering the puppet higher from his ground."

Glenda

The poetry of Glenda has always been an integral part of her therapy. When Glenda first entered the group—I have seen her only there—she said little for months, although clearly she was following everything with greatest interest. An early poem was:

> We sat in a room
> Selma, Jean, Jessie, Jack
> Some others
> And me
>
> We played the game
> I feel, I feel, I feel
> I feel anxious—
> You do?
> I do, too.
>
> And how can I tell you
> What it was like,
> I don't know.
>
> But I'll go and I'll go
> And I'll go and I'll go,
> And so, so, so, so
> What.

These verses depict much of Glenda, how she experienced the group: hoplessness, meaningless, futility—but not quite. For she permitted me to read this poem to the group, and the next one.

It expresses her hostility, again, and something of the grandiose wishes that most of us experience in a group situation, when we hope that others will recognize our brilliance and intelligence.

> If the world were my oyster,
> And my cup of tea,
> I'd make those shitheads
> Bow down to me.

During the following group sessions, she began to speak more freely.

One of the members of the group did all the things suggested in Glenda's poem "Joan." Though Glenda was annoyed, she said not a word; she did write this verse, useful to her in understanding her own behavior.

> **JOAN**
> I bounce in late
> For my Tuesday date
> My hair is long
> My skirt's up high
> So you can
> *See me, see me*
> Make me
> Be.

Glenda was separated from her husband, had a small child, and suffered loneliness. So strong was her determination not to spill over orally that she held all her complaints in, but had her say in this poem:

> My universe is small, you see
> There's only me—and me and me.
>
> No one to touch,
> No one to hold,
> No one to keep me from the cold.
>
> Oh, yes, there is a gentleman
> Who comes and quickly goes again.
>
> And though I say that's not enough.
> Maybe there's nothing more.

In this as in previous poems, her feeling of hoplessness is clearly expressed. But in contrast to the others, her next poem reveals a new insight concerning the neurotic's desperate search for happiness.

> No man is an island,
> Is he a sea?
> No, he's a personality.
>
> A coddled self
> Who wants to pick
> The pimples of his inmost quick
> Traveling endless psychic paths
> To find—true happiness at last.
>
> *Happiness:*
> Our endless quest
> Our heart's desire.
> Our egos, ids, and selves conspire,
> To flush him out
> To catch him quick
> To make Hap-Happy stick and stick.
>
> But his elusiveness outruns
> Our analysts on fatted bums.
> It makes them rich,
> While we go round
> Seeking what cannot be found.

Glenda here succeeded in verbalizing an important but rarely stated truth about neurosis and therapy: that of a promise, too often implied by therapists, that happiness is what they have to offer. Freud's answer to a neurotic patient's question whether he could promise that therapy would result in happiness was negative. He held forth the promise not of happiness, but of a sharing in the general unhappiness of humanity rather than in the special unhappiness of the neurotic. Seeking to recapture the Lost Eden days of infancy, the neurotic is searching for a kind of happiness that does not exist for the adult. Glenda's phrase, "seeking what cannot be found," is a clear statement that neurotic methods lead not to happiness but to an increase in pain and suffering.

As most patients do, Glenda also refers to the problem of transference—this in her gallows humor:

> Harold—
> Your heart is as big
> As the borough of Brooklyn,
> Yet I find that your tactic,
> Flamboyant didactic,
> Is not too attractive
> To me, poor me.

That I did, in fact, live in Brooklyn is readily discernible in my speech, hence the charming second and third lines. The rest of the poem is a criticism of my lack of sensitivity and a clear statement that I should change my tactics.

In one session, a younger woman had occupied much of the group's attention, describing what she labeled her severe depression. Glenda said nothing during the session, but went home and wrote the following:

> I wanted to ask Nancy
> Where's your hidden greatness,
> Your secret fancy?
>
> What are you underneath and inside,
> What is it you have to hide?
>
> I know my answer
> My hidden vice:
> Never to want, need, give,
> Or seek advice.
>
> Arrogance is the name,
> Denial—they tell me—is the game.
> No one will ever tell me what to do
> Not even you, bubby, not even you.
>
> Underneath
> Is not grief.

The next of Glenda's poems was written following my suggestion that she use poetry for her therapy. In it, she describes the reason she refrains from speaking in group.

> I never say
> What I want to say.
> It never sounds
> How I want it to.
> Talking to you,
> Talking to Stan,
> Talking to any other man,
> Or woman, too.
>
> I want to say
> What can I do?
> But I'm afraid.
> You'll tell me.

She is indicating to the therapist that he should make no great effort to change her. If she were to ask: "What can I do, what can I do?" and the therapist were to tell her, the therapeutic relationship would be destroyed and her dependency become more pronounced. As she points out, letting her be is the better alternative.

Glenda's poem about Nancy indicates considerable identification with her and is expressive of many of her own feelings. Again referring to the therapist, she writes: "No one will ever tell me what to do/ Not even you, bubby, not even you." Although still concealed, the rage that has kept Glenda immobilized is clearly hinted at in, "Underneath/ Is not grief." The task is made much clearer for the therapist in these two poems. She seems to indicate that to try to help her would bottle up her rage and not permit its expression. Only grief, sorrow and appeals for help would appear, when what has to be released is her aggression. It would seem then that Glenda sees in Nancy a kindred soul; that both of them are sitting as if paralyzed while hiding their grandiose fantasies, their omnipotence, from the world. They are in a fury because they have been deprived, and still the world does not bow down to them; therefore their determination to "turn off and drop out."

These examples from the poetry of patients may indicate how valuable poetry can be as a communicative device in the context of therapy. I think that readers will be able to understand a good deal more through reading the poetry cited here than I have had the temerity to venture.

The most important function of poetry as therapy consists in the opportunity given the patient to express his emotion in a socially acceptable form—that of a poem, which is not a direct unconscious expression as the dream is. Something more than a spurting forth of raw feeling is created through its transmutation into poetry. T. S. Eliot has said:

> In expressing what other people feel, he (the poet) is also changing the feeling by making it more conscious; he is making people more aware of what they feel already, and therefore teaching them something about themselves. But he is not merely a more conscious person than the others; he is also individually different from other people, and from other poets too, and can make his readers share consciously in new feelings which they had not experienced before. That is the difference between the writer who is merely eccentric or mad and the genuine poet. The former may have feelings which are unique, which cannot be shared and are therefore useless; the latter discovers new variations of sensibility which can be appropriated by others."

Eliot's statement is particularly appropriate to group therapy, in which patients read their poetry to other group members. It contains an implication regarding the diagnostic value of poetry, i.e., unlike the writer who is eccentric or mad, the genuine poet can share his sensitivities with others. A wonderful goal for all of us: to share our sensitivities with others, so that they may make use of them.

REFERENCES

1. Eliot, T. S.: On Poetry and Poets, New York, Farrar, Straus and Cudahy, 1957, pp. 7–9.
2. Hogan, P., and Alger, I.: The Impact of Videotape Recording on Insight in Group Psychotherapy, presented at the 24th Annual Conf Amer Group Psychotherapy Assn, New York, January 28, 1967.
3. Robbins, B. S.: Insight, activity and change, J Robbins Institute 1:(#4) 1956.
4. Berne, E.: Transactional Analysis in Psychotherapy, New York, Grove, 1961.

CHAPTER 13

Poetry as a Therapeutic Art
In the Resolution of Resistance in Psychotherapy
ROLLAND S. PARKER, PHD

*Formerly Consultant, The Police Athletic League, Inc.,
Private practice, New York*

THIS CHAPTER WILL CONSIDER the contribution made by poetry and the other therapeutic arts to our knowledge of the theory and practice of psychotherapy, and also suggest a strategy of Poetry Group Therapy as an extension of dynamically oriented group psychotherapy. My first contact with poetry therapy occurred when, overcoming my skepticism, I accepted Dr. Jack Leedy's invitation to participate in a conference at Cumberland Hospital, Brooklyn, in 1964. The poetry therapy session there, led by Dr. Samuel Spector and the late Eli Greifer, was genuine therapy, with deep expression by the participants. It reached a heterogeneous group of patients that would have proved discouraging to those of us who practiced more conventional techniques.

Poetry and Therapy

That poetry is therapeutic says much of the therapeutic process. It is a sobering idea how little poetry there is in the lives of most patients. By poetry, we shall mean in this chapter "The expression of beautiful or elevated thought, imagination or feeling, in appropriate language, such language containing a rhythmical element and having usually a metrical form ... extended to creative art in general." (*Ruskin* [18]) This extended definition enables us to consider the other therapeutic arts, also—music, dance, painting.

Therapy is more than a verbal exchange: it is a healing experience. The therapeutic use of poetry, in its various phases, includes creativity, enhancement of self-expression, and development of insight. Psychoanalytic theory, as well as the introspective reports of creative and re-creative artists, helps us to understand aesthetic experience and thus to make possible the utilization of poetry as a systematic therapeutic modality.

Freud [10] suggested that the writer's world of fantasy is invested with a great deal of affect, while being sharply separated from reality. The activity of fantasy is linked with three periods of ideation: first, an intense desire from the present; then, an early experience in which this wish is fulfilled; finally, a future situation representing fulfillment. Whereas we would be indifferent to or repelled by the fantasies of the daydreamer, poetic art creates pleasure, overcomes the feelings of repulsion and the barriers erected between human beings. "The writer softens the egotistical character of the day-dream by changes and disguises, offering aesthetic pleasure. The true enjoyment of literature proceeds from the release of tensions in our minds." Subsequently, Freud [11] felt that poetry was the step by which the individual separated himself from the group. The poet invented the hero myth, who represented, indeed, himself, and this way he alternated between the levels of reality and imagination. His hearers understand the poet, and, "in virtue of their having the same relation of longing toward the primal father . . . identify themselves with the hero." Conscious wishes awake unconscious wishes, in turn receive reinforcement from them, and thus become dream-instigators.[9] These unconscious wishes are ready for any opportunity to ally themselves with conscious impulses and transfer their own greater intensity to them.

Wilhelm Reich [28] indicated that the psychoanalytic therapy evolving in the nexus of these ideas "was that of uncovering and eliminating resistances, not that of interpreting the unconscious directly. . . . There was not only one layer of ego defense to be broken through. . . . Instinctual desires and defensive functions of the ego, closely interwoven, permeate the whole psychic structure." Free association is hampered by the conflict between unconscious drives and ego-defenses; furthermore, symptoms persist even when the unconscious content is made conscious. This led to emphasizing interpretation in the order of the stratification of the transference resistances. Calabria [4] found evidence in poetry for this idea of stratification. Analysis of Abbe's poem "The Lamb," by means of the author's free associations, "revealed several distinct though interpenetrating, latent levels of meaning in the poem."

Kris [14] (in collaboration with Abraham Kaplan) states that poetry may tolerate or require ambiguity. This is reminiscent of the personalized response elicited by projective tests.[21] Multiple meanings exist in the preconscious of both artist and audience. In contrast to the self-imposed limitations of the scientist, the poet "explores the full range of responses to language including imagery and excitation. . . ." Metaphor serves as a stimulus to functional regression because of its similarity to the primary process. Furthermore, communication "lies not so much in the prior intent of the artist as in the consequent recreation by the audience of his work of art. . . . The person . . . contributes to the stimuli for his response."

The poet George Abbe states that the basic element in poetry is imagery, since "without metaphor, without the pictorial, the poem would descend into the limbo of prose." He believes that the healing, purging, and exalting quality of poetry (Donne, Blake, de la Mare, Wordsworth, Coleridge, Poe, Dickinson) is attributable to its symbolic qualities. These writers "crossed over and took us with them into the nuances of ultimate reality, the subtleties, elusive fragrances, colors and stunning beauty, the unexpected and daring images that shift and change and flourish beyond rational meaning, and yet remain the same imperishably."[2] The poet transforms the subliminal world into a "world of invention or make believe." As he does, he experiences the surprise of self-awareness. "And that is why poetry is the great therapy."[1] He believes that the best poetry has been written from subconscious sources under compulsion to relieve inner tension. This is achieved by attaining the introverted attitude described by Jung, with its withdrawal of emphasis from the external world (the world of consciousness), and its awareness of the subjective factor (the background of consciousness). The subconscious is "loaded with images trying to reach us (see Jochum, below), trying to tell us something we ought to know. . . ."[1] To write, he tells us, he sits at a desk or lies down, and lets his mind go "in a definite guided direction—backwards, as far as possible. A conscious effort may be necessary to put it in a receptive mood, to allow images of earlier years—particularly of childhood or adolescence—to crystallize and take hold. . . ."

Let us consider the ways in which poetry effectuates therapy.

1. THE PROCESS OF CREATION:

We will use Beethoven as an example because of his deep devotion to poetry (e.g., after decades of consideration, composing Schiller's *An die Freude* as the last movement of his *Ninth Symphony*.) This revolutionary composer had a drunken grandfather and father. His father would pull the nine-year-old boy out of bed late at night and, together with a sottish organist, give him both piano lessons and blows until dawn. The boy developed a unique talent and a Herculean, though flawed, ego.

During his career as performer and composer occurred what might have been a disaster: gradual and complete deafness. Beethoven developed suicidal impulses as a reaction. Nevertheless, the result of coping with this impairment was an incomparable increase in the expressive elements of his art commencing with the "Eroica" symphony. The cathartic value of writing is illustrated by these brief excerpts from the "Heiligenstadt Testament"[29]:

O you my fellow-men, who take me or denounce me for morose, crabbed, or misanthropical, how you wrong me! . . . Born with a fiery lively temperament, inclined even for the amusements of society, I early was forced to isolate myself. . . . Not yet could I bring myself to say to people, "Speak louder, shout, for I am deaf." Oh how should I then bring myself to admit the weakness of a sense which ought to be more perfect in me than in others, a sense which I once possessed in the greatest perfection, a perfection such as few assuredly of my profession have yet possessed it in. . . .

This material is atypical of the depressive in its poetry, length, and intensity. We may surmise that catharsis and externalization, together with his philosophy of "Man, help thyself," caused Beethoven to experience added strength. His character, molded by inner struggles against his defect and loneliness and external conflicts with the aristocracy for the independence of the musician, developed depth of experience and compassion, together with a deep vein of anger and suspiciousness. Nevertheless, these weaknesses were transcended by his artistic powers, as suggested by these quotations from Schlauffler's famous biography.[29]

Against his thoughtlessness towards Bettina, however, one may balance his delicate kindness to her sister-in-law. At this time Madame Antonie was often so ill that she had to keep to her room and refuse all visitors. Beethoven had discovered the science of musical therapy a century or so before it received more general recognition. He used to call regularly on the invalid, go without a word to an adjoining room, open the piano and improvise—then leave the house as silently as he had come. . . . He accomplished far more for his privileged patient than all the drugs and all the doctors.

Baroness Dorothea von Ertmann told Felix Mendelssohn that "when she lost her last child Beethoven at first did not want to come to the house. At length he invited her to visit him, and when she came he sat himself down at the pianoforte, saying simply: 'Now we will talk to one another in tones.' More than an hour he played without stopping, and as she remarked, "he told me everything and at last brought me comfort." Since then for how many sorrowing millions has he performed a like service.

In 1812, when he was almost completely deaf, Beethoven said: "A musician is also a poet, and he can feel himself suddenly transported by a pair of eyes into a lovelier world where greater spirits amuse themselves with him and set him right suitable tasks. . . ."[29]

2. INSIGHT AND EMPATHY:

Bruno Walter, a great Beethoven interpreter in the romantic tradition and himself called "the poet of conductors," helps us to understand the empathic and insightful concepts of the aesthetic response. A victim of both anti-Semitism and Nazism from 1933 on, he had to flee Germany, Austria, and France, and then to live to experience a daughter killed by her husband,[26] his wife's death, and later the loss of beloved colleagues far younger than himself. Maestro Walter writes that[36] "the end of the funeral march in Beethoven's *Eroica* can only become my own if my heart is in sympathy with that unique tragic darkness." He quotes Friedrich Schlegel: "Through all the sounds of this motley life-dream there sings one soft note for him who listens intently," and comments that amidst all this elemental turmoil, however, the 'intent listener' hears a sound from spheres beyond this earth."

The process of contact with the audience is elucidated by the distinguished conductor Eugen Jochum,[13] who describes a work of art as "a living thing, from which the creator detaches himself after creation like the mother from the child." As the thinking mind excludes the possessive, forming will, "the deeper layers of consciousness are vibrantly awake, straining towards the work, so that an emotional field of tension is formed in which 'the spark leaps over.'"

Poetic forms seem to reorganize mood and perception. They simultaneously sensitize the person to his "soft note," as well as to the emotional essense of the art. What has been described for music [12] is surely true of poetry: It enhances expression of otherwise unvoiceable feelings and the externalization of deep feelings; it has a universality in the conveyance of meaning.

3. EXPRESSION AND CATHARSIS:

Personality and its creative outcome in poetry tend to be organized in strata. Bion [3] helps us understand the significance of this in working with groups. He differentiated between levels of group functioning that were preverbal, involuntary, and inevitable ("Basic Assumption"), and those that were cooperative and utilized words as symbols ("Work"). By relating his theory to Melanie Klein's concepts of internal objects, projective identification, and failure in symbol formation, he provided a bridge to another school of thought whose descriptions are appropriate for particular processes occurring in poetry therapy. The "paradigmatic school" of psychotherapy lays stress on repressed feelings. Therefore, the therapist must create opportunities for the patient to understand his behavior, and to reexperience deeply buried emotions and memories. Coleman and Nelson [5] believe that "borderline patients need help in identifying what they feel, rather than why they feel." While paradigmatic technique is defined as "a setting forth by example,"[17] this could easily describe those feelings that a patient recognizes in himself after reading an appropriate poem.

How may these concepts be applied to poetry therapy? Ezriel [8] discusses the opening of a group psychotherapy session in terms reminiscent of the complex interaction between the poem and reader (or listener). Remarks are offered until a particular response matches the unconscious fantasies of another member of the group. If the latter responds, a common problem is identified and the group process evolves. It is likely that great poetry has elements corresponding to the conflicts of a large proportion of individuals.

Kris [14] discusses the "aesthetic illusion," that denial of reality which permits the audience to enter the world of make-believe and enhances the experience of poetry. To release unconscious tensions (catharsis), the ego searches for outlets. If it cannot find a point of identification with the artistic creation, or if there is insufficient incentive for energy discharge, the result will be detachment and "over-distance." With a successful "aesthetic illusion," there occurs a type of vicarious participation. Then "the pleasure is a double one, in both discharge and control. The maintenance of the aesthetic illusion promises the safety to which we were aspiring and guarantees freedom from guilt since it is not our own fantasy we follow."

Strategy of Group Therapy
With Special Reference to Poetry Therapy

We may now consider a strategy of poetry group therapy.[23] The assumptions and techniques were evolved from dynamically oriented group therapy experience in a hospital,[20] out-patient clinic,[22] and private practice.

ASSUMPTIONS

A. The therapeutic encounter is but a small proportion of the entire week. Art is long and life is short. The therapist assumes the obligation to help his patients utilize their treatment time efficiently.

B. Observation teaches that disturbed behavior is largely inflexible, despite the varieties of emotional pain and maladaptation that bring a patient into therapy. Furthermore, information generally does not change disturbed adaptation. Therefore, psychotherapy is often a lengthy process even with so-called well-motivated patients.

C. *A therapist must cope with the patient's favored style of adaptation.* This is revealed in large measure through his hereditary and dynamic forms of resistance,[24] including his self-concept, social role, and inappropriate transferences of earlier experiences. These adaptations mediate inner stability and integration with the environment in ways which may be not only inconsistent but productive of anxiety and other forms of disorder.

The poetry therapist may be warned that creativity may serve the process of resistance. Sinsheimer [31] offers an interesting example of resistance and reaction formation (with perhaps therapeutic failure). Shakespeare, resentful of the Calvinists and Puritans (with their Old Testament orientation against the theater), revenged himself upon them in the form of the moneylender Shylock. However, "as we know, the man Shakespeare ... thought and acted in a different way. He lent out money and filed suits against negligent debtors. He was, paradoxically, nearer Shylock than the Venetians of his day."[31] Edgar and Hazley [6] point out that a student used poetry to enhance his self-esteem rather than to alter his behavior.

D. *Variability in groups enhances the process of therapy.* Differences among patients provide the material for surprise, deep emotions, and a wide variety of transferences from authority figures and parents of both sexes, siblings, and children. The poetry group therapy session is an excellent opportunity to observe and further understand the individual patient (as well as himself) in both verbal and nonverbal behavior.[25] Even on a single hospital ward, narrowly defined as "maximum security," patients can vary in degree of intellectual contact, social integration, and quality of expressed affect.[20] Edgar and Hazley [6] observed differential reactions to poems based on IQ differences, and speculated whether treatment results might be related to transference reactions based on the sex of the therapist. Spector [32] demonstrated differential responses to poems according to diagnostic types, with alcoholics showing extreme reactions. His finding that schizophrenics reacted positively to a pessimistic poem that had been reacted to negatively by normals, is similar to the finding by Parker,[21] concerning the reactions of somewhat similar groups to their own projections of the human figure onto the Rorschach inkblots. Thus, the poetry therapist is warned to anticipate paradoxical reactions to dysphoric materials by severely disturbed individuals.

E. *The distinctive aspect of group psychotherapy is interactions between patients.* If, as our observations suggest, adequate group therapy can be conducted by therapists who put some social and emotional distance between themselves and their patients, then it must be assumed that the essence of therapy in groups is the activity of the patients themselves. Therapeutic patient activity consists of free expression of feelings within certain limits; acknowledgement that they need help and that they add something to their own difficulties; careful listening; support for the maturing attitudes of their colleagues; moderate discouragement for self-defeating attitudes in others; and neither active nor passive interference with their own treatment or that of others.

F. *The optimal therapist.* Such a perfect human being must be capable of free participation with minimal neurotic distortions and countertransferences. He should be able to set an example of acceptance of negative feelings and to resolve disagreements about his role. Exercising maximal alertness, he must understand the history and momentary dynamics of both the group and its individuals. He ought to be able to withstand the anxieties and pressures that the group will stimulate in him. Finally, he must develop certain practical techniques for recruitment, administration, and therapy of the individuals, and of that cohesive unit, the group itself.

NINE PRINCIPLES

1. Resistance should be the therapist's chief target. Since therapeutic impact is relatively brief (*Assumption A*), therapist activity ought to be directed towards reduction of resistance to change, thus encouraging maturation and flexibility. While we have recommended elsewhere (for conventional groups) that the therapist ought to be vigorous, directive, and confronting rather than passive, accepting to an excessive degree, and overly patient,[22] this model ought not to be applied indiscriminately in poetry therapy. An active therapeutic approach, conceived for patients able and motivated to withstand anxiety, will cause others to drop out and seek other forms of treatment.[27] When progress has been made towards reducing resistance in the group, the therapist ought to defer his own activity in favor of the patient's therapeutic activities (E).

Poetry group therapy may be particularly helpful in reducing resistance, insofar as it aids insight, encourages, and suggests new forms of behavior. Writing poems can be viewed as sublimation and symbolic externalization closely associated with dreams.[7] Thus, barriers to awareness are circumvented and resistances are broken down, since the poem appears to be objective (i.e., external and impersonal). Leedy [15] calls attention to the spell-weaving, hypnoidal, or hypnotic effects of such poems as Coleridge's "The Rime of the Ancient Mariner," wherein the patient has his attention drawn to the sound rather than to the content. The isoprinciple (reading mood-related poems) overcomes resistance and adds to the feeling that others share the reader's experience. This may be a unique contribution to the theory of resistances, since ordinarily anxiety would be aroused by confrontation with conflict-arousing ideas. In fact, poems selected according to the isoprinciple "were used as levers to involve the patients in discussion of their feelings."[7]

2. *Patients should be trained to do therapeutic work.* In the writer's VA Outpatient Clinic and private practice groups (college students and adults), it has proved feasible to train patients to eliminate or cut to a few minutes the so-called warm-up period (A), although this is a continuous effort. We consider the time saved as more valuable than waiting passively until expression of the "focal group conflict"[23] permits underlying common issues to be made available for interpretation. Indeed, the warm-up period may be by-passed: poems should be so chosen that "they can provide a continuity and a progression. . . ."[7]

Budd Schulberg [34] has utilized poetry and creative writing successfully to reach some members of the Watts region of Los Angeles, the scene of rioting in 1965. "Even more than by the vivid quality of the work produced by his class, Schulberg is impressed by the way his writers cooperate and encourage one another. 'I wouldn't have believed that they would listen so intently to each other's work,' he says; 'they listen and are moved.'"

3. The therapist creates an appropriate emotional climate. To enable patients to confront their emotional difficulties directly (*A*, *B*) and reduce anxiety and anger after attack on defined areas, the therapist has to be committed to group therapy as a technique of value, and must encourage a positive transference and group cohesion through shared experience. Otherwise, the anxieties, hostilities, deprivation, embarrassments, and negative transferences will drive the patient from treatment.

Fultz [12] sees the patient as "one who must become engaged in a 'doing' rather than a 'being done to.'" Schulberg [30] refers to a young man in his Watts experience who was considered to be a type of village idiot, yet who was "strongly dependable.... Luke was not writing but he seemed proud to have little jobs to do on behalf of the writers." Naumberg [16] indicates that as the patient understands the meaning of his own symbolic art, "he is able to help actively in his own psychotherapy ... and his dependence on the therapist is gradually reduced." Leedy [15] concurs that members of poetry therapy groups are enthusiastic about group-reciting..., (which) increases their ego strength, decreases the duration and intensity of their anxieties...." Edgar, Hazley, and Levit, [7] who consider poetry a vehicle for therapy, feel that it "can help to create a mood or tone by which emotions can be shared by the group, responded to ... and therefore can stimulate interpersonal relationships." In this group atmosphere, patients are more spontaneous and critical, and as a result there is more emotional responsivity with less aggression. Therapeutic interpretations are made with more ease and safety since the relatively unthreatening interpersonal relationships pose a minimum of threat. Even when a college group had become cohesive after twelve hours, there were appropriate times for an individual to be the focus of attention rather than the group.[6] There arrived "the precise moment to communicate the repressed meaning of a series of symptoms or the hidden sense of some attitude of mind."

4. Groups should be reasonably homogeneous in ego intactness. Homogeneity in intellectual contact and integration are required for adequate group cohesion.[20] Sufficient variability in pathology and dynamics (*D*) is generally present to prevent antitherapeutic overidentification and allow for beneficial multiple transferences. Different approaches to group activities are indicated according to the average level of ego integration, i.e., a "therapeutic smorgasbord." However, it may be that the technique of poetry group therapy permits group cohesion and therapeutic results with a more heterogeneous group than is possible with conventional techniques.

5. The therapist emphasizes "the here and now." It follows from A, B, and E that the emotions and interactions of the group session ought to have priority over historical reviews, early memories, and dreams, particularly if these serve the cause of resistance.[88] (See *3* above.)

6. The therapist keeps group activity in a state of flux. The therapist's activity ought to maximize change (B, D, and E) though not at the expense of thorough and beneficial exploration where appropriate. It should be different from that of the group (supporting or confronting as indicated), and his interventions may stir up feelings through surprise. They should be appropriate to the stage of development of the individual or group.

7. Personal responsibility is the chief therapeutic goal. It follows from the frequent difficulties of involving important family figures in treatment, as well as resistance manifested by feelings of weakness, tendency to blame others, and manipulation of the therapist to fulfill archaic needs,[24,25] that the patient's assumption of personal responsibility is the chief goal of therapy. We emphasize the importance of employment and familial responsibilities, education for one's own needs not those of parents, reduction of scapegoating, and so on.

Poetry may contribute to such goals, since it possesses, according to Abbe,[1] spiritual and ethical qualities that people need to satisfy. The most moving poem "is the one that stirs us at that psychic-ethical depth where we live most intensely." Nevertheless, to achieve the healing quality of poetry, the reader must take an active attitude, trying to comprehend the poet's intended meaning by drawing upon his richest imaginative powers. "Poetry can assist patients to develop a philosophy of life" that will aid their adjustment, inspire them to constructive action, and help make their disorders easier to bear.[15] And there may be healthful egointrojects from memorized "psycho-grafts" (Greifer) of poetry, displacing the patient's destructive self-signaling systems.[7,24]

8. *Group therapy may increase motivation by providing insight.* It has proved useful to invite patients who deny the nature of their psychosomatic and other conditions to participate in group therapy, in order to observe carefully their own reactions. While they may become aware of psychological factors (D, E), insight is considered to be only a preliminary to change (B).

The contribution of the therapeutic arts to the resolution of resistance may be understood in the words of Naumberg.[16] Since "most academic and professional training has emphasized verbal forms of communication ... it has become difficult for some ... to recognize the promise that creation of spontaneous images has to offer as a means of frequently projecting the unconscious conflicts of patients into pictures before they are able to describe them in words." Art therapy expands the patient's power of expression in both words and pictures. Art permits forbidden impulses to form "outside the patient's psyche," from which he gains detachment, thus enabling him to examine his problems objectively. It is interesting that the content of original poems has been most consistently related to Carl Jung's concept of archetypes.[2,4,6] Winston[37] claims that movement exercises may be used to stimulate image-production to produce a desired kind of movement. Specific patterns of relating, reflected in the movements and sensations stimulated by imagery, may be approached therapeutically through exaggerated and opposite movements. New material often is elicited in the verbal therapy or old material is reexperienced more vividly. With freer movement and expression, the patient appears more genuine and spontaneous, inspiring a realistically warmer response in others.

9. *Combined individual and group psychotherapy has value.* Those problems requiring unimpeded introspection or analysis and synthesis of complex events are probably not efficiently resolved in the intensity, disruption, and rapid shifts of group sessions. But in group therapy the therapist obtains a relatively complete and less distorted view of some samples of the patient's behavior, which can be subsequently explored in the individual session. Therefore,

the therapist must discriminate between resistance and legitimate questions of confidentiality. In many cases the treatment of choice is combined group and individual therapy, preferably with the same therapist, although this latter is not essential where mutual esteem and communication exist.

The poetry therapist cannot avoid the questions of confidentiality, correct timing of emotional interactions between patients, and intrapsychic upsets, which may or may not be easily apparent. He therefore must obviously be an individual of mature clinical judgment, since poetry group therapy seems to have many of the characteristics of the usual psychodynamic group therapy with the added goal (and potential hazard) of rapidly eliciting unconscious material.

Discussion

Obviously, not all psychotherapists have the interest, knowledge, skills or aptitude to develop a useful program utilizing poetry or the other therapeutic arts. We will have to rely on an increasing supply of specially trained therapists. These will be recruited primarily from among persons who wish to assist others yet cannot or do not wish to complete full professional training. Poetry therapists ought to possess that degree of dispassionateness and freedom from excessive interpersonal anxiety characteristic of successful psychotherapists.[35] Group therapy will be an important part of their training.

An important technical problem requires research. Wilhelm Reich [27] has stressed the importance of interpretation in the order of the stratification of the resistances. Since the order of unconscious material elicited by poetry therapy may be less under the control of the therapist than his option of interpreting or not interpreting during psychoanalytically oriented psychotherapy, what is the implication for therapeutic results? The possibility remains that those integrating aspects of character serving as a guard against forbidden impulses and screening out anxiety-arousing stimuli may remain to plague the patient. Or the catharsis and insight achieved may alleviate the dysfunctioning and thus eliminate the necessity for therapeutic attack on nuclei of neurotic character structure. It is apparent that this tool will be a powerful one in research and practice, providing as it does a new dimension for approaching the emotionally disturbed individual.

ACKNOWLEDGMENT

The author acknowledges with thanks the helpful comments of Julius Barasch, MD, Chief, Psychiatry and Neurology Service, and Melvin Wiederlight, MD, Chief, Mental Hygiene Treatment Section, the VA Regional Office, New York City.

REFERENCES

1. Abbe, G.: Poetry: The Great Therapy, A Statement of Faith, American Weise-Whetstone Pub, undated.
2. ———: You and Contemporary Poetry, Peterborough (N.H.), Richard R. Smith, 1965, p. 105.
3. Bion, W. R.: Experiences in Groups and Other Papers, London, Tavistock, 1961.
4. Calabria, F.: The Free Association Method and Interpretation of Poetry. Abstract of paper delivered at Ann Convention, Amer Psychol Assn, San Francisco, 1964.
5. Coleman, M. L., and Nelson, B.: Paradigmatic psychoanalysis in borderline treatment, Psychoanal Rev 5:28–44, 1957.
6. Edgar, K. F., and Hazley, R.: Validation of poetry therapy as a group therapy technique, this volume.
7. Edgar, K. F., Hazley, R., and Levit, H. I.: Poetry therapy with hospitalized schizophrenics, this volume.
8. Ezriel, H.: A psychoanalytic approach to group treatment, Brit J Med Psychol 23:59, 1950.
9. Freud, S.: The Interpretation of Dreams, New York, Basic, 1955.
10. ———: The Relation of The Poet to Day-dreaming, Collected Papers, IV, London, Hogarth Press, 1950.
11. ———: Group Psychology and The Analysis of The Ego, New York, Bantam Books, 1960, p. 88.
12. Fultz, A. F.: Music Therapy, Psychiat Opinion 3:32–35, 1966.
13. Jochum, E.: On the phenomonology of conducting, *in* Bamberger, C., ed.: The Conductor's Art, New York, McGraw-Hill, 1965.
14. Kris, E.: Psychoanalytic Explorations In Art, New York, Internat Univ Press, 1952, pp. 39–47.
15. Leedy, J. J.: Some principles of poetry therapy, The Brooklyn Psychologist, September, 1964.
16. Naumberg, M.: The nature and purpose of dynamically oriented art therapy, Psychiat Opinion 3:5–19, 1966.
17. Nelson, M. C.: The effect of paradigmatic techniques on the psychic economy of borderline patients, Psychiatry 25:119–134, 1962.

18. The Oxford Universal Dictionary Prepared on Historical Principles: Rev and ed. by Onions, C. T., ed. 3, London, Oxford Univ Press, 1955, p. 1531.

19. Parker, R. S.: Principles of the psychodiagnostic examination; tests in common clinical usage, *in* Cammer, L., ed.: Outline of Psychiatry, New York, McGraw-Hill, 1962, pp. 309–319.

20. ———: Patient variability as a factor in group activities on a maximum security ward, Psychiat Quart *39*:264–273, 1965.

21. ———: The acceptability and expression of attitudes associated to the Rorschach Human Movement Response (M), J Project Techn *29*:83–92, 1965.

22. ———: Therapist activity in the resolution of resistance in out-patient group psychotherapy, Psychiat Quart Suppl Part I, *41*:86-98, 1967.

23. ———: A strategy of group therapy consequent upon certain assumptions, unpublished manuscript, 1966.

24. ———: The varieties of resistance in group psychotherapy considered from the viewpoint of adaptation, Psychiat Quart *41*:525–535, 1967.

25. Parker, R. S., and Wiederlight, M.: The integration of non-verbal behavior and the subject-examiner interaction in diagnosis, unpublished manuscript, 1966.

26. Pinza, E. (with Robert Magidoff): An Autobiography, New York, Rinehart, 1958, pp. 159–161.

27. Reich, W.: Character Analysis, New York, Orgone Institute Press, 1949, pp. 33–36, 66.

28. ———: The Discovery of the Orgone: The Function of the Orgasm, New York, Farrar, Strauss, and Cudahy, 1961, pp. 4, 33–36, 115–116.

29. Schlauffler, R. H.: Beethoven: The Man Who Freed Music, New York, Tudor, 1944, pp. 90–93, 210, 283, 285.

30. Schulberg, B.: The New York Times, August 14, 1966.

31. Sinsheimer, H.: Shylock: The History Of a Character, New York, Citadel Press, 1963, pp. 85–90.

32. Spector, S.: Research in poetry therapy, unpublished manuscript.

33. Stock, D., and Lieberman, M.: Methodological issues in assessment of total group phenomena in group therapy, Int J Group Psychother *12*: 312–325, 1962.

34. Time Magazine: July 22, 1966, pp. 53–54.

35. Tyson, F.: Therapeutic elements in out-patient music therapy, Psychiat Quart *39*:315–327, 1965.

36. Walter, B.: On Music and Music-making, New York, Norton, 1961, p. 28.

37. Winston, S.: Dance and movement therapy, Psychiat Opinion *3*:26–29, 1966.

38. Wolf, A., and Schwartz, E.: Psychoanalysis in Groups, New York, Grune, 1962.

CHAPTER 14

The Use of Poetry in Individual Psychotherapy

SMILEY BLANTON, MD*
Cofounder and Director of Psychiatry, American Foundation of Religion and Psychiatry, New York

BEREAVEMENT IS A UNIVERSAL emotion. Solace at such times is frequently drawn from poetry and from passages in the Bible such as the challenge flung by St. Paul in the face of fate when he cried "O death, where is thy sting? O grave, where is thy victory?" Robert Louis Stevenson, writing in the same vein, has brought comfort to many sorrowing hearts by testifying to man's unconquerable spirit.

> RESURGENCE
> He is not dead, this friend—not dead
> But, in the path we mortals tread,
> Got some few, trifling steps ahead
>   And nearer to the end,
> So that you, too, once past the bend,
> Shall meet again, as face to face, this
>   friend you fancy dead.
> Push gaily on, strong heart! The while
> You travel forward mile by mile,
> He loiters with a backward smile
>   Till you can overtake,

---

* Dr. Blanton died before he quite completed this chapter. In *The Healing Power of Poetry* (New York, Crowell, 1960, page 11), he had observed: "I write from long experience in using poetry as a specific means of therapy."

At the American Foundation of Religion and Psychiatry, Mrs. Helen Margalith is organizing the Smiley Blanton Poetry Therapy Collection in connection with her work as Consultant to the Library of the Foundation.

> And strains his eyes, to search his wake,
> Or whistling, as he sees you through the brake,
> Waits on a stile.

For over forty years I have made use of poetry's faculty for healing the distressed. Among the many I have reached in this way was a woman whose mind was almost unhinged by the death of her 18-year-old son. She found comfort in Stevenson's poem. It told her something she wanted to hear, that her son's dying was not the end of the story. The poem revived her hope and restored her faith so that she was enabled to accept the tragedy of her son's death.

A very useful poem to help the depressed is one by Algernon Charles Swinburne. A young woman, 38 years of age, found herself deserted by her fiancee after an engagement that had lasted two years. The man married another woman. She developed feelings of worthlessness, lost her interest in the world about her, and fell into a deep depression. When other admonitions failed, these lines from Swinburne seemed to revive her:

IN HARBOUR

> We have drunken of Lethe at length, we have eaten of lotus;
> What hurts it us here that sorrows are born and die?
> We have said to the dream that caressed and the dread that smote us
>   Goodnight and goodbye.

She subsequently met another man. Her marriage with him has proved successful, and she has been most happy for the past ten years.

Confronted with a need to make a major change in their lives, some people wishing to hold onto the past discover that their rigidity inhibits new ways. This conflict at times leads to depression. I have found the following poem by James Russell Lowell most valuable in such cases:

> New occasions teach new duties; Time makes ancient good uncouth;
> They must upward still, and onward, who would keep abreast of
>   Truth:
> Lo, before us gleam her camp-fires! we ourselves must Pilgrims be,
> Launch our Mayflower, and steer boldly through the desperate winter
>   sea,
> Nor attempt the Future's portal with the Past's blood-rusted key.

I have read poems to those who find themselves tense, nervous, irritable and unable to relax. The soothing and relaxing influence of these poems has helped many patients to slough off their troubled state of mind. The following lines from Swinburne's "The Garden of Proserpine" have a quieting effect on disturbed people:

> From too much love of living,
>   From hope and fear set free,
> We thank with brief thanksgiving
>   Whatever gods may be
> That no life lives for ever;
> That dead men rise up never;
> That even the weariest river
>   Winds somewhere safe to sea.

These lines, from Robert Browning's "Epilogue to Asolando," are very helpful in encouraging people to meet their responsibilities and to cope with their problems, even though their spirit has begun to ebb:

> One who never turned his back but marched breast forward,
>   Never doubted clouds would break,
> Never dreamed, though right were worsted, wrong would triumph,
> Held we fall to rise, are baffled to fight better,
>   Sleep to wake.

For those suffering from tension, I have recommended these verses by Swinburne:

> **LOVE AT SEA**
> We are in love's land to-day;
>   Where shall we go?
> Love, shall we start or stay,
>   Or sail or row?
> There's many a wind and way,
> And never a May but May;
> We are in love's hand to-day;
>   Where shall we go?

And for those who suffer unrequited love, this song from Browning's *Pippa Passes* has proved its value:

> *You'll love me yet! — and I can tarry*
> *Your love's protracted growing:*

> *June reared that bunch of flowers you carry,*
>   *From seeds of April's sowing.*
>
> *I plant a heartful now: some seed*
>   *At least is sure to strike,*
> *And yield — what you'll not pluck indeed,*
>   *Not love, but, may be, like.*
>
> *You'll look at least on love's remains,*
>   *A grave's one violet:*
> *Your look? — that pays a thousand pains.*
> *What's death? You'll love me yet!*

Browning points out that patience and tolerance are most needed and that love will be reciprocated ultimately, if not in the present then at some time in the future.

For those who are bewildered, fearful, and afraid to take a chance, I have prescribed this magnificent sonnet by William Shakespeare (29):

> When, in disgrace with Fortune and men's eyes,
> I all alone beweep my outcast state,
> And trouble deaf heaven with my bootless cries,
> And look upon myself and curse my fate,
> Wishing me like to one more rich in hope,
> Featur'd like him, like him with friends possess'd,
> Desiring this man's art, and that man's scope,
> With what I most enjoy contented least;
> Yet in these thoughts myself almost despising,
> Haply I think on thee; and then my state,
> Like to the lark at break of day arising
> From sullen earth, sings hymns at heaven's gate;
>   For thy sweet love rememb'red such wealth brings
>   That then I scorn to change my state with kings.

In my experience, this sonnet has been most effective in restoring to troubled patients their faith in love's capacity to make survival possible.

For many of us, the most difficult thing in the world is to allow the one we love to harbor thoughts that we are not permitted to share. Many husbands and wives believe that they should be as one and must participate together in everything. This is not possible, of course, and that it isn't proves to some a most disillusioning discovery. These salutary verses, from Emerson's "Give

All to Love," have restored balance to some of my patients. The final verse is especially appropriate to people who find deep unhappiness when their children grow up or apart from them, or when husband and wife have feelings apart from each other.

GIVE ALL TO LOVE

Give all to love;
Obey thy heart;
Friends, kindred, days,
Estate, good-fame,
Plans, credit and the Muse,—
Nothing refuse.

Leave all for love;
Yet, hear me, yet,
One word more thy heart behoved,
One pulse more of firm endeavor,—
Keep thee today,
Tomorrow, forever,
Free as an Arab
Of thy beloved.

Though thou loved her as thyself,
As a self of purer clay,
Though her parting dims the day,
Stealing grace from all alive;
Heartily know,
When half-gods go,
The gods arrive.

Poets understand love. Euripides' *Hippolytus* describes loving and being loved in this fashion:

Phaedra. Nurse, what is this thing that men call love?
Nurse. The sweetest thing in the world, my dear, and the bitterest.

In *Romeo and Juliet* (I,1), Romeo beautifully expresses ambivalence in love:

    Rom. Alas, that love, whose view is muffled still,
Should, without eyes, see pathways to his will!
Where shall we dine? O me! What fray was here?
Yet tell me not, for I have heard it all.
Here's much to do with hate, but more with love.
Why, then, O brawling love! O loving hate!
O anything, of nothing first create!
O heavy lightness! serious vanity!
Mis-shapen chaos of well-seeming forms!
Feather of lead, bright smoke, cold fire, sick health!
Still-waking sleep, that is not what it is!
This love feel I, that feel no love in this.
Dost thou not laugh?
Ben.   No, coz, I rather weep.

Rom. Good heart, at what?
Ben.   At thy good heart's oppression.

One of the poet's functions is to help us see what life is and ourselves as we really are. A beautiful example of a poem that shows the deeper, hidden part of life is this sonnet by Richard Realf:

THE WORLD

O Earth! thou hast not any wind that blows
Which is not music; every weed of thine
Pressed rightly flows in aromatic wine;
And every humble hedgerow flower that grows,
And every little brown bird that doth sing,
Hath something greater than itself, and bears
A living Word to every living thing,
Albeit it hold the Message unawares.
All shapes and sounds have something which is not
Of them: a Spirit broods amid the grass;
Vague outlines of the Everlasting Thought
Lie in the melting shadows as they pass;
The touch of an Eternal Presence thrills
The fringes of the sunsets and the hills.

I continually see teachers and parents who complain that children are doing less than their best in school. Even though the boys and girls are bright, they do not seem to be interested in school or learning. This is often caused by poor teaching or poor concepts of what teaching should be. This poem of Browning's should be engraved in the minds of parents and teachers everywhere.

From PARACELSUS

Truth is within ourselves; it takes no rise
From outward things, whate'er you may believe.
There is an inmost centre in us all,
Where truth abides in fullness; and around,
Wall upon wall, the gross flesh hems it in,
This perfect, clear perception—which is truth.
A baffling and perverting carnal mesh
Binds it, and makes all error: and, to KNOW,
Rather consists in opening out a way
Whence the imprisoned splendour may escape,
Than in effecting entry for a light
Supposed to be without.

Some people seem to be in a constant state of anger, resentment and irritation. They feel (owing usually to some conflict in the unconscious mind) that they are being frustrated at every turn and that their efforts are unappreciated. The first step such people must take is to learn to understand themselves: they must have self-knowledge. Many of us who think we know why we behave the way we do are only fooling themselves. Shakespeare's Isabella makes this point to Lord Angelo, the Deputy, in *Measure for Measure* (II, ii):

> . . . but man, proud man,
> Dress'd in a little brief authority,
> Most ignorant of what he's most assur'd,
> His glassy essence, like an angry ape,
> Plays such fantastic tricks before high heaven
> As makes the angels weep. . . .

A recent patient of mine is typical of scores of others. He was very discouraged and felt there was nothing he could do to make life interesting. He sold his business at the age of 54, and now had nothing to do. I made some specific suggestions: he could start another business—if not the same line, then some other line. I told him that I had found Tennyson's "Ulysses" to be a great help when I was discouraged. No matter how discouraged one may be, how hopeless one feels or how lacking in faith, this poem has never failed to refresh and revive hope and faith. Ulysses, an old man in the poem, speaks to his mariners:

> There lies the port; the vessel puffs her sail;
> There gloom the dark, broad seas. My mariners,
> Souls that have toil'd, and wrought, and thought with me,—
> That ever with a frolic welcome took
> The thunder and the sunshine, and opposed
> Free hearts, free foreheads, — you and I are old;
> Old age hath yet his honor and his toil.
> Death closes all; but something ere the end,
> Some work of noble note, may yet be done,
> Not unbecoming men that strove with Gods. . . .
>   Come, my friends,
> 'Tis not too late to seek a newer world.
> Push off, and sitting well in order smite
> The sounding furrows; for my purpose holds

> To sail beyond the sunset, and the baths
> Of all the western stars, until I die. . . .
>   and tho'
> We are not now that strength which in old days
> Moved earth and heaven, that which we are, we are,—
> One equal temper of heroic hearts,
> Made weak by time and fate, but strong in will
> To strive, to seek, to find, and not to yield.

The main problem with most people is anxiety. People are afraid of failure, of losing their jobs, and of many other things as they go through life. One man came to me with tremendous anxiety because he was afraid he was going to lose his money. The money was well invested, but he was afraid he would not be able to do his work well because he had reached the age of 55 and thought he was getting old. Actually he was in excellent health, well developed and an intelligent man. I found this poem by Christina Rosetti, especially when read aloud in a whiny voice, effective in alleviating this man's anxiety.

UPHILL

> Does the road wind uphill all the way?
>   *Yes, to the very end.*
> Will the day's journey take the whole long day?
>   *From morn to night, my friend.*
>
> But is there for the night a resting-place?
>   *A roof for when the slow dark hours begin.*
> May not the darkness hide it from my face?
>   *You cannot miss the inn.*
>
> Shall I meet other wayfarers at night?
>   *Those who have gone before.*
> Then must I knock or call when just in sight?
>   *They will not keep you standing at the door.*
>
> Shall I find comfort, travel-sore and weak?
>   *Of labor you shall find the sum.*
> Will there be beds for me and all who seek?
>   *Yes, beds for all who come.*

The philosophy inherent in great poetry will enable one to face with courage and intelligence whatever comes. I remember seeing a woman who suffered from a progressive disease of the nervous system. She had been a very effective secretary, and she found

Individual Psychotherapy

a place where she could work a few hours a day. She had a collection of small cards, which she could turn from one side to the other on a ring. Written on them were verses from the Bible and other poetry. She told me: "If I didn't have these passages to read each day, I don't think I could go on." She lives cheerfully and courageously. One of the poems she used was this old 13th century hymn.

> Art thou weary, art thou troubled,
> Art thou sore distressed?
> "Comt to me," saith One, "and, coming,
> Be at rest."

In my own case, when I feel discouraged, I like to read Shelley's "Ode to the West Wind," which ends with these beautiful lines

> O, wind,
> If Winter comes, can Spring be far behind?

CHAPTER 15

Poetry Therapy in a "600" School and in a Counseling Center
Creative Writing As A Therapeutic Instrument

DOROTHY KOBAK, MSW

Psychiatric Social Worker, Bureau of Child Guidance, Board of Education, New York, and Associate Director, Mid-Way Counseling Center

CREATIVITY, WHEN APPRAISED AS AN INBORN or natural tendency, can be used therapeutically in the healing of emotional disturbances and disordered attitudes. It builds on the innate facet of every person's inheritance, *Eros*, the will to live. For to create is in some sense to be born again.

Creative writing can be a therapeutic vehicle that offers the client an opportunity to turn his attention inward towards repressed and unconscious material, without having this material modified or camouflaged. Through it, first thoughts are expressed, which in oral expression are often censored, edited, or distorted because of the presence of a listener (therapist). Thus in writing resistance is lessened, and the most flagrant fantasies may be more freely expressed with less danger of conversion from their raw form by the need for approval or fear of disapproval. We have studied the therapeutic efficacy of this process in both a group setting and individual therapy.

The "600" School

We programmed poetry and story writing in the group setting at a "600" school, a specialized educational facility operating within the framework of the New York City Board of Education, for the socially and emotionally maladjusted pupil. Since we were working with many boys whose inner controls were weak or minimal, structured conditions appeared advantageous. Thus, rather than have them write on anything they chose, the therapist encouraged them to amplify their thinking for the broadest possible response offered the topic. The paucity of the boys' inner resources was a determining factor in this. To burden them with choice of subject matter might have reinforced their always painfully present sense of inadequacy. A set topic added security and comfort to the process and gave them a springboard from which to develop their ideas.

The four boys chosen for this pilot group were of the passive-aggressive type, with clinically revealed diversity as well as similarities in their problems. Their conduct changed significantly as familiarity with this new mode of self-expression increased. At the beginning, attention span in writing was short, but there was never any resistance to writing. Both during the writing and discussion sessions, however, great anxiety was manifested by immediate body movements. At times, their scrawls and pencil doodlings over their own writing often rendered it illegible, indicating an unconscious self-deprecating mechanism as well as an attempt at concealment. Gradually, both of these conditions diminished. Initially, writing was sparse, both in quantity and depth, and the group often attempted to escape into generalities.

Written while the group was in session, the following poem illustrates the endeavor of one boy. It served as a springboard for discussion of "sentimental" material hitherto frowned on by the boys as "square."

A FISHERMAN

There once was a fisherman who lived at sea.
He had a boat, it sailed so free.
He knew some sailors big and strong
Who sailed with him the whole day long.

One day they went out for a swim,
And found a rowboat neat and trim.
It was piled with flowers red and white,
Roses, and violets shining as light.

> They pushed the boat up to the shore.
> They hoped that they could find some more.
> But there was no more to be found,
> Even though they searched around.
>
> So they went back to their own big boat.
> They set the sails and went afloat.
> They ate a meal and went to bed,
> Thinking of flowers all white and red.

The next was achieved in the manner of a "Round Robin" enterprise; that is, each boy added a sentence until the poem was completed. It afforded a tremendous "togetherness" for the boys, who, mostly self-centered loners, rarely gave of themselves in cooperative ventures. Their sense of satisfaction in building something with others corroborated this method. The end goal was the stressed factor, not the immediate satisfaction of contributing a line. The project was an "instant success," despite the need to contain themselves until the poem was finished. When it was, there was a mirthful boast of mutual congratulation at the success of their common effort. This was particularly gratifying, in that these boys hitherto had always evidenced low frustration tolerance.

> THINGS WE LIKE
> I like trees because they are green,
> I like to eat especially beans.
> I like the sky but I don't know why.
> My hair is black and I am shy.
> I like the sea because it is blue.
> I like you because you are true.
> I like a boy who has a gun.
> But to have a gun would spoil our fun.

The introverted boy offered the lines about the "green trees" and the "blue sea," yet he added the hostile line on the gun. Our obese member contributed the line about "eating beans," but gave the concluding lines about the gun "spoiling the fun": he had sublimated his angers through eating. The rejected boy, who desperately craved a relationship both from peers and therapist, described his shyness and pointed to the therapist when he gave his line, "I like you because you are true."

Although the writing activity was structured, the talking periods following the writing were free and always animated. In reading their material, the boys only rarely seemed embarrassed to reveal their productions or to expand on them. The discussion would often digress far from the original written material, very much in the manner of free association. A small point mentioned by one member would often touch off a tangential train of thought in another and then be further developed by the group.

In one discussion, one boy said, "We get love in this group." Appraising what this meant, one boy thought that he must mean that the therapist "likes him better than his own mother does." Another said that the therapist acts like a nice mother, and this could be what he meant. A third, who had a deep hostility towards his mother, moved on to say he wished mothers could be changed. The discussion wound up with comments concerning the killing of parents, the role of punishment, aspects of life the boys would like to see changed. Much of the undercurrent of the conversation reflected hostility and personal deprivation.

The therapeutic effect of these talk sessions following the writing lay in the fact that one boy's ability to express his feelings overtly often would free another boy to discuss a sensitive area that had previously been too threatening for him to discuss. This form of "derivative insight and spectator therapy" had therefore more than a small element of emotional contagion. It led to a lessening of resistance towards self-revelation and to decreased feelings of isolation.

In terms of their story writing, their fantasy lives were exposed and unrealistic flights into unattainable goals discussed. Writing a "Round Robin" *story*, which again required that each member add a sentence until the story was completed, the boys unleashed hostility to authority and angry expressions of violence. They introduced certain questions of morality, and evidenced a need for sheer revelry in make-believe adventurous escapism. Yet their *poems* showed a melancholy search for beauty, a pathetic loneliness, and sometimes a hopeless depression. In contrast to this, they wrote a *play* in which they experienced a vicarious identification with a hero who was a millionaire tycoon of the toilet paper industry!

By creating something, the boys saw themselves eventually as participants in a socially valuable or "building situation" rather than in the antisocial "breaking down" arena, which had previously characterized their lives. For boys who had rarely experienced recognition or success, acknowledged accomplishment here tasted sweet, and feelings of inferiority diminished.

The peak of emotional impact came when a boy read his "own work" to both therapist and fellow members. He was "on stage" with his own creation, making his contribution to the group process. By tapping his own creative potential, he had opened new avenues of responses, hitherto unused, which, as they became second nature to him, equipped him more fully for even rougher encounters with these emotions in future experiences. If once he had been an isolate, a failure with no sense of belonging, he was now back in communication with his fellow man. By creating—by giving of himself—he was no longer "different" but now was contributing. His own thoughts, from his depths, avenues of estrangement before, now, by writing and expressing, had become *the avenues of permission* to rejoin the society as a person committed to its functions.

The Mid-Way Counseling Center

At the Mid-Way Counseling Center, a religiopsychiatric clinic, poetry therapy was practiced in a joint endeavor with Dr. Joseph H. Gelberman, Director. In individual therapy with adults, writing poetry became an effective tool for uncommunicative and constricted clients impotent to express their feelings. The creative efforts illustrated below had the therapeutic effect of releasing on paper thoughts that clients had difficulties saying—difficulties due to a damaged ability to relate, originating from early insecurities that prohibited trust in people, especially with emotionally charged material. Written between one session and the next, this poem represents a dialogue with self as the "listener" and thereby lessened the resistance to expression of feeling.

> Because you have paved the way,
> I now know the gift of life
> And see light in every day.
> I now have the strength,

To face each day
And I know I will prevail.
I now can hope,
And I know I will find success.
I now can share—
My thoughts, my dreams, and fears.
I now feel life—
Its sorrows and its joys.
I now have patience.
And know, that in time
I will give, and receive,
The blessings of love.

Examination of this poem with the client suggested honest self-appraisal, delineation of problem, ambivalence, despair, but hope for the goals that she herself defined: "And know, that in time/I will give, and receive,/ The blessings of Love." We could then establish with the client that when this had occurred, healing had taken place.

The following are excerpts from poems written by a client who "could not feel" and "could not love." Sessions would usually elicit only arid, factual, question-like relating. However, her poems revealed the depth of the transference, the therapist as ego ideal, and a testing-out need for trust.

SESSION WITH GOD

What a sweet repast
To sit and behold
The still, small voice
Of God speaking through you.

TO YOU WHO ARE

She is dear to me,
Dearer with each step up.
To be as loving as she,
Could I but become.

FEELINGS PREVAIL

I want your understanding;
To be near as I ascend.
Sharing with you the joys
As once we shared pain.

Later, when there was much improvement in relating feeling, she wrote the following excerpt seeking the therapist's praise and approval.

> It is Love that shows me how.
> It gave me Soul to speak now.
> Please look at me anew,
> See how much I grew.

Another client, who sought withdrawal from people for fear of his own impulses and of failure, describes his loneliness and self-imposed exile.

LONELINESS

> As an old friend, you walk in,
> Ever ready to taunt,
> Always accompanied by tears—
> Yet you bring me joy.
> You are silent, and strong,
> I am glad that you are with me.
> Yet—I hear a knock at the door
> I will open—good-bye—
> Good-bye loneliness—don't rush back.

However, the confrontation that followed a discussion on the ambivalence between the enjoyment of the loneliness and the desire to be rid of it prompted the following poem, in which, at last, he asked himself the decisive question and answered the regression that he evidences in the middle of the poem.

WHO AM I

> Will someone
> Tell me who I am?
> I seem quite unable
> To find myself.
> There is a certain Power
> Driving me to uncertainty
> And to me that seems like my security.
> But then—
> That same old voice
> Trying, never tiring
> But always inquiring
> Who I am.

A highly immature client with great dependency-needs could

not verbalize, for shame and guilt, her own narcissistic egocentricity. When asked to write a poem about herself, she described what she "saw" and added her own goal—which, ultimately she achieved:

THE FIGHT IS ON

I have taken flight from preoccupation with man
Compassion and sympathy—just two words!
Poverty and pain—just too bad!
I have taken flight.
A deed undone, a smile forgotten.
A thought of hate—who cares!

But a fight goes on in me.
I must stop the flight.
I start within, and work without.
The fight is on!
I shall arrange my Soul
Now I am ready for man.

In summing up the experience of clients who have been involved in creative self-expression, as in writing poems, there appear to be some far-reaching gains in this process in therapy. As the client writes, talks, and reacts to his own written word, the material produced serves as a therapeutic tool, which, when added to the traditional therapeutic process in individual or group therapy, enables the client to accelerate his healing.

To create is to build, little by little, until a completed or whole entity is achieved. This emerges with a new form—a re-creation, a rebirth. Thus creativity is a natural companion to the therapeutic process, which builds step by step, until mental health *wholeness* is attained.

CHAPTER 16

Why Poetry?

S. SUE ROBINSON, MSS, ACSW
*Director of Social Service,
Institute of Pennsylvania Hospital,
Philadelphia*

JEAN K. MOWBRAY, MS
*Guidance Counselor,
Bryn Mawr Hospital,
Pennsylvania*

A LITERARY PROJECT, *The Tatler*, was initiated at The Institute of the Pennsylvania Hospital in 1960. The idea for it was hardly new to this private psychiatric hospital. As far back as 1843, *The Illuminator*, a hand-written literary journal, was published here during the administration of Doctor Thomas Kirkbride. Reflecting his enlightened approach to the treatment of mental illness, this small magazine contained poems and articles by patients.

Practicing his philosophy of "moral treatment," Doctor Kirkbride had a basic guideline for therapy: if you treat the patient as a human being, he will behave as a human being. Within the patient community, which simulated life outside the hospital, the focal point for therapy was participation in the activities of daily living. The patient was encouraged to do for himself, think for himself, be himself. His own capacities to give and to contribute, to lift his experience to a plane of creative fulfillment, were the springs that contained his recovery.

Geared to this philosophy of adjunctive therapy, the hospital program supported expression in art, music, and poetry. Not only the creative activity of writing, but the feat of turning out multiple copies of *The Illuminator* by hand might be called occupational therapy today. Whether creative writing was considered therapeutic is not recorded. History tells us only that a few years later the journal no longer existed.

A hundred and twenty five years later, patients again write poetry at The Institute. Although an outgrowth of the program

Why Poetry?

of resocialization, the emergence of writing poetry was not the result of a plan contrived to yield certain outcomes. The project evolved out of a normal sequence of events. At a meeting of the patient government, the patients requested a newsletter of their own to announce time and plans of all hospital events open to patients, such as movies, sports events, card parties, and special activities featuring outside entertainment. Before this newsletter, information about the organized program of activities within the hospital community was announced to the patients by the nurses. In a psychiatric setting, where participation needs specific encouragement, the weekly printed record of hospital activities served as an added stimulus to the withdrawing patient. When the announcement of events came from the patients rather than from authority, attendance increased.

As psychiatric social worker, representing the staff at patient governmental meetings, I was asked to act as "counselor" for this new publication. An exciting and rewarding experience followed. At that time, none of us could have predicted the birth of a literary project. Informal weekly meetings took place with a representative from each ward of the hospital. Forming the editorial staff, the committee gathered schedules of those activities of the hospital that were of potential interest to patients. When the materials were assembled, the newspaper staff typed, mimeographed and distributed the newsletter to every patient. In this simple way, a newspaper began.

In the next few months, the project took on new dimensions. The newsletter was named *The Tatler* after the original Addison and Steele periodical (1709–1721). Other staff members—from occupational therapy, the recreation department, and the nursing department—were asked to join the committee. Most important from a therapeutic standpoint, a resident psychiatrist was added to the already augmented patient committee, with his skills and his own enthusiasm for the project. The character of the group changed with the introduction of each new member. *The Tatler* now represented the whole hospital community.

In the mechanics of publishing the newsletter, now six mimeographed pages, ideas for content burgeoned. Encouraged to use their own initiative, the patients introduced the ideas for content, weighed their merit, and accepted or rejected them. All patients and staff were asked to submit their contributions for publication. As *The Tatler* flourished, the patients who contributed items, as well as those who read them, became more involved with the activities of the hospital. Soon an editor was elected, and an editorial appeared. With this beginning, the evolution of the newspaper became apparent.

It was not long before a patient submitted a poem. The committee decided to print the verse, not so much for its value as for the pride and pleasure of the contributor. Not only had the patient used her own creative energies, but approbation, so much needed by psychiatric patients, was implicit in the publication of her work. Many contributions of poetry were submitted to *The Tatler* office during the next few days, and continued in the weeks that followed. Any type of literary work was accepted by *The Tatler*; however, the contributions were predominantly poetry. Rarely were short stories or essays submitted. Although a relatively small percentage of patients contributed poetry at any given time, the productions were not the offerings of a prolific few. Most hospitalizations here are of short duration, the average stay about six weeks. The turnover in patients made the contributors a varied, changing group. Success bred success, and the poetry production continued. With this new source of material, a literary supplement was added to the newspaper.

So *The Tatler* again changed character. A professional poet was invited to join the group. An acquaintance of the resident psychiatrist, this writer was willing to give his time and talent to promote the literary project. Available to offer criticism for the patient's work, he read poetry aloud, including his own, led discussions on techniques, and probed for deeper meanings in the materials discussed. The poet's natural sensitivities to the patients' feelings created an immediate rapport. Moreover, his professional guidance gave serious status and dignity to the project. With the "poet in residence," the patients' writing became more disciplined, more artistic, more mature. Poetry itself became therapy. Another weekly meeting was scheduled as a literary seminar for all patients who were interested.

The success of *The Tatler*, now a monthly journal of twenty to

Why Poetry?

thirty pages, was evident in many ways. The hospital staff allocated to the publication a room of its own, the editor's office, and a meeting place for the seminars on poetry. A typewriter and mimeograph machine were contributed for the journal's own use. A small charge was made for each copy to help defray expenses; any profit was used to buy supplies needed for publication. The number of readers expanded, for the mailing list included not only patients but the medical staff, the Board of Directors of the hospital, members of the women's auxiliary, and other community organizations. Among others, a newspaper editor and an English professor became regular subscribers.

Reflecting the inner feelings of the patients, the poems opened a new source of understanding for the medical staff. The residents' orientation manual now contains a patient's poem, written during an acute phase of his illness, the brief lines revealing inner conflict more poignantly than an objective case history.

In the course of a year, a newsletter became a literary journal. Retaining the original purpose, *The Tatler* still published the news, but the literary section became its most prominent feature, evidence of the patients' growing enthusiasm for creative writing. The hospital staff, always alert to new therapeutic approaches, promoted an optimal atmosphere for the literary project and at every level supported and encouraged the patient's natural interest in writing poetry.

Although the significance of poetry as therapy was never formally discussed, its healthy effects were apparent. The opportunity to read and analyze poetry in a group setting and to discuss ideas at the weekly seminar provided a constructive experience for the patient. Important as this outcome was, however, group discussions of this kind have long been accepted as part of milieu therapy. Writing poetry seemed to have a deeper consequence. As a verbal and imaginative art form, poetry appeared to be uniquely suited to serve the psychotherapeutic goal.

Regardless of diagnosis, the patient hospitalized for mental illness has often slipped along the continuum from well to sick. In crucial areas of his development, ego functions are impaired. In all cases, the goal of psychotherapy is to bring about a more mature integration of personality. Poetry seems to be geared to this integrative purpose. The etiology of poetry and psychotherapy both involve unconscious and preconscious materials, including dreams, daydreams, and fantasies. Both employ the defense mechanisms of condensation, sublimation, displacement, and symbolization.

Basically, the production of a poem may be considered a problem-solving activity. The poet's motives are conscious and deliberate, his productions the result of a skillful use of his tools to express rather than to conceal. He uses fantasy to elicit meaning in a fresh context; he distorts in order to clarify; he symbolizes in an effort to illuminate. To translate feelings into a verbal unit suggests an awareness of self. To probe for insights requires experimentation with language and economy of words. To give form to thought represents a maturity of effort, a growth-producing experience compatible with therapeutic aims.

The therapeutic values of poetry, however, scarcely explain the appeal of this activity among so many patients. In order to develop into such proportions, the poetry project must have been inherently satisfying for those who participated. The patients at The Institute did not write poetry because it was prescribed as therapy. They expressed themselves in poetry because that seemed a natural thing to do. This creative outlet seemed to touch a need of contributing patients more sensitively than other media. Why? The answers are neither simple nor conclusive. *The Tatler* and the seminar may have encouraged some patients to try to write. In trying, there was the interest and stimulation of writing a poem, receiving professional criticism, and seeing the finished work in print, a satisfying creative sequence. At another level, writing poetry may have provided ventilation, a helpful release for the lonely, the depressed, the hostile.

At a deeper level, writing poetry might have offered an even more intrinsic satisfaction. The patients' poetry in *The Tatler* seemed to confirm some of the theories of Freud and his successors on creative writing. Freud described the poet as a "professional daydreamer" [1] whose unconscious wishes are fulfilled by sublimation. Creativity or poetry is similar to neurosis but is not neurotic. Art may even be described as a substitute for neurosis. The poet has the sensitivity to be aware of his own and others' impulses, dreams and fantasies and the courage to express them verbally.

Many psychiatric patients, both in and outside the hospital, have this same sort of sensitivity, as well as some degree of awareness of preconscious material.

In another comment on creativity, Freud observed that art (or poetry) is "an activity to allay ungratified wishes—in the first place in the creative artist himself and subsequently in his audience or spectators." [2] This may account for the therapeutic value for those who participated in the literary seminar but who did not write poetry themselves.

Neither Freud nor his immediate successors—such as Ernst Kris, who wrote about art and psychoanalysis—were suggesting that poetry might be used as therapy. Their stated purposes were to explore the mind and personality of the artist in an effort to understand the "special qualities" [3] that produce creative artists. To summarize briefly Freud's theories on the qualities necessary for creativity, the artist must have *1.* a strong instinctual drive; *2.* an extraordinary capacity for sublimation; and *3.* laxity of repression.[3] The poet, in addition, must be able to verbalize. Poetry, then, of all the arts, comes closest to the therapeutic hour in psychoanalytic terms. The similarity is striking. Both use preconscious and unconscious material to probe for inner meanings. Both employ words to expresss this material in conscious form. Both seek a solution to resolve inner conflict.

In addition to sublimation, the defense mechanisms most frequently used by poets are condensation, symbolization, and displacement, which turn the frightening unconscious into something acceptable. Metaphor is used by both poetry and psychiatry in similar ways. Catharsis of emotion by both poet and reader, a philosophical concept, Freud accepts and explains. When basic emotions are turned into aesthetic form, the sexual or aggressive impulses are gratified in a pleasant and satisfying way. Relief is obtained from tension. This may be an explanation for humor, another form the poet uses, as illustrated in contributions to *The Tatler*. Humor adds another dimension to poetry and to psychiatry, allowing the writer to see a situation in another perspective or from another view point.

To carry the analogy a step further, myths may be termed the collective unconscious fantasies of whole groups of people. Their universal acceptance must signify a universal need of wish-fulfillment in the acceptable terms of imagination. For another viewpoint—from a layman, not a psychiatrist—Glenn White, a freelance writer, attended a *Tatler* staff meeting. He read many of the patients' poems and wrote an article about his experience.[4] His apt title was "The Healing Muse."

Some of the poems are of such excellence that it is obvious they are not the work of mental patients who just happened to express themselves poetically; they are the creation of persons of poetic talent who happen, for the moment, to be mentally ill.

The themes which recur in these poems are loneliness, the search for love, the search for self and for self-understanding. This is a type of self-revelation generally characteristic of lyric verse, but as the expression of mental patients it has unusual poignancy and, often, surprising, incisive humor. I found much to be learned and enjoyed, and some of the experience of anguish, in these poems; a psychiatrist may see even more, and see it differently. But it is always best to let a poem speak for itself, so that psychiatrists and other mortals may hear what they can hear and see what they can see.[5]

ALONE

How can one bear the awful loneliness
That makes the child shriek in the darkness for
   his mother,
That forces the hollow laughter of adults at
   cocktail parties
And gnaws at the heart of the aged as they sit, sit,
   sit, and rock, rock, rock?

Oh, we may dress the fearful ghost in activity
And by disguising it, forget for a while that it
   haunts our busy footsteps
As we hurry and scurry, push and shove, race, pant,
   strain, work, work, work, keeping busy, busy, busy.

But when we return at night to our empty rooms,
There sits the unwelcome guest with its hollow eyes
   and gaping mouth, beckoning to us with a bony finger,
So that we run into the bedroom, slam the door,
   and fling ourselves upon a solitary bed
And weep, weep, weep, cold tears, tears, tears.

SOUL

There is a dark place where sometimes
   no one dwells;
It is called my soul.

It is lonely and cold there;
   and far away from the warmth of the sun.
It is a lonely place;
   and few come there to visit.

It is a quiet place,
   because no one talks above a whisper.
It is a place where one can think
   if one dares to face the fearsome things
that are conjured when one meets self.

CANTE FLAMENCO

I sank into a well
   Of deep despair.
It was so deep, so icy
   Sunken there.

There was no rope, just walls
   That gleamed with slime
And echoed back the endless
   Screams of time.

The psychiatric staff were more aware of the therapeutic value of writing, while White noticed the literary excellence of some of the poems: "And here is light verse of a quality to rival Phyllis McGinley's or Ogden Nash's—written in One North, an open floor of the Pennsylvania Hospital for patients nearing discharge." [6]

BLUES IN THE NIGHT,
or WAITING FOR THAT DAMNED
SEDATION TO WORK

Environment, heredity,
beast's nature and so forth . . .
I lie and ponder on the whys
that brought me to One North.

Was I a docile little gem

or an obnoxious sibling?
Did I say yes and no on cue,
or spend my time in quibbling?

When falling in and out of love,
did I avoid the pitfalls?
Was I murmuring honeyed words,
or were they really spitballs?

What kind of complex have I got?
There's quite a list to choose from—
is my bête noir a sense of guilt,
or do I get the blues from

that C in Math that shot to hell
my straight-A dream diploma?
that time the Pullman bed collapsed
did I sustain berth trauma?

Environment, heredity,
beast's nature and so forth...
I lie and ponder on the whys
that brought me to One North.

Here is a description of the shattered state in which so many mental patients find themselves.

MALLEABLE AS YOU ARE

Move and change,
Sleep and wake,
Flex and bend,
Malleable as you are

You break—
Not as a dish,
In two or three pieces,
But as a goblet
Hurled upon the hearth
After a toast.

If you were to count
The tiny fragments,
You would contract a job
Equal to counting
The stars,

Or all the words of men,
Or all the second-long bits of time.

Me, who am I?
My one-way mirror-mask
Is shattered.
I can't see!
Someone fix my eye!

Move and change,
Sleep and wake,
Flex and bend;
Malleable as you are,
You break.

"Many of the patients displayed in their poems poetic craftsmanship of a high order; some showed the kind of sensitivity and insight that sometimes results in literary art. If a college professor of creative writing were handed poems of the quality of these two by B. C., he might feel he had discovered another Edna St. Vincent Millay": [7]

2:00 AM

Then sleep, your dark head warm
Against my heart,
Your fingers slack upon my own
Which move to trace
Lightly, with love, the eyebrows' curve
The line of cheek, the quiet mouth.

The record spun out long ago,
The glasses emptied, talk was done;
Time is the one sound left,
Each honed and delicate tick
Chiselling our flesh and bone to death's dimension.

My own, a stranger and beloved,
When have I known you, when have I found you?
Time like a torrent roars between us,
Death like a meadow grows between us,
The serried stars fling through the silent night
And we on our separate star;
We are lost in the lurch of stars.

Then sleep, my love:
And I will hold the pity and the wonder in my arms
And let me for a little have this breathing-space
That spans the meadow and the torrent;
Let me touch this silence with tentative fingers
And see in your lost and sleeping face
The heartbreak of a world.

SONNET

As petals open one by one, asserting
The perfect sudden purity of bloom,
Or as a child thrusts into light, deserting
The chaste, archaic haven of the womb,
The guarded spirit struggles, frets, travails
To open, leaf by leaf itself, unclose
And flower, quickened, fed by truth, assails
Imponderable darkness; labouring, grows
Toward some mighty knowledge and intent,
Pursuit primeval as the blood's old surge,
The balance of negation and consent
That love at last may brilliantly emerge;
    So phoenix-like the spirit moves through flame
    To give itself a passage, home, and name.

"This is loveliness, but for those of us who are old-fashioned and like verse with a moral, here is a modern one, as old as time":

God is Godot and God is time
I am as much Godot as anyone.
  We are all our own connection;
Our own Man.
  There is a spark in each of us
That if we would but kindle
  Would burn eternally.

"Some of these verses seem to me to contain much of an age-old wisdom that enables all men and women who make it their own to endure and enjoy the day."

"Having read them, I feel stronger." [8]

In reading the patients' poetry, those of us from the professional staff could not help feeling that we too had learned from the *Tatler* project. It is not a coincidence that the patient publication is now named *Insight*.

REFERENCES

1. Freud, Sigmund: Creative writers and day-dreaming, The Standard Edition of the Complete Psychological Works of Sigmund Freud, London, Hogarth, 1953, p. 147.
2. ———: The claims of psychoanalysis to scientific interest, Gesammelte Werke VIII, London, Imgo Publishing, 1940–1942, p. 416.
3. ———: Creative writers and day-dreaming, *op. cit.*, ref. 1, p. 156.
4. White, Glenn: The healing muse, Psychiatric Reporter, Philadelphia, Smith Kline and French, May-June, 1964.
5. ———: *Ibid.*, p. 11.
6. ———: *Ibid.*, p. 11.
7. ———: *Ibid.*, p. 12.
8. ———: *Ibid.*, p. 13.

CHAPTER 17

The Use of Poetry in a Private Mental Hospital

AARON KRAMER, PHD

Associate Professor of English, Dowling College, Oakdale, Lecturer, Queens College, Flushing, New York

IT HAS BEEN my good fortune to participate in a long-range therapy program, which, because of its novelty and success, may interest others. In the summer of 1956, I was invited to give a poetry recital at Hillside Hospital, in Glen Oaks, New York. The Group Activities Department admitted some trepidation, since no such evening had ever been attempted there, or (so far as we know) in any other US mental institution. Nevertheless, the staff approached the event as a possibly entertaining experiment, and publicized it widely.

It was explained that Hillside, along with only one or two other US hospitals in this field, operates on a more or less voluntary basis for both admittance and release. Most of the patients, I was told, are above average in intelligence. Their generally relaxed and normal appearance before strangers might fool me into forgetting how deeply disturbed they actually are, and might lead me to introduce material or make statements of a nature violently discomforting and painful to some of them. I was warned in particular not to read long or "heavy" selections, and to shy away from the theme of death. It was pointed out that several months earlier a pianist had destroyed the effect of her musicianship by playing several elegiac numbers, which disquieted and depressed a large section of her audience. As a result, some patients had requested that she not be invited to perform there again.

The publicity bore surprising fruit. I was told to be ready for

Private Mental Hospital

as many as 50 people—some of whom were expressing, in advance, a great enthusiasm for poetry; others who were frankly curious about seeing a "live poet"; still others who hoped to have a good laugh at his expense. I was reassured that enough matrons would be on hand to cope with any disturbance that might arise—of which there had usually been one or two. A hundred patients showed up. This represented half the entire hospital population. Of the 100, about 75 were between the ages of 16 and 25. I operated on the premise, right or wrong, that most of my audience were unfriendly to poetry: they had come because they preferred "an evening out" to remaining alone in their wards. My aim was, therefore, to surprise and convert them.

I planned to spotlight the widespread disregard and contempt for such "luxury" items as poetry in a crassly materialistic society, aided and abetted by the generally poor teaching of literature in our public schools. I hoped to prove, as dramatically as possible and with ample illustration, that at many times and in many places poetry has not been a luxury but has played most useful and dynamic roles. To lessen their feeling of difference between me, as a two-hour entertainer, and them, as year-long prisoners, I dispensed with both microphone and stage, stood in their midst, and addressed them very plainly in terms of my own creative problems, experience and credo. In general, I followed the admonition of the staff, choosing mostly short, light-hearted poems, and avoiding all morbid themes.

However, while discussing the special role of poetry in evoking the proud past of subject peoples and inspiring them to rebellion, I decided on the spur of the moment to exploit the attentive silence by reading a very long excerpt—with its share of gloom—from Poland's nineteenth century epic, *Pan Tadeusz*, explaining first the historical background and various obscure allusions. Midway through I heard, for the first time, conversation in the back of the auditorium, and looked up in dismay, thinking my choice had been a blunder. The conversation, however, involved three matrons; with a rather electrifying unanimity, the audience turned 'round to "shush" their police! This ten-minute selection won more applause than anything else.

An animated discussion followed, in which perhaps a dozen

persons participated, centering chiefly on the Polish excerpt and on remembrances of poetry as "an instrument of torture" in the lower grades. Two young men rose to admit that they'd come with the expectation of mocking poetry, but now—for the first time in their lives—felt that poetry might have value for them. Others asked for advice on follow-up reading.

Afterwards, the hospital informed me that doctors had noted a marked "uplift" in the mood of numerous patients, and asked me to visit regularly, not as a guest artist, but as a workshop leader for those who now wanted to specialize in reading and writing poetry. At the next appearance, however, there were about 50 people, although another activity was offered at the same time. Because like numbers attended each time, the hospital finally decided not to offer any other activity on the nights of my appearance, and to publicize these poetry readings as a regular monthly feature. The average attendance has been 100. On every occasion, more than two thirds have been 25 or younger.

I've kept no journal of these evenings, and have discarded my preparatory notes. To think or write of my activities and experiences at Hillside Hospital in terms of therapy might have had a harmful effect on my behavior toward the patients: I've always avoided considering them anything other than my peers—at the least—both in intellectual capacity and social potential, and I believe their awareness of this is an important factor in the continuing welcome they extend. For the purposes of this report, however, I will set down the aspects—favorable and unfavorable—of my two-year program at Hillside, and certain incidents that needed no journal to be remembered.

Among the problems to be dealt with, I would list the following: *1. Shifts in audience:* no steady attendance, as in a classroom, but always many new faces present and old faces gone; the need is, therefore, to maintain a certain continuity, while avoiding repetition and staleness.

2. Shock treatment: the staff has, perhaps mistakenly, allowed certain patients to attend only a few hours after they've received shock treatment. In many cases, particularly among the more mature people, there is no visible effect except a loss of memory (one lady, who'd come to hear me four times, addressed me as Mr.

Copland the fifth time, then apologized and explained that she was under shock treatment). Among the very young, though, particularly girls, the effect is heartbreakingly clear—one youngster of about 16, in mannish garb, could not restrain herself from moving around and giggling at several references to sex; the other patients strained nobly to disregard her, but the giggling was contagious.

3. *Moments of upheaval:* besides shock, patients occasionally attend while under great emotional stress, and endanger the mood of the evening. An incident of this kind took place recently, involving two 17-year-old girls who've developed a strong attachment. Both are poets, the feminine partner displaying a rich lyric gift. The month before, both had approached me with poems in tribute to Anne Frank, and I had read the poems at the outset of the evening, announcing their authorship. This time, a few minutes before the program was to begin, I heard a commotion in the hallway. The mannish partner, eyes bloodshot and eyelids swollen with weeping, was arguing violently with other girls. She finally came in, walking past me without sign of recognition, and seated herself at the piano, where she leaned forward and played violent combinations of notes with her left hand, again and again. I strolled over to say hello. Before hearing me, she blurted: "I'll stop playing if you're ready to begin." I asked the fate of the Anne Frank poems, and she responded: "Hers was accepted, mine was rejected." I asked whether she'd written anything new. She told me she'd finished a long series of "wonderful" dialogues—and rapidly indicated the content of each, becoming so absorbed that soon she stopped her nerve-wracking shrieks from the piano. She hoped I'd read some of them.

Then she whispered that her girl friend had escaped from the hospital an hour ago, with the words: "I must go to the sea—if I live, I'll see you again." None of the attendants knew about the escape, and she begged me to say nothing. "That's why I'm acting this way—" she explained, and emphasized that no one besides this girl had ever loved her, and that she feared the possibility of suicide. By this time she was all talked out and rather calm. Another patient gently asked for the use of the piano, and I walked this girl to her seat. She kept thanking me for having listened to her, and having shown an interest in her poems. I urged her to concentrate on the Shakespeare reading, which was about to begin, "since these people have rehearsed for two weeks and deserve your full attention." One of the girls in the cast also seemed most upset; guessing the reason, I suggested that she beg her friend not to keep the secret any longer: it was urgent that the search for the escaped girl begin at once. A few minutes later she returned, whispered in my ear that the attendants had been informed, and went onstage to give a fine performance. The other girl sat through the entire evening without any visible sign of disturbance.

4. Educational differential: this is faced by all lecturers, to some extent, but is especially marked at Hillside. The audience ranges from the extreme of lifelong poetry enthusiasts and even specialists to the opposite extreme of those who've never paid attention to a poem before, except perhaps in hostility or bewilderment. It is difficult—well-nigh impossible—to prepare and carry through a program that will satisfy all: to find poems, and to speak in a language, capable of striking home on many levels. The discussion period gives those more advanced an opportunity to introduce more subtle nuances and more advanced concepts, and to draw the kind of answers from me that will satisfy their intellectual needs; in this "give and take" form, the material is livelier, and those less advanced listen with a good deal of interest.

Sometimes an individual either is or fancies himself to be beyond the lecturer in knowledge of his field. One such case was a Greek boy of about 18, very well-read, and himself a prolific poet. When he failed to attend, it was interpreted, by me and others (perhaps incorrectly), as a criticism of the program. When he did attend, there was no satisfying him; he always requested that I read the longest and most difficult poems imaginable—wonderful choices for a graduate school course, but impossible in terms of the educational differential here. Among his requests were Keats' "Hyperion" and the entire Book of Job. While praising his taste and expressing enthusiasm for his choices, I read only tiny passages from these works. The patients regarded him with awe; had he prevailed, however, he might have crushed both program and their self-esteem. (The hospital, incidentally, instructed me in strong terms not to cater to this boy's requests.)

5. Sensitivity to sex and death: some patients are particularly touchy on one or both of these subjects, tabooed in childhood and thrust suddenly upon them during adolescence. While not ignoring death, one may advisably shy away from too violent and vivid descriptions. As for sex, my method thus far has been to deal with it whenever appropriate. Though occasionally someone squirms, or giggles uncomfortably, or even stalks out, muttering "This is too much for me!" the general effect is so wholesome, in terms of audience gratitude for being handled without kid gloves, that a few minor disturbances may be overlooked.

6. *Exhibitionism:* this constantly looms as a frightening possibility. Very few of the adolescents indulge in this activity—on the contrary, their problem is usually a self-imposed silence and self-abnegation. Several adults are more likely to demand attention. However, there have been a number of such cases—mostly before the program begins, or at the very outset. I've tried at least to neutralize those who make a threateningly noisy entrance: teasing, singing, or complaining—by engaging them in brief conversation beforehand, and focusing my eyes on them in a kindly way from the beginning of the evening. These "bursting" individuals will usually make more than their share of comments during the discussion period; I try to praise their comments and questions whenever merited, and to treat them respectfully. This seems to give them the attention they really crave, and afterwards they are often among the most stalwart listeners. Twice, at the close of rough evenings, it was heartening to have groups of patients come and apologize for the exhibitionist, explaining that he "didn't know any better" and assuring me that my visit had been greatly appreciated.

7. *Presence of attendants:* this, I think, may have a harmful effect on the patient's ability to concentrate and to enjoy the event; it reminds him of his true status, continually. Being commanded to leave at 9 PM sharp, and sometimes bodily removed while in the midst of a thought, has a most demoralizing and embarrassing effect, dampening the mood of the whole evening. Very few of the attendants, however, perform this function harshly.

8. *Choice of words:* while not seeming careful, one must take great care with one's vocabulary at all times. Patients mentally ill are most keenly alert to hidden or double meanings—even to smiles

and gestures. They observe at least as thoroughly as they are observed, and draw subjective conclusions, often unfounded, which cause them to feel "insulted and injured." Words pertaining to mental or emotional disturbance should, if possible, be avoided. In preparing for a reading from *Hamlet*, I carefully circled four or five references to "madness" that were to be omitted. This particular event drew the largest audience ever; I saw at once that a number of patients had supplied themselves with copies of the play, in order to follow my performance, and realized that others in the audience, considering their backgrounds and the nature of their illness, might know the play better than I. Deciding that it would be worse to omit the circled lines than to read them, I went ahead without any deletions. The response was unusually good; a first-rate discussion ensued, centering on the question of Hamlet's "madness." Most gratifying was that none of the comments had subjective overtones, so far as I could observe.

9. *Lecturer's status:* there is always an undercurrent of awareness that the guest is about to leave for home and work "out there" —while the audience is about to march back to their wards "in here." At first, this separation was more intense, since the hospital, for good reasons, refused to allow any personal conversation after the program. Several times, more recently, there have been opportunities to converse, personally, with those patients who seek me out (usually to obtain my opinion of their poetry).

Following the success of *Hamlet*, I prepared a reading of some Falstaff scenes, from *Henry IV* Parts I and II, and suggested that patients volunteer to take on some of the other roles, so that I could concentrate on the character of Falstaff. An SOS phone call came from the hospital a week before the scheduled performance. The volunteers were resentful: there wasn't enough for the girls to do, and some of the fellows hankered after the colorful role of Falstaff. We worked it out by giving Falstaff to one of the boys, and by choosing another scene in which the girls played an important part. Everything went off smoothly. Giving the spotlight to seven patients meant a great deal, not only in terms of their own healing, but as a flesh-and-blood symbol to the onlookers of their own possible flowering. Two of the girls have begun writing "floods" of poetry, and one of the boys is working on a drama "in Shakespeare's style." All seven actors have established a team-relationship, with one another and with me.

10. Self-centeredness: this ranges from the egocentric variety, which resents my holding the spotlight and actively attempts to usurp it (as in exhibitionism), to the daydreaming variety, which resists my efforts to intrude and make contact and which maintains an even pitch of soul-crushed silence despite all the enthusiasm and debate raging around it. Not being members of a school class, they cannot be confronted or tested, and it is impossible for the lecturer to gauge the extent—if any—of his influence. Yet they return, month after month, applaud limply with the rest, and sometimes a few in this category unexpectedly join the "thank you" line shaking hands with me at the close of the program.

Along with the problems, however, are several factors that have contributed to the success of poetry therapy at Hillside Hospital.

1. A creative figure: the fact that the lecturer is a published poet fills many of the patients with genuine awe and interest. A very large number of these people have hoped, at one time or another, to play a creative role in the art world—as painters, writers, musicians; one suspects that, in some cases, lack of creative success has been a factor in their emotional deterioration; but they are excited by the presence of a poet, and ask no end of questions about the practical problems faced in a creative career.

2. A semi-classroom atmosphere: these youngsters, many of whom probably enjoyed their only brief success and sense of safety within the classroom, perhaps feel a nostalgic stimulus and security in the mood of lecture-discussion. At the same time, there is no danger of examination or forced recitation, and the down-to-earth, nonesoteric treatment of literature is an intriguing change from their classroom experience, leading them to reassess earlier attitudes.

3. Variety of format: the nature of the evening is not consistent. There have been many surprises that tend to keep and develop interest: national programs: Negro, Jewish, modern Greek, American; media programs: dramatic monologues, ballads, lyrics; theme programs: satire, humor, social protest, love, anonymous poets of the world. Occasionally there is a complete break in the pattern:

an evening of poetry recordings, or performances of scenes from Shakespeare, or an all-request program, or a program of my own favorite poems (with explanations why they are my favorites).

At one time, a small group of poetry-lovers became so fervent that they decided to form a Poetry Committee, to help me prepare new programs, take care of the publicity, and meet afterward for an evaluation of the evening. Although the initiation of this group was considered a very wholesome development, unfortunately, so much dissension arose among the members over what should take place the following month that the committee soon disintegrated. With closer supervision, it might have enlarged and thrived, with interim activities between my appearances.

4. Freedom of discussion: generally the most vital part of the evening, usually lasting half an hour, is the discussion period. Even those too timid or benumbed to participate seem animated when their more vocal wardmates take the floor. The questions and comments often show originality of thinking as well as erudition. Having nothing to lose, they are all remarkably candid, and accept equal candor from me. Some who participate preface their remarks with a statement that they've "never spoken up before."

5. Voluntary basis: that there is no compulsion or pressure about either entering or remaining contributes to the mood of relaxation. Naturally, the patients will give more wholehearted and friendly attention to a speaker whom they have *chosen* to hear. It would be even more effective, I imagine, if attendance were not taken—though taking it is probably a necessity. Once, at the last moment, the supervisor in charge became ill and asked whether I would mind being at the helm alone, without her introductory remarks or her authoritative presence at the front of the room. Except for a little difficulty in bringing order at the beginning, the evening worked out exactly as well as if she had been there.

6. Original work: a highlight of several evenings has been the reading of poems written by patients. This deserves to be a therapy activity in itself—and a creative writing workshop should eventually be initiated. A sizable number of Hillside people, mostly teen-agers, are making poetry their means of self-expression. Few, however, have been courageous enough to let me read their self-revelations before 100 acquaintances—fewer still would face the audience and read the poems themselves. But those few constitute a real triumph. From time to time, the most extreme cases of apparent introversion will amaze their fellows by rising and reading. Even when the poems are too cryptic for general communication, or when the embarrassed poets mumble their lines almost inaudibly, the listeners are consistently polite and warm in their show of approval. That one of them *has* managed to verbalize his or her feelings in an artistic way, and is participating in a respectable poetry recital, has inspiring significance for the others.

At one such event, in response to an invitation for original verse, a fellow came forward and read several satirical rhymes which, while slightly bawdy, displayed real wit and deftness of style. The audience loved it, particularly as a "breather" after an hour of serious material. The supervisor, however, did not laugh—and privately expressed the suspicion that this patient was guilty of a consciously insulting intrusion, intended to poke fun at my program. The next month, along with others, our humorist brought a sheaf of additional verses. Unfortunately, the supervisor adamantly refused to call on him, though he kept waving his hand. The audience became restive; a cry arose: "Let him read!" At my urgent request she finally, rather ungraciously, gave him the floor, limiting him to a couple of minutes. Again, his verses were really clever and not without ironic content; I praised and thanked him when he was done. The audience laughed and applauded heartily, yet it was apparent that a certain bitterness had been engendered as a result of this strategic blunder. Possibly the supervisor, a veteran on the staff, was basing her attitude on some prior experience; certain patients have a history of public destructiveness. Her effort to control this young man, however, turned many patients against her as the symbol of authority.

A similar situation was narrowly averted several months later. One of the middle-aged patients marched in belligerently, carrying a volume of Nick Kenny "poems" with a dozen threatening pagemarks. He announced that he hadn't ever come to these programs before, and didn't know what I was doing there, or what right I had to decide what poems should be read. Opening the book, he said he'd found some beautiful verses, which he intended to share with the audience. I invited him to read his four favorite poems.

Many patients had to turn their faces away so that he would not see how close to laughter they were because of the sentimental and banal lines. However, all applauded politely when he'd concluded, and I thanked him. We utilized the unexpected entry of Kennyism by developing a good discussion on the difference between rhyme and poetry. He then boisterously complimented my reading style, and nearly shook my arm out of its socket.

7. *The nature of poetry:* this, more than any other factor, has been decisive in the success of the program. Were the lecturer weaker, the frequency and attendance might diminish; were the lecturer stronger, more success might be attained. Of one thing I am certain: a considerable nucleus of interest, even enthusiasm, existed from the outset, and is permanently dependable. For reasons that professional psychologists could surely state with more confidence and clarity, a large number of mentally disturbed people at Hillside Hospital have made reading poetry a favorite pastime from the days of early adolescence—and, of this number, possibly half had attempted versification as a means of personal expression and emotional release. Even if no new adherents had been won during my two-year campaign, this nucleus of old-time poetry addicts would have welcomed the program, and it would have been worthwhile as a timely stimulus both for reading and writing poems.

Even more than music, poetry has been an instrument by which especially sensitive individuals, in all lands and ages, record their emotional upheavals and imaginative wanderings. Poetry is the most concentrated and vivid language of both pulmonary and nervous systems; poetry is a challenging outcry from those who refuse to conform and who are in eternal revolt against the status quo; poetry seeks for meanings under meanings; poetry insists on finding a way of saying what is forbidden or impossible; poetry resounds through a silent world, sings arias in a theatre of stammering conversation. These are not scientific or scholarly definitions, but the sum of them may indicate why adolescents who are out of tune with their daily lives, and who are moving with frightful speed toward mental and emotional disturbance, may attempt to take refuge in poetry: a language closer to them than the language of mothers, newspapers, or doctors.

Besides, there is a widespread old portrait of The Poet as a figure aloof and misunderstood, yet ultimately victorious over his time. Intellectually keen adolescents, rejected by society and in turn rejecting society, find in this legend of The Poet a convenient and romantic pattern to emulate. To qualify the "success" of Hillside's poetry program, it must be pointed out that the question has been raised whether it might be better for the disturbed adolescent to begin speaking and thinking socially, rather than jotting down his egocentric thoughts for his own satisfaction. However, I have stressed the role of poetry as a communicative and deeply social art—and, even in those cases where the patient is too timid to make his rhymes public, the consensus of opinion seems to be that by putting his most urgent thoughts down on paper he has taken a long step forward toward self-clarification and eventual health.

It would be presumptuous of me to make definitive statements based on my particular observations and experiences. Hillside Hospital, to begin with, is a most unusual place; what succeeds there might fail elsewhere. Then, too, its intellectual level is probably beyond that in most mental hospitals. That most of the patients come from Jewish middle-class homes should also not be discounted. Finally, I've had little direct contact with the medical staff, which is in a far better position to gauge the effects of my poetry program. Nevertheless, the fact that poetry has had, and continues to have, considerable therapeutic success at Hillside should mean something to those who are looking for every possible instrument of therapy.

Poetry Therapy in a Self-Help Group
AFTLI and/or Poetry Therapy

SAMUEL ALVIN GREENBERG, MD
Founder of AFTLI and of the Institute of Theopsychosophy, Brooklyn

In 1961, we founded a self-help organization and called it the Association for Feeling Truth and Living It (AFTLI). It has grown by leaps and bounds, expanding in size far beyond our original intention. That was to serve as a social center where people in individual or group therapy could let down their hair, air their gripes, exchange thoughts and, in general, grow together through social contact. It was designed to be a place where people could be free and spontaneous with one another, and it was hoped that in an atmosphere free of the usual pressures and in which people could exchange both positive and negative currents within them, creativity would flow, with its curative release of dynamic psychic and social power. We hoped to bring out the unique quality in each individual and, through a number of activities, to provide a means for him to make his unique contribution. To do so, an atmosphere had to be provided where the blocks holding members back would automatically be removed.

We set our members to work with each other in skits, research projects, audience-participation sessions, musical, dance, and poetic innovations, and, what has proved very important, discussions in groups, soon known as DIG. As an adjunct to activities, these sessions were of the highest importance in allowing members to communicate with one another, no holds barred, on deeper and deeper levels.

AFTLI is run by its members, with president, vice-president, secretary, treasurer, executive secretary, and a judicial committee, who are voted on by the general membership. An advisory board includes three ministers and four doctors, all interested in human relations. As with our DIG sessions, the meetings of the officials in committee are not formal but charged with emotion that, in expending itself, clears the air for rational discussion. The organization is growing. Many who come to our open meetings have gone away enthusiastic and vowing to start a similar place for free human exchange in their communities.

Soon after we commenced, members of our members' families expressed a desire to join, even though they were not under psychiatric care. They were accepted gladly. Now once a month our sessions are thrown open to the public; its folk come and join enthusiastically in our programs. Often, indeed, they apply for membership and are accepted.

AFTLI membership consists presently of 53 members. Attendance at meetings averages around 125. There are 3,000 people on the mailing lists. The ages of the members range from 16 to 60 years. Members and nonmembers are in all walks of life: teachers, social workers, housewives, executives, salesmen, technicians, doctors, lawyers, businessmen, high school, college and postgraduate students, printers, plumbers. There are membership dues, donations, a convention journal, raffles, dances, and donations as a result of demonstrations: monies are being accumulated. The members wish to have their own building, a foundation of self-help groups with other specialty groups, and after their growth in the specialized group, to move into the AFTLI setting.

What we work toward is an atmosphere of freedom. The freer the individual, the greater the spontaneous flow; the more spontaneous, the more natural and poetic our members become, whether acting, dancing, delivering humorous skits, or creating a poem. Many come to our meetings withdrawn and afraid to become involved with other people. But the important thing is that they attend. For after several meetings in AFTLI's spontaneous atmosphere, these people come alive and begin to flower. Robert Frost has said that "poetry is a small miracle." At AFTLI, we see many small miracles happening, as inhibited individuals release the poetry in them as comedians, actors, or creative writers.

At AFTLI, we see poetry serving as therapy for the poet, as a resolution of the disease within, a facing of a conflict. Through the creation of a poem or the expression of one's problem in poetic lines, an alteration is achieved in the unconscious of the individual. There is a dumping of a psychic unconscious conflict, after which creative energy again commences to flow. The therapeutic impact of this process is undeniable.

> Sweet are the uses of adversity,
> Which, like the toad, ugly and venomous,
> Wears yet a precious jewel in his head;
> And this our life, exempt from public haunt,
> Finds tongues in trees, books in the running brooks,
> Sermons in stones, and good in everything.
> Shakespeare: *As You Like It* (II, 1)

Most of our members have never attempted to write a poem in their lives. Many believe that they hate poetry, saying they could never "see" it. When, however, poems by various members are read back and forth without self-consciousness, there is a distinct stimulus to try one's hand. The poems are often not such as those that would be presented in a literature course. But their creators haven't that purpose in mind. Very often, they start writing without any forewarning and are unable to stop until the wind of creativity, which may not be of the highest order, spends itself. At AFTLI we encourage the wind of creativity. In such an atmosphere, resistances to the act of creation are more easily overcome. The members are themselves all attempting to do something creative, if only to express themselves to one other person.

Activities relating to poetry include the members' readings of their poems; discussion of poetry by Marguerite Harris, member of the Poetry Society of America and of AFTLI's Advisory Board; creation of music to accompany the reading of poems; singing of Shakespeare's songs in groups, such as "O Mistress Mine" from

Twelfth Night, "Who Is Silvia" from *Two Gentlemen of Verona*, "Hark! Hark! The Lark" from *Cymbeline*, "Spring" and "Winter" from *Love's Labor's Lost*, "Songs of the Greenwood" from *As You Like It*, "Sigh No More" from *Much Ado About Nothing*, "Seals of Love" from *Measure for Measure*, and "Fear No More" from *Cymbeline*; listening to records of Shakespeare's songs, the music having been written by Elizabethan composers and by Schubert; listening to other Shakespearian songs from the plays composed by Arne Harker, Loomis, Gould and La Forge while backgrounds for the dramas have been supplied by the incidental music and overtures to *A Midsummer Night's Dream* by Mendelssohn, *Romeo and Juliet* by Gounod and Tschaikowsky, *Othello* by Verdi, *Hamlet* by Ambroise Thomas, *Macbeth* by Richard Strauss, *The Merry Wives of Windsor* by Nicolai, and *Twelfth Night* by Erich Korngold; the group-reciting of poems in which sounds are dominant as "Romance" by Walter James Turner, "Quod Semper" by Lucy Lyttleton and "The Song of the Shirt" by Thomas Hood; experiments with the use of the refrain as a "chorus" in which all the members join as with Shakespeare's "With a hey, and a ho, and a hey nonino!"; interpreting poems by sketches, paintings and dances; poetry contests; and discussions and recitations of poems by a poetry therapist.

All of our activities are designed to encourage the unloading of tensions and the release of positive and creative flow. The accounts of feeling disturbed and restless before writing, of being unforewarned that they were going to write, bespeak something in them that must out. Where a troubled boy on the outside might slash the tires of a truck to get rid of the "feeling," at AFTLI a member can dance, act, or write a poem. Afterward, the "poets" speak of feeling cleansed, relieved, relaxed, as after sexual catharsis. Much of the relief here is the sense of having been the almost impersonal bearer of a message from the Beyond-within, from the ocean of the unconscious on which our conscious selves sail—a message from the deep for which one has been merely the vessel. One cannot help feeling personally enlarged to discover pouring through him creative energy that seems both personal and yet to derive from a vaster, more cosmic "Self." So new are some to the creative process that they will tell you: "I thought I was going out of my mind," or "Something happened to me that's never happened before," or "This can't be me, I never did this before." One member was consumed in a big way; he produced 77 poems in four months. "I can't seem to stop them coming," he confessed with wonder. "In the middle of my work in the office, I have to set aside my work and write down these poems as they come to me. I don't look for the words; the words come to me."

Our approach at AFTLI is that the creation of the poem holds in it the active principle of therapy. The release in the dumping of energy and simultaneous intake of positive energy, especially when the poem accomplishes the resolution of a conflict, proclaims the poet his own self-therapist. Through it, unconscious strength is converted for conscious use. Above all, there is the sense of having broken through to an accomplice within who is anxious to help and to whom one can turn.

Many of the members of AFTLI submitted poetry to help illustrate the latter point. I have chosen to use here the written communications of Jean. Jean clearly relates how she felt before, during and after the creation of her poems. My primary interest lies in the experience and the nonverbal change that occurs.

July 30, 1965
I am sending you what I've written during my recent sojourn in hell. It was a period of depression and rebellion triggered by my feelings of rejection and neglect from you, Frances and Sidney, AFTLI, and the world in general, I guess. The hate was directed at Frances and Sidney, and I felt that I could no longer belong to AFTLI because it would throw me in contact with them. Pain, anger, and hate came in waves and lasted for several weeks. Communication appeared futile, and only escape remained, and with that I called Morris and resigned from AFTLI with anger. After separating myself, these poems came without effort and gave me a deep feeling of satisfaction and release. The whole thing seems like a nightmare and . . . . Frances and Sidney were here to dinner last night.

PRIDE
Today I poisoned my life,
Today I gave up strife.
Today I hung out a shroud,

Today I chose to be proud.
My pride strikes
A dagger it hides,
In darkness it hides,
In darkness it fights,
Devastation it lights,
In death it delights.

HATE 3

The night was dark and dreary
  And nothing was any good,
Nothing remained but reasons
  For waging a personal feud.
Just can't turn to one
  Who's ever understood.

DESPAIR

Tonight will be dark
  Life is no lark
How do I know?
  Yesterday I found it so
    Because
I lived in nightmare alley
Walked the labyrinth of grief
Drank a cup of nothing
  Chased a ghost on every street.

Today I can hardly believe that it happened at all. I feel just fine now. Best regards to Evelyn.

JEAN

The poems were clearly of great value for Jean. Her creative storm was like a sermon to herself. It was her symphony for herself and her growth. She became optimistic, and realized what she had to do with her life. She has grown emotionally and spiritually in the act of creation.

I received another communication from Jean:

May 20, 1966

I was aware for a long time that I was burdened by feelings of hate, anger and hostility, but it was like a distant cloud that became ominous only when I felt rejected or overlooked.

However, each time it had happened, I managed to either reason it away or just push it down. This time I could do nothing about it but

I felt a strong inner need to retreat. Then like a cloudburst, hate, anger and pain enveloped me. I felt that no one could possibly understand or help, that I did not belong, and that the only way out was to close the door on everyone and everything associated with that feeling of rejection and neglect. Then, seemingly from nowhere, abruptly words began to fashion of themselves and into shapes that are entitled "Pride," "Hate #3," and "Despair."

While setting these words on paper, I had the feeling of being face to face with some important reality from which I could not retreat or hide. I felt an intense need to communicate on paper immediately and directly. Sometimes I had the feeling that I went through all this before, long ago. Was it not the way I felt as a child when my siblings were treated with more respect and consideration, and were preferred to me?

After that things began to get brighter and fell into place again. I felt clean and more alive again. The revitalized Jean expressed herself freely in the poems. I still feel relaxed within myself and with people around me. It is as if I went through an emotional pregnancy and have emerged from the pangs of my own rebirth. I am now a new Jean.

To use a "computer age" expression, most of us enter the world and become wrongly "programed." Right or wrong, the disturbances of parents are passed on to their children; ministers, teachers, society in general all contribute to this conformist patterning. The child wants to laugh, he is told he must not laugh; he is crying, he is told to stop crying. He wants to run and sing, he is told not to run and sing. He is dependent on these "gods" who are programing him, so he buries his resentment with his spontaneity. The love-hate ambivalence sets in. Seemingly he grows up as he is programed to do, and for many the programing is suitable and adequate. But for countless others there is the agony of feeling squashed and of demanding to find a way to "be oneself." That is where AFTLI can be of service. For a man "hypnotized" in early years by "programing" and miserable, a process of de-"hypnotizing" and de-"programing" must be undergone. Psychotherapists are in practice largely to help such people in their reeducation. AFTLI was founded to further that work.

Everyone at AFTLI is striving for a healthier adjustment. In the process of creative acts, they find out about their inner selves much that they did not know or "see" before. As their inner reality becomes realer to them, so do their feelings about themselves in relationship to people, things, and the *totality*. For this attempt of ours at AFTLI to integrate psychology and religion in a program to help our members toward insight, I have coined the word Theopsychosophy. The goals of organized religion and psychology are the same, in that both aid man in getting to his creative core, or soul, in order to find and feel meaning and purpose in life. In the search, finding that others are no different, he loses fear of them. When through the revelations that come to him through his own creative process, he begins to feel like someone and starts again to love and respect himself, then anchored and secure, he can move on to the great, ecstatic sensation of giving of himself, gratis, to help others in the world outside himself. And being secure inside, he is not affected one way or another by acceptance or rejection in his efforts to serve.

Man's development depends on his inner reaction to outer stimulus. This entails unending conflicts, to the resolution of which a knowing use of the creative process provides the most satisfactory day-to-day approach. The wise man attempts to become more and more aware of his unconscious processes. Socrates' admonition, *Know thyself*, says it all.

In the heat of creativity, many immaturities and petty conflicts are killed off. Symbolically, Cain, the growing self, kills off Abel, the younger self, who is holding him back. By the same token, the "programed" self is broken through by the creative self's searching for freedom. He breaks through the programing that love is good and hate is bad, to all as furrow and crest of the same wave. The energy of hate can be used constructively or destructively. Driven outward and faced in the constructive resolution of a conflict, it is harnessed positively. Handled fearfully by a person who feels low in himself, it can only plunge him deeper into the churn of his sadomasochistic morass of psychosomatic symptoms, depressions, or conversion reactions.

The same goes for anger, aggression and many other tendencies tut-tutted by the establishment that has done the programing. All such drives, properly handled with insight and proportion, can be handled in a constructive way. A good fight clears the air, but the man who chronically swallows his anger because of his programing is in for trouble.

Without beating about the bush, let us say: Man is the vessel of God, who is there at all times for man to make the "connection." He will always be there and He can be depended on. It is the job of a man to learn how to work with Him, the first great lesson to master being that the Kingdom of God is within. If it is your project to dehypnotize or deprogram yourself toward greater maturity, He will be your prime ally while it is toward Him that you move.

It is the job of a man to experience the reality of God in an inner encounter. Once experienced, no one can shake you of its reality. To sense the unity of the Creator, the Creative Process, and the Creation is to be integrated in an experience of unity with yourself and outer reality. This is the bridge that makes these two one, and the creative process (that we encourage above anything else) is our link to this knowledge, our invitation to ever-expandable maturity.

If the creation of poetry is therapeutic, as we have seen that it is, it is so because in the act of creating the poet is moving toward wholeness. He has found a way through to his deeper powers, the deeper sources of his being. But he hasn't drowned; he has come back to the surface impassioned for others to share with him and find their own way to this incalculable wealth. Poetry therapy may be an active or passive experience: at AFTLI we do not think of poetry therapy as being confined to the written word. It comes through the spirit of the meeting, with the freedom in the air, with people given the chance and the place to be free. There is a catalyst out of which poetic experiences evolve.

Because of the warming success we are having, we can only express the hope that organizations like ours will spring up in many communities, for it is clear that they are badly needed, and they would immediately contribute, as we are doing at AFTLI, to making the brotherhood of man a deeper reality. Thus AFTLI is "AFTLI and/or Poetry Therapy."

It would seem appropriate now to include some of a poetic view of AFTLI seen through the eyes of one of our members, Aaron.

AFTLI—A SEQUEL

AFTLI is a blithe spirit
Embracing people of religion
And of no formal faith.
AFTLI is a moment of truth
Presenting you with reality,
Flowing, fusing, fulfilling soul's
    yearning
For comprehending, for feeling,
For knowing—for living.

AFTLI is a significant experience:
Awakens the near dead
Quickens the pulse
Affirms the ego
And challenges the adventurous,
Allowing the weak to stumble
And rise again,
In total compassion.

AFTLI is the means
Yet becomes the cause,
A firm foundation
For structuring personality,
Allowing self to bloom—
Spurring the conscious ego
To venture, to experiment,
To be unafraid.

AFTLI provides a key
To the unconscious:
To the revelation of self
To the flowering of emotion,
Giving speech to feeling;
A glorious combination
Having the capacity
To alter the person.

AFTLI is a sigh and a tear:
A confrontation with yourself
Etched in murals of the heart
Subjecting the self
To search for substance
A trumpet call to action
A revelation
Moving you outward and inward.

AFTLI is a song in the heart:
A unique experience
A reality tied to a dream
Wherein you are absorbed
Challenged and changed
Transmuting positive from
    negative
Building bridges
To the world of reality.

To summarize, through poetry therapy people can cure themselves of their inner turmoil by resolution of their conflicts in the creative experience. Man has a natural desire to grow and move towards the ultimate truth. Given the chance and place in a free atmosphere such as occurs at AFTLI, a person can deprogram himself, change his value system, and bring the nonself into the conscious in various creative experiences. It is of extreme necessity for man to be able to integrate within himself the religious (creative, peak, etc.) and the analytic orientation in a humble experience of oneness with the Totality and reality of God, or to have the God experience.

We can now understand the Cain and Abel story, and how it

relates to the risings and fallings that occur in psychosomatic symptomatologies: the depressive phases during the killing of Abel (programed self, or immaturities) and thus the penance (depressive phase) period in which self-punishment or destructive action brings forth the creative dumping. A new look must also be taken at mental dis-ease. It may now be seen as a growth feature leading to mental health. As Dr. Menninger put it: "We can become weller than well." The perfect examples of William James, Abraham Lincoln, John S. Mill and many others bear out the factor that depressions can be a step towards a creative dumping, and these men thus became "weller than well."

Thus at AFTLI each person lives the experience of caring and becomes his brother's keeper. Each is physician in the sense that he ministers to his brother by sharing his experiences, caring for his fellowman with concern, and giving his love. Perhaps Robert Frost has a suggestion of all this in his

THE SECRET SITS

We dance round in a ring and suppose,
But the Secret sits in the middle and knows.

CHAPTER 19

The Double Door
Poetry Therapy for Adolescents

ROBERT E. JONES, MD
Clinical Director, The Institute of the Pennsylvania Hospital, Philadelphia

NORMAL ADOLESCENTS have more poetry in their lives than any segment of the population other than English professors. Their exposure to it comes mostly in popular songs—simple direct insights made memorable by simple retainable tunes. Every crop of adolescents supports some idol poet-singer, who addresses himself to their problems.

Consider the current hero, Bob Dylan.[1]

What he is saying is getting an unbelievably intense reaction from a generation thirsting for answers other than those in the college textbooks. Students may very well learn more from Dylan today than from the obsolete educational system, structured by another epoch. . . . In schools all over the country, students are copying down lyrics of Dylan's songs from records and insisting that the English class study them. A Jesuit high school in Sacramento devoted most of an English class one semester last year to the study of Dylan as poetry, and the University of California, like numerous other colleges and universities, has seen students get together themselves to hold unofficial seminars on his poems. . . . He has taken poetry out to the streets and put it on the juke boxes and brought it into the lives of everyone. . . . He has discovered how to speak to youth.

Psychiatrists need to speak to youth, too, and therefore must be able to assess the role of poetry in normal adolescent life as well as to use poetry as a therapeutic technique.

The problems common to all adolescents—identity, security, acceptance—seem to find expression in such metaphor as Dylan's. Adolescents entering mental hospitals bring with them this normal interest in poetic forms. It may even be that nervous adolescents have a more intense interest in poetic forms than their better-adjusted peers. "I am handed sheaves of poetry by our patients," said C. Robert Rubenstein, MD, research director in the adolescent program at Yale Psychiatric Institute, "and I try to make use of it whenever possible in therapy."

Theory

What is the theoretical basis for the use of poetry—both reading and writing it—in the treatment of emotionally disturbed adolescents? Searching for therapeutic constructs, we can turn to Freud. In "The Poet and Day-Dreaming," [2] Freud relates creative writing and the use of fantasy to the imaginative play of childhood: "The writer does the same as the child at play; he creates a world of phantasy which he takes very seriously; that is, he invests it with a great deal of affect, while separating it sharply from reality. Language has preserved this relationship between children's play and poetic creation." The child, in his course toward adulthood, learns to conceal his fantasies as being "childish" and "prohibited," because he learns that as an adult "he is expected not to play any longer or to day-dream, but to be making his way in a real world." But the pleasure of fantasy life persists, even in adulthood, and can be indulged only in certain acceptable ways. Imaginative writing is one of the ways. "Imaginative creation, like day-dreaming, is a continuation of and substitute for the play of childhood," and the artful writer can put us "into a position in which we can enjoy our own day-dreams without reproach or shame."

On the pathway from childhood to adulthood, then, the child learns to convert his wish-fulfilling play into the private exercise of daydreaming, which he can legitimately enjoy as an adult in the form of literature, poetry and song. The period of learning to conceal daydreams and to deal with them in mature ways is, of course, adolescence. For normal adolescents, poetry has a universal appeal because it provides an obviously acceptable means of dealing with fantasy. The disturbed adolescent has an even greater need for techniques to deal with impelling id wishes and fantasies. Freud said: "If phantasies become over-luxuriant and over-powerful, the necessary conditions for an outbreak of neurosis or psychosis are constituted; phantasies are also the first preliminary stage in the mind of the symptoms of illness of which our patients complain."

Poetry can serve as a two-way door, opening toward the world of fanciful childhood play or toward the reality-oriented fantasy-concealed world of adulthood. As a therapeutic tool with adolescents, therefore, poetry has two potentials: to uncover and reveal the wishful dreams of childhood, and to convert these dreams into socially acceptable yet pleasurable adult forms.

That poetry provides a pleasurable means of dealing with fantasy is important. Many childhood experiences are painful and traumatic, and the means of uncovering and dealing with them must be kindly and pleasant. "The art of the writer," said Freud, "lies in the fact that he can soften, change, and disguise the character of the day-dream by offering it in a pleasurable form. . . . Many emotions which are essentially painful may become a source of enjoyment to the spectators and hearers of a poet's work." The act of writing or reading a poem, then, can provide a way of translating a distressing experience into a pleasurable form.

Not only does poetry offer a means of communicating with childhood fantasy life; it also offers a means of communicating with the emotions attached to particular events. "Poet and novelist," said John Dewey,[3] "have an immense advantage over even an expert psychologist in dealing with an emotion. For the former build up a concrete situation and permit *it* to evoke emotional response. Instead of a description of an emotion in intellectual and symbolic terms, the artist 'does the deed that breeds' the emotion."

Practice

That poetry can work in both directions, that it is a double door, allows it to be used in a variety of ways in the therapeutic setting. At the Institute of the Pennsylvania Hospital, the use of poetry therapy with adolescents takes four forms, in all of which participation is voluntary.

Poetry seminars are conducted two mornings a week for an hour and a half, by Mr. David Fetterman, an English instructor at Temple University. Procedure at the seminars, quite informal, varies from session to session. Usually Mr. Fetterman reads contemporary poems, of his own choosing, and invites comment and discussion from the patients and nurses present. Sometimes he selects prose pieces with marked emotional impact, such as an indictment of Eichmann, or an essay on psychedelic drugs by Ginsburg. Patients may read their own selections or original verse. On occasion they have studied the compositions of guitarist Bob Dylan and heard songs written by their fellows.

Mr. Fetterman sees his role as a poetry therapist as that of activating and guiding the group. He does not offer meanings for poems, but will suggest alternate meanings from which patients can select. "I represent someone who has done this before, a person they can trust, so that they can feel free to associate to the poems." Mr. Fetterman has his own ideas about the value of poetry to the patients. "A poem is a *commune*—a place where things can participate. More than anything else, a poem is the most immediate form of relations between things, an agent for making reality concrete, a model for relationships. A poem is not hopelessly abstract; it clarifies the act of knowing the things that the mind deals with." Most important, he believes, is that the poem provides a way of "dealing with something on satisfactory terms." Mr. Fetterman quotes William Carlos Williams: "A poem is a vision of the facts," he says; "adolescents have to deal with the facts to form convictions about things." For adolescents, he sees a poem as "an adventure with an idea. Kids fantasize, and the fantasies can take over. They can see the reasoning of the poem and see how unreal their own fantasies are. Furthermore, they can identify with a poem. They can say, 'I correspond with this poet.' For them, it's a personification, a step toward a sense of dignity."

The emotional value of poetry has importance for Mr. Fetterman's philosophy also, as a group and as an individual experience. "Poems give a dignified release of emotions, and also a direction, a form." Thus, the poetry seminars are a group experience in the form of a discussion, usually—but not always—using the poetry of professional poets. It permits the exchange of associations to the poetry among the patients. The group is able to correct and modify the interpretations of its individual members.

Adolescent patients are invited to participate with adults in publishing *Insight*, a monthly news and literary hospital magazine, called *The Illuminator* in the 1840's and the *Tatler* in the 1950's. At twice-weekly staff meetings, patients read articles and poems that they have written, criticize one another's efforts, and select the best for publication. The character of these meetings changes with the patient population, at times being very businesslike, at other times resembling the poetry seminar, with emotional sharing. The editorial staff is at times very tolerant of "crazy" poetry, selecting poems that have emotional impact without necessarily having logical meaning.

Being advisor to such a publication can provide a stimulating experience for a volunteer. Over the past seven years at the Institute, several gifted people have held the post. A young poet who donated his services found the job stimulating to his own creative work. The post was filled for another year by a housewife and mother, who had retired from a magazine editorial job to raise her family. When the patients learned that she would have to give up her position as advisor to the publication, they decided to sell the magazine at 15¢ a copy in order to pay for a baby-sitter, so that the young mother could continue to volunteer her services to the hospital! Both volunteers made ample use of professional poetry in group discussions. Resident physicians are required to attend *Insight* meetings for one month in order to acquaint them with the use of creative literary work in a mental hospital. Occasionally, a resident will thereby become interested in this therapy and choose to sponsor the activity himself. When a volunteer or resident has not been available, the post has been occupied by a social worker or a music therapist, but any interested person, such as an occupational therapist or nurse, would qualify if available. As with poetry seminars, the character of the meeting is determined by the personality of the advisor and by the patients present. Of course, the patients elect their own editor and production staff. At *Insight* meetings, adolescents have an opportunity to work with adults and to share with them the experience of writing poetry, thus verifying poetry's reality-testing function.

The Institute's school unit, with its literature and creative writing courses, offers a third exposure to poetry in the therapeutic setting. The approach of the teacher is usually oriented much less toward uncovering pathologic fantasy-life and more toward structure, comprehensible meaning and good writing. Miss Julia Johnson, a teacher of disturbed adolescents at the Yale Psychiatric Institute, points out the difference in approach of the teacher from that of the psychiatrist. With his interest in the unconscious, "a psychiatrist can reinforce their writing bad poetry. By encouraging too many autistic associations, the doctor encourages bad writing rather than good." Thus, the teacher is interested, more than the doctor, in the patient's ability to organize his thoughts and feelings and to give logic and meaning to his work. The teacher, she says, "can confront the student with his craziness, with his statements that don't make sense."

Another aspect of writing poetry is the achievement of the patient. Generally, achievement is praised. For the patient, this may pose a dilemma, because he may assume that the teacher or therapist feels as his parents felt and communicated, "If you achieve, you are competing with me, and I do not want that." The use of an abstract poem may permit the patient to "find numerous ways to get away from it. If concrete, the poem can be a direct stimulus," Miss Johnson says. It is always important for the teacher to work closely with the therapist and to be as familiar as possible with the patient's history and pathology. Miss Johnson gives examples of a patient's blocking on the meaning of a poem because of family pathology. In general, the teacher is a more reality-oriented, ego-supportive user of poetry in the mental hospital.

The use of poetry by individual therapists varies from doctor to doctor. In general, the psychiatrist is interested in a patient's productions as expressions of unconscious conflicts and feelings, although this generalization should not be applied universally, because the therapist's problem is not only to analyze the patient's inner struggles but to develop in the patient the capacity for creative synthesis. The business of making the unconscious conscious is only part of treatment; maturation into an integrated person is the aim, especially with adolescents.

This synthetic process and the importance of metaphor in it are the subjects of a paper by John C. Sonne, MD: [4] "Has the effect of our scientific study of schizophrenia been to diversify our materials and forms rather than to create an organic synthesis? Do we not need poetry in the psychotherapy of schizophrenia, in addition to our new-found knowledge about the unconscious and communication?" In one example of the treatment of a schizophrenic family, Dr. Sonne capitalized on the father's use of the "illusion" of love. "In treating families such as this, or in treating their offspring, one must bear in mind that, at times, rather than being analytic, one must be poetic, for the poetry is the reality." The metaphor has a healing power, because it can translate a pathologic unconscious idea into healthy meaning.

The metaphor contains surprise, similarity and contrast, relationship, and power. An apt metaphor can link unconscious, conscious, and interpsychic levels and more, and can be as powerful in health as a dream, a delusion, or a symptom can be in sickness. One might speculate that not until we say something metaphorical do we have a human relationship. Metaphors are the reservoirs of relationships and the instruments for relating. In psychotherapy, the psychotherapist endeavors to establish a poetic and permanent organic unity with the psyche of his patient, and shares with his patient in participating in the experience of composing metaphors. 'You'll live in my mind forever' is a poetic or metaphorical statement, which is meaningless if taken literally, yet to live in each other's minds is a requirement of psychic life, if we are not to live alone.

To Sonne, the metaphor is important for its quality to synthesize and unify a relationship. He quotes Aileen Ward on Keats[5]:

This taking part in the existense—or, as he later called it, the identity—of other beings was one of Keats's most important insights as a poet. What he called "essential Beauty" was a sudden realization of the innermost character of a person or thing, won by imaginative identification with it; and through this insight a new universe was revealed to him. So he could become one with the intense absorption of the sparrow picking for its food in the dirt, or with the loneliness of the oyster asleep in its shell at the bottom of the sea; he could even feel his way, as he once said, into a billiard ball delighted with its own smooth motion and perfect roundness. What he described to Bailey was, of course, a quality which he had often achieved in his poetry without being quite aware of it, when his focus shifted from his own response to an object to the imagined inner life of the object itself: the sensations not only of the astronomer discovering a new planet, but of the star itself gazing down on the earth, or of the lazy power of a breaking wave and the delight of the rock weed swirled about in its foam.

Sonne's statements about the unifying quality of metaphor confirm the usefulness of poetry as a maturing influence. The individual therapist has a choice of using it as an uncovering or as a unifying technique.

Poetry provides a two-way treatment for adolescents, who find themselves, naturally and by virtue of their illnesses, at a period in life when the fantasies of childhood need to be mastered. In an adolescent treatment center, poetry can be utilized both to explore fantasy life and to master it: by group-sharing experience; by reading, writing, publishing, and studying it; and by using it in individual psychotherapy. Because of the nature of adolescence, poetry's use with adolescents seems particularly apt.

REFERENCES

1. Gleason, R. J.: The children's crusade, Ramparts, March, 1966, pp. 29-34.
2. Freud, Sigmund: The poet and day-dreaming, Collected Papers, vol. 4, London, Hogarth Press, 1953, pp. 173-183.
3. Dewey, John: Art as Experience, New York, Capricorn Books, 1958, p. 67.
4. Sonne, J. C.: Metaphors and relationships, Family Process 3:425-427, September, 1964.
5. Ward, Aileen: John Keats. New York, Viking, 1963, pp. 137-138.

CHAPTER 20

The Patient's Sense of the Poem:
Affinities and Ambiguities

DAVID V. FORREST, MD
New York State Psychiatric Institute, New York (Now Military Psychiatrist, Vietnam, Visiting Lecturer in Psychiatry, University of Saigon)

> *They sought it with thimbles, they sought it with care;*
> *They pursued it with forks and hope;*
> *They threatened its life with a railway-share;*
> *They charmed it with smiles and soap.*
>
> LEWIS CARROLL: "The Hunting of the Snark"[43]

PATIENTS PURSUE THEIR DEMONS (or seek their snarks) in many ways, but all use language to justify their need of the hunt. All link and define words and beliefs in various ways unlike most people (including therapists). Therapy aims to teach these differences to the patient while easing his estrangement by accepting him, without passing judgment as most people do. The more varieties of shared meanings there are, the greater the patient's feeling of acceptance and his trust in what is taught.

I wish here to consider the possibilities and problems of poetry as one variety of meaningful language to be shared with patients. I propose to explain some ways in which poetry differs from ordinary, workaday language; to suggest some similarities of poems to the patient's thoughts, and some differences; and to demonstrate some problems of understanding that will be encountered with poems from and for patients. Finally, I shall describe some advantages of poetry for the patient and for the therapist.

1. How Poetry Differs from Ordinary Language

I. A. Richards has described a difference in the *justification* or *verification* of statements in prosaic or scientific discourse and poetic statements, and has called the latter "pseudo-statements":

> A pseudo-statement is a form of words which is justified entirely by its effect in releasing or organising our impulses and attitudes (due regard being had for the better or worse organisations of these *inter se*); a statement, on the other hand, is justified by its truth, i.e. its correspondence, in a highly technical sense, with the fact to which it points.[1]

R. P. Blackmur describes poetic language as *gesture*, in which words used poetically exceed their dictionary meanings, their meanings in discursive prose:

> Gesture, in language, is the outward and dramatic play of inward and imaged meaning. It is that play of meaningfulness among words which cannot be defined in the formulas in the dictionary, but which is defined in their use together; gesture is that meaningfulness which is moving, in every sense of that word: what moves the words and what moves us.[2]

E. E. Cummings has poetically embodied this special force of poetic language in his (pseudo-) statement, "2 plus 2 is 5"[3]; that is, poems are organic wholes in which synergism occurs, making more of their parts than their sum.

This extra force in part arises from the presence in poetry of a *phonetic order* as well as the *semantic order*. The sound of poetry is so salient that, as Richards has said, "It is possible to enjoy poetry for its sound alone, prior to and independent of understanding." The sound in poetry comprises rhymes and other harmony, and the variations in meter, which are rhythm. Ezra Pound has said "Rhythm is a form cut into time,"[4] but, aside from its formal and sculptural qualities, rhythm has a profound *emotional* force, well explained by Roethke.[5] Discussing Blake's poem

A POISON TREE
I was angry with my friend:
I told my wrath, my wrath did end.
I was angry with my foe:
I told it not, my wrath did grow.
. . . . .

Roethke states:

The whole poem is a masterly example of variation in rhythm, of playing against meter. It's what Blake has called "the bounding line," the nervousness, the tension, the energy in the whole poem. And this is a clue to everything. Rhythm gives us the very psychic energy of the speaker, in one emotional situation at least.

But there are slow rhythms too, for we're not always emotionally high.

The extra force of poetic language also arises from its figures of speech and imagery, which are integral, and not merely accessory, to the total meaning of the poem. Brooks shows, in fact, that rhythm and imagery add *complexity* and *conflict* to the "simplest" poem:

The relationship between the intellectual and the nonintellectual elements in a poem is actually far more intimate than . . . that of an idea "wrapped in emotion" or a "prose sense decorated by sensuous imagery."[6]

For the imagery and the rhythm are not merely the instruments by which this fancied core-of-meaning-which-can-be-expressed-in-a-paraphrase is directly rendered. Even in the simplest poem their mediation is not positive and direct. Indeed, whatever statement we may seize upon as incorporating the "meaning" of the poem, immediately the imagery and the rhythm seem to set up tensions with it, warping and twisting it, qualifying and revising it. . . . To illustrate: if we say that [Wordsworth's "Ode on Intimations of Immortality"] celebrates the spontaneous "naturalness" of the child, there is the poem itself to indicate that Nature has a more sinister aspect—that the process by which the poetic lamb becomes the dirty old sheep or the child racing over the meadows becomes the balding philosopher is a process that is thoroughly "natural."[7]

Brooks and the formal critics have shown *that* the rhythm and imagery of poems make their sense, but there are aspects of *how* and *why* this is done that I think are of particular interest to psychiatry.

Poetry proceeds largely by comparisons and identifications of imagery, but does not justify them according to scientific logic. The reasoning of secondary process does not govern all that occurs in a poem, but yields to primary process when the poem most works upon us.[8] Poetic thought resembles that of children, of dreamers, and of patients, especially schizophrenics, in that it proceeds by *paralogic*. Paralogic allows that "a single emphasized feature possessed in common by objects is sufficient warrant for connecting together the most heterogeneous things."[9] Von Domarus echoes this principle in what has become known as his Law: "Whereas the logician accepts identity only upon the basis of identical subjects, the paralogician accepts identity based upon identical predicates."[10] (It could be put more precisely: that all identification of subjects must proceed by identification of predicates, but that the logician requires *all* predicates to be identical, and the "paralogician" only one.[11]) Arieti, who uses the term *paleologic* in place of paralogic, adds: "Why a certain predicate, out of numerous possible ones, should be selected as the identifying link can be found out only by the study of the emotional factors involved."[12]

Samuel Johnson remarked a similar way of thought among poets, whose wit could be "considered as a kind of *discordia concors*; a combination of dissimilar images, or discovery of occult resemblances in things apparently unlike." He went on to complain that, with the seventeenth-century English "metaphysical" poets, "The most heterogeneous ideas are yoked by violence together...."[13] The heterogeneity and violence vary in degree, but the discovery of resemblances in unlike things is a fundamental act of poetry. I have illustrated elsewhere [14] with poems that poetic resemblances, like resemblances seen by schizophrenics, are justified paralogically. Again by example, I have shown that the logical process of argument in a poem is a trite exercise somehow missing the point, accounting for a fraction of the thought and none of the work of the poem. T. S. Eliot has said:

... the chief use of the "meaning" of a poem in the ordinary sense, may be ... to satisfy one habit of the reader, to keep his mind diverted and quiet, while the poem does its work upon him: much as the imaginary burglar is always provided with a bit of nice meat for the house-dog.[15]

What the logic misses is again paralogic and, in fact, another argument the recognition of which *involves a participation in paralogic by the reader.*[16]

The evidence for the presence of this other argument is the

pleasure of the poem, which derives from the fulfillment of wishes in poems, as in dreams, by paralogical manipulations of rational reality. Poetry is written to fulfill wishes in the imagination. Poets argue by loose and false analogies that are established by paralogical connections and compressed into metaphors; schizophrenics do the same but are unaware that they are analogizing; or, as suggested by Bateson, they use *unlabeled* metaphors.[17] Thus Arieti gives schizophrenic identification by metaphor the name of *metamorphosis*.[18]

2. Similarities of Poems to Patient's Thoughts

> *When the language of words fails we resort to the language of gesture. . . . when the language of words most succeeds it becomes gesture in its words. . . .*[19] R. P. BLACKMUR

Poets share with schizophrenic (among other) patients a reliance upon paralogic to establish the links that fancifully satisfy their whims in the world of words. But a creation made in the world of words needs reinforcement if it is to withstand the competition of the world of things, which, by the wishful nature of poetry, is to varying degrees contradictory. Something must be done to the language to increase its inner consistency, harmony and inevitability, and decrease the appearance that it arose by chance, so that the language itself may grant an air of *authority* to what is said, thereby increasing the sense that the wishes *are* fulfilled. What is done to seek order at the surface of the language to echo and amplify the wishful statement. Pope expressed this well:

> True Wit is Nature to advantage dress'd,
> What oft was thought, but ne'er so well express'd;
> Something, whose truth convinc'd at sight we find,
> That gives us back the image of our mind [20]

explaining that:

> True ease in writing comes from art, not chance,
> As those move easiest who have learn'd to dance.
> 'Tis not enough no harshness gives offense,
> The sound must seem an Echo to the sense. . . .[21]

Dr. Johnson thought this false wit, that Pope's definition "reduces" wit "from strength of thought to happiness of language."[22] But Pope scorned those who "to church repair,/Not for the doctrine, but the music there,"[23] and his "wit" seems more generally applicable as the contribution of language itself, especially its sound, to the making of paralogical links among images to fulfill wishes. This creation to rival the real world, this making of a linguistic order for the authority it may confer to statements, I have called *poiesis*,[24] after Aristotle, for whom poiesis in an act of art meant the making of an imitation of nature.[25]

If, then, to gain authority for wish-fulfillments, poets and patients seek order in language, it follows that their processes of thought become limited by preexisting possibilities of order inherent in the language, which in part then contribute an *extrapsychic* element to the expression of poets and patients. This presents a difficulty to the poet and a danger to the patient. Thus, John Crowe Ransom has said of poetry that "extravagant exercises with language are not the rule by which logical men have arrived at their perfections of thought. The composition of the poem is an operation in which the argument fights to displace the meter, and the meter fights to displace the argument."[26] And Arieti has said of schizophrenic thought that "often mental processes occur which are stimulated only by verbalization."[27]

With his increased preoccupation with the form of the words, the schizophrenic, like the poet, finds it more difficult to speak his mind, and may sometimes use his words to fill out a form at the expense of not having them express his thoughts. In other words, sometimes the meter displaces the argument. At this point the poet may revise his poem, or else be satisfied with the thought it says, although he did not intend to say it. He may even convince himself that the thought the words say was what he had in mind all along, and in this he may resemble the schizophrenic whose thoughts are derailed by the accidental relationships among words which have no relation to their meaning, as in clang associations. The submission to language may be at the level of the sound of words or their literal meaning, involving identifications in which the verbalization is the identifying link. . . .[28]

Noyes and Kolb present an example of such linking:

One patient with a rapid flow of thought, when asked if he were sad, replied, "Yes, you have to be quiet to be sad. Everything having to do with 's' is quiet—on the q. t.—sit, sob, sigh, sin, sorrow, surcease,

sought, sand, sweet mother's love and salvation. This is my first case—
I am kind of a bum lawyer or liar—too damned honest to be a lawyer,
so had to be a liar.[29]

And a patient of mine wrote the following:

Playing games with people had been my idea to turn deterioration into socialization.

A banjo clock that says tick-tock, which is all in the recitation, is what spells reverberation. Also, a banjo clock that strikes is a denotation of reverberation.

Other similarities between poetic and schizophrenic expression involve rhetorical devices and the development of words.[30]

(1) METONYMY

Fowler defines metonymy as: "'name change.' Substitution of an attributive or other suggestive word for the name of the thing meant, as when *the Crown, Homer, wealth,* stand for the sovereign, Homer's poems, & rich people."[31] Storch reports a patient for whom a bird was "le song," and the summer "le warm."[32]

(2) SYNECDOCHE

Related to metonymy, synecdoche is defined by Webster's *Collegiate Dictionary* (ed. 7) as "A figure of speech by which a part is put for the whole (as *fifty sail* for *fifty ships*), the whole for a part (as *the smiling year* for *spring*), the species for the genus (as *cutthroat* for *assassin*), the genus for the species (as *a creature* for *a man*), or the name of the material for the thing made (as *willow* for *bat*.)"[33] Thus when Storch's patient saw

... the cellar as "le spider" or "le torn" (the torn spider-web), we are able to understand this kind of substitution of a part of the thing for the whole from the point of view of thinking in complexes, in which there is no differentiation between the sign for the part and the sign for the whole. We find a substitution of words of this same sort both in the language of children (the sun is sometimes designated as ça brûle) and in the so-called "symptom metaphors" of primitive peoples (Werner). Thus for example, the crocodile is designated "divided teeth". . . .[34]

Even scientists have resorted to such substitutions to a limited degree in developing space jargon, for example "*eyeballs in* and *eyeballs out* (describing conditions of extreme acceleration and deceleration respectively)."[35] But patients may distort synecdoche itself and "misuse the principle of *pars pro toto*, in such a way that its least essential component is chosen to represent the total concept."[36] These distortions are probably purposive as much as they are misperceived; I can cite a patient who, when she wanted to tease, would call me "Dr. Stump," diminishing my stature by making a Forrest into one sawed-off tree. And if there is an unlabeled metaphor, one might expect an unlabeled metonymy and synecdoche in schizophrenic language.[37]

(3) POLYSEMIA OR POLYSEMY

Polysemia is the extension by radiation or multiplication of the meaning of a word, as when *head* as a part of the body can come to mean the top of anything, a chief or leader, a side of a coin, or a division of a theme—all independent senses of the word.[38] Poets extend and stretch the meanings of words by using them in new contexts, as when Shakespeare for the first time said "cudgelling one's brain" and "beggaring all description,"[39] and E. E. Cummings wrote "but if a look should april me."[40] Patients develop peculiar and personal senses of words, which may have no relation to the words' histories. Thus my patient Richard, whose poems await us, thought dadaism, the 20th century art movement, referred to things his father did.

(4) BLENDS OR PORTMANTEAU WORDS

Schizophrenics, when fusing and condensing images by paralogic, may condense words as well. This may occur by hyphenation or the production of compounded substantives, such as "elbow-people," who tormented Bleuler's patient,[41] and "stethotypoallegation," a neologism by which one of my patients denoted "talk worth getting off the chest." A further extension of the process telescopes the elements, as when Bleuler's patient who "owns Algiers" suffers from "neuralgiers,"[42] and a blend results. Poets and other groups also innovate blends, as when Lewis Carroll created "slithy" from "slimy" and "writhe" and "frumious" from "fuming" and "furious," [43] and Los Angeles created "smog" from "smoke" and "fog."

Other processes are used by poets and patients in common, and it seems to me that the patients' usages should be dignified by the precise terms from poetics or general usage, because to do otherwise is to suggest that patients are being peculiar, a suspicion they have enough of.

The schizophrenic, whose quest in language is in many ways the poet's quest, may find the poet's answers; and the reverse is also true. In the oeuvre of E. E. Cummings appear a great number of the possibilities of external order, of order at the surface of language, that could be evolved by anyone in search of such order, had that person the motivation and talent to do so. I have shown[44] point for point that the peculiarities of schizophrenic writing as described by Kraepelin, Bleuler and others are used *poetically* by Cummings in expressive aberrations of spacing, capitalization, punctuation, and word division and agglutination; changes of spelling and syntax; use of dialect and slang; new uses of words; and coinages. Despite these similarities, Cummings' language is poetic and not schizophrenic, for all of the reasons which follow.

3. Differences Between Poets and Patients

Lest anyone protest, let me say at once that poets and patients are overlapping categories of people, and that emotional disorders and creativity sometimes get along famously. But the integrated poet and the disorganized or schizophrenic patient are different, and illness interferes with creativity as with other human functions.[45] Here are four differences:

(1) The poet realizes that what he does with the words for things is not thereby done to the things themselves; and the schizophrenic does not always realize this. For the schizophrenic, the word for an object may acquire the properties of the object, "and may be substituted for the object when the latter is not available."[46] This is called *word magic*, and the result is that for the schizophrenic, things may be no sooner said than done.

(2) The poet is a master of language, and the schizophrenic, even

more than everyone else, is a slave to language (Dr. Hilde Bruch suggested this distinction to me). The poet's purposes are triumphant in language, but the schizophrenic's purposes are often lost in or originate in language, to a greater degree than most people's.

(3) The poet consciously or preconsciously manipulates levels of abstraction in arriving at metaphors, but the schizophrenic tends to have difficulty distinguishing levels of abstraction [47] and differentiating concrete from metaphorical.[48]

(4) The poet expresses emotional attitudes clearly and movingly (albeit subtly and complexly) in the tone of the poem; whereas the schizophrenic's emotional attitudes are confused and contradictory, and the tone of schizophrenic utterances seems flat or inappropriate, rather than moving in any direction.[49]

4. Problems in Understanding: Poems From and For Patients

One purpose, perhaps underhanded, of this chapter so far has been to show that poetry is complex language, and that its use in therapy may pose problems. Now I shall be more aboveboard and try to show this with my patients.

A. POEMS FROM PATIENTS

With the more profound degrees of emotional illness, such as bring people into hospitals, understanding the patient becomes more problematic but is therefore more vital as his estrangement from others has been more profound. Acceptance of the patient becomes less a matter of suspension of judgment and more resembles the "willing suspension of disbelief" of Coleridge, who agreed for his part of the *Lyrical Ballads*

> ... that my endeavours should be directed to persons and characters supernatural, or at least romantic; yet so as to transfer from our inward nature a human interest and a semblance of truth sufficient to procure for these shadows of imagination that willing suspension of disbelief for the moment, which constitutes poetic faith.[50]

Perhaps there is also a therapeutic faith, that people can be understood. The following poems by patients test that faith, because they are confusing, conflicted, and partaking of William Empson's seventh degree of ambiguity or beyond. This seventh type of ambiguity

... occurs when the two meanings of the word, the two values of the ambiguity, are the two opposite meanings defined by the context, so that the total effect is to show a fundamental division in the writer's mind.

Of course, conflict need not be expressed overtly as contradiction, but it is likely that those theories of aesthetics which regard poetry as the resolution of a conflict will find their illustrations chiefly in the limited field covered by the seventh type.[51]

The patients' poems are further afield, and more ground is covered in conflict. In general, poets in their poems are able to surmount conflict and express a unified vision; patients are not. As E. E. Cummings once wrote me,[52]

finally,let's remember what no mere rationalist possibly could realize—that(as Hermann Keyserling brilliantly observes via"The Travel Diary Of A Philosopher")

"In practice no one ever gets beyond dualism;it is impossible to think,wish,strive for,act at all without postulating duality.   Why then deny it? ... On the other hand,the practical insurmountability of dualism does not mean that it belongs to Being;in all probability it depends rather on the nature of your instrument of recognition" (I,256–257)[53]

or as Heinrich Zimmer succinctly if dogmatically states ("Philosophies Of India" p 380)[54]

"Perceived pairs of opposites reflect the nature not of things but of the perceiving mind"

And Cummings' perceiving mind has unfailingly seen that

> one is the song which fiends and angels sing:
> all murdering lies by mortals told make two.[55]

The following four poems were written by Richard, an 18-year-old high school junior, whose personality had become disorganized with catatonic traits. While falling apart, he had become adept at gymnastics, which he felt "absolved all failure." He learned to stand on one hand and to do a back flip from a standing start, landing on his feet. But he preferred the high bar, because "in tumbling there was nothing to hold on to and I was afraid." The poems, too, are improbably balanced, turn life upside down, and perform contradictory reversals in midair. There is frequent mention of falling, a fear of infants and acrobats. The reader is not given the comfort of a solid high bar to grasp and swing around, but must share a feeling of being lost in space.

The patient handed me the first poem and said he "would like to write and be numb the rest of the time."

> Had you not the greater beauty
> Host to all my plays and taunts
> Had you not the straighter duty
> Of denial of my haunts
> Then I would fall, O rapture, to
> An uncrowned sailor, prince of seas,
> Victor of celestial launch.

I might willingly have taken the first quatrain as a statement of the patient's admiration and respect of me, of his gratitude because I was putting up with all his raillery and helping to limit his supernatural preoccupations. "Had you not" this capacity, the patient continues, "Then I would fall"—a clear thanksgiving, if the poem did not now suddenly turn all upside down and express *rapture*, at the prospect of a "fall" by which the patient becomes an uncrowned but princely sailor of celestial seas, the rapt victor by a voyage into private realms beyond my ken. Meter echoes the argument adroitly as the dutiful and regular trochaic foot dissolves after the quatrain into rocking, maritime rhythms as impossible to scan as swells at sea. I was left feeling I had been sincerely praised for denying my guest rapture, and was perhaps a trifle seasick. The night after he had brought me this poem, the patient dreamt his older brother died of an infection of an arm or limb. This brother, the patient told me months later, used to strike and kick him, saying he was the disgrace of the family. The patient commented, "I don't tolerate anger, a large anger sweeps me up into its course." I guessed that the brother and I had been killed together in his dream for denying him his "haunts."

But things were not so simple, and two days later the patient resurrected us for another attempt at reconciliation with his private realm. He dreamt that his brother came from across the country to visit him, appearing more handsome than he had remembered ("Had you not the greater beauty"). In the next session the patient appeared rather forlorn, and brought another poem:

No one cares, I think
Not one soul with my soul shall ever link.
Of armor stripped, I stand a man of steel
Protected from life's gifts, untouched, untouchable, untouching,
A man of men remiss.
This was what I chose, a self-perpetuating choice
In whose bent I, fallen, rent my garments with loud voice.
Give me knowledge of my ways so that I may in going find
My soul revived with age.

In this poem, counterbalanced figures again tend to check any momentum that might result. Unlike the first poem, this one begins by lamenting how alone and uncared for the speaker is. The poem contends with itself throughout. The semantic sense that no soul shall link with his is countered phonetically by numerous internal *pairings* of words and sounds besides the two end rhymes "think, link" and "choice, voice": "No one, Not one; soul, soul; man, men; chose, choice; ways, may." Unsatisfied with this, he *triples* the sound in "untouched, untouchable, untouching" and "bent, rent, garments." Then he ends with a matter-of-fact prayer for aid from the listener who presumably *does* care after all. Paradox abounds: stripped of armor, he is made of steel; though no one cares for him, it is he who is remiss; he must be steel to be *protected* from life's *gifts*. His illness was his *choice*, which yet compels him to continue unwilling and protesting in its bent. Given knowledge, he is immediately *going* from the giver. Age is *reviving*. This poem left me bewildered whether the patient was helpless or resolute in his aloneness; in it I am asked to give him self-knowledge, knowing he will be protected from the gift, which therefore is injurious and will cause him to flee. Lastly, in spite of my efforts, only time will heal.

Five days later he again brought a poem, first telling me of a word he had invented, *carstegial*, which meant "birth out of darkness from a broken baby carriage."

As out the flowers bloom deathwards
Their petals rising fall earthwards
And smell their fragrance to the dust
Like unleashed winds who tarry now
Round about the all-encircling out
Breath of hate, abomination standing stout.

In this third and more obscure poem, the strongest emotions appear to need the strongest contradictions and the most schismatic thought, so that a feeling results of impediment and even paralysis. Ideas do not persist beyond contradiction in the same line. The flowers *bloom deathwards* and in *rising fall*. The afferent sense of *smell* is used in reverse as an efferent of scent, which is lost instantly in dust. Winds *unleashed* without prior warning in the poem as suddenly *tarry*, then encircle their source, an abomination who is breathing hate, but standing stout rather than acting out. The patient could give little direct exegesis of this poem, and said he did not know what "abomination standing stout" meant. "It sounded right to me—I just wrote it down," he said. Yet he became annoyed when I asked if perhaps it had no meaning but its sound, and insisted it had "an unconscious meaning." Some may wish to add the bodily significances of tumescence and flatus to these images, with constraint of genital and anal urges; but the overall impression is that of paralysis in the experience of hate. The meter is regular and does not risk with rage what it did with rapture.

Hatred of whom? In the same session the patient said, "My folks are away." He then opened a book of poems by Dylan Thomas, and delivered a quite passable exegesis of the rather difficult poem, "The force that through the green fuse drives the flower,"[56] with emphasis on the idea of dumbness therein. Then he said, "I feel forced, consciously capable of insulting a person in a blind torrent, but I am afraid to express anger." He was tempted to unleash this torrent on another of my male patients on the ward, but could give no explanation of this, as he felt he had always liked the other patient. I concluded that his parents were the implied objects of rage for their faulty nurture (the "broken baby carriage") supposedly causing his illness, and now their going across the country to visit the older brother, for whom my other patient stood. I stood in lieu of his parents, and thus received the poem simultaneously expressing hatred and turning it back into hatred of self (as abominable).

It seemed that Richard's transference toward me had shifted with these poems from thinking of me as a disapproving older brother to thinking of me as an unsupporting parent, with the result that in the next several sessions with support of his anger the patient was able to complain about his parents in a less covert way, and further to state that "Rage was denied in my family." Surely one did not require the poems to comprehend that the patient was confused and had difficulty with anger; but the poems allow the reader in some part to experience for himself the patient's confused and topsy-turvy viewpoint, and the qualities of contradiction, frustration, and paralysis in the patient's own experience of anger. The poems allowed the patient to share cautiously, in a covert way, emotions that consequently he felt safe to share openly. Understanding, and thus therapy, were advanced by the poems.

> My day of innocence is past,
> Those leaf spun hours gone for good
> Now time is making them like flowers
> Turn to poison
> As all ancient flowers should.
> Oh, hell embalmed inherits now
> Those early days that would not stand
> And finds me sered and hastening
> As best I can. As best I can.

This last poem, written several months after the others, betrays a sadder, soberer Richard who had relinquished some of his numbness and "rapture" and was struggling to do his schoolwork despite his thought disorder. He explained that "My day of innocence is past" meant that he was "more in touch"; that the hours of numbness (in which he was "innocent" of feelings) had turned to poison in that "their remembrance frustrates me because I can't have them back." "Hell embalmed" is an odd and tortured idea, which, the patient said, applied to himself. I took it to reflect hellish feelings in a state of cold preservation and thoughts of suicide that appeared fleetingly at that time. "Those early days that would not stand" (that is, "last") tormented him, and he felt "sered" ("burnt"), that is, he had begun to feel his inner hell. He was hastening "anywhere away from them" (the remembered days), and the poem asked me to recognize the great suffering this effort cost him. It repeated that he was doing all he could so that more would not be asked of him. After I had restated this to assure him that I got the message of the poem, he said that he was beginning to take himself seriously because I took his suffering seriously. By this time, his ability to understand and paraphrase his own poetry had grown. But he paradoxically (and typically) added that he wished he could "realize" himself the suffering in the poem, thus telling me he could not yet fully express it otherwise than in poetry.

The following poem was written by Lois, a 16-year-old high school graduate, whose intellectual precocity was outweighed by her emotional immaturity. She had led a chaotic artist's existence in bizarre dress smeared with dirt and paint, and her rebellion had featured day-night reversal, sexual acting out, fasting, and a rather paranoid disorganization of thought on and off amphetamines and marijuana. She maintained all this was merely "seeing what kind of life I want to lead," and was overtly opposed to hospitalization, running away at one point to her old habits. Back in the hospital, again looking like a brushed puppy, she wrote:

> what's it like??
> what's it like??
> they lock ya in padded cells,
> throw ya in straight jackets,
> gag ya
> beat ya,
> putcha in ice packs, huh? huh?
>
> nah—it's nothin'
> as good as that—
> yuh just sit in
> a room for a couple of years
> and then they let ya out
>
> that's all.

The poem, although metrically free, is intensely rhythmic and strongly stressed. Its tempi, stanzas and sense reminded me of two other strongly rhythmic poems:

> (will you teach a
> wretch to live
> straighter than a needle)
>
> ask
>   her
>   ask

Patient's Sense: Affinities and Ambiguities 247

                    when
                        (ask and
                        ask
                        and ask
            again and)ask a
            brittle little
            person fiddling
            in
            the
            rain
            . . . . .
                    —E. E. Cummings [57]

Hinx, minx, the old witch winks,
The fat begins to fry,
There's nobody home but Jumping Joan,
And Father, and Mother, and I.
                    —Mother Goose [58]

The half poem from Cummings is unlike the patient's poem in being regularly trochaic, but her first stanza recalls his poem by its similar breathless urgency to know. There is an additional violence, not in Cummings' poem, expressed by her pounding accents of "lock ya," "throw ya," "gag ya, beat ya," and "putcha." The Mother Goose rhyme matches in mischief the mayhem of the patient's poem. Roethke reads the rhyme as a drama of a secret tryst with a minx, Jumping Joan, while "the fat begins to fry, literally and symbolically."[59] Both poems begin with pounding accents, as in "huh? huh?" and "hinx, minx," and employ slow anapests toward the end to delay the reader: cf. "yuh just sit in/ a room for a couple of years" and "There's nobody home but Jumping Joan,/ And Father, and Mother, and I." The delay creates anticipation, both of the tryst and of getting out, which the patient renders in a brisk iamb that seems to skip: "and then they let ya out."

The contrast between the patient's first and second stanza suggests alternative responses she might have had to our teaching her "to live/straighter than a needle," and it is made clear she would prefer the first, paranoid version to the second, depressive alternative. Thus she dreamt of me as a menacing Batman brandishing a syringe of "mind-bending drugs." Placed in confinement unless on good behavior, a situation intolerably boring and depressing to her, the patient rapidly earned privileges and attended art school from the hospital.

There seems to be little question that, when presented with a poem by a patient, the therapist should try to understand it. Whether to continue to encourage communication by poetry is another matter. The foregoing poems suggest that some patients with severe conflicts may be able to communicate in poetry or in poetic speech some of their confusion and anguish which they cannot as yet express directly. But one ought to be prepared to relinquish poetry, however interesting or beautiful it has been, in favor of direct speech when the patient is able.

B. POEMS FOR PATIENTS

When poems flow in the other direction, other problems appear, primarily of understanding. Let us begin not with patients but with a group that might be selected for the ability to understand poetry. For intelligence with flexibility and impressionability, let us choose undergraduates, at a highly respected university, say, Cambridge. Let there be equal numbers of men and women. Let the majority in our group be "reading English with a view to an Honours Degree." I. A. Richards lectured such a group, whom he described as "the products of the most expensive kind of education.... I would like to repeat, with emphasis, that there is no reason whatever to suppose that a higher capacity for reading poetry will be manifested by any similar group anywhere in the world."[60]

Richards submitted to his students printed sheets of unidentified poems by such traditional authors as Rossetti, Donne, Millay, Hopkins, Lawrence, Longfellow, and Hardy, and asked them to submit their comments. The group was further selected in that "those who took the trouble to write—about 60 per cent—may be presumed to have been actuated by a more than ordinarily keen interest in poetry."[61] Richards presents their replies which are entertaining but sobering to the prospective poetry therapist. He concludes:

The most disturbing and impressive fact brought out by this experiment is that a large proportion of average-to-good (and in some cases, certainly devoted) readers of poetry frequently and repeatedly *fail to understand it*, both as a statement and as an expression. They fail to make out its prose sense, its plain, overt meaning, as a set of ordinary intelligible, English sentences, taken quite apart from any further poetic significance. And equally, they misapprehend its feeling, its tone, and its intention.[62]

As soon as metaphorical or figurative uses of speech are introduced, and such writings can rarely avoid them, these dangers become much increased. I have made, since the bulk of this book was prepared, some further experiments with the paraphrasing of fairly simple and semi-allegorical passages. They more than corroborate what was shown by the protocols here given. Not nearly 30 per cent of a University audience are to be trusted not to misinterpret such language.[63]

Introduce metaphor, and the dangers increase. Introduce an audience who think in unlabeled metaphors and tend to take metaphor literally, and one becomes something of a daredevil.

Searles has described clearly the schizophrenic's problems of understanding. One problem is *desymbolization* of "once-attained metaphorical meanings" so that "the individual reacts to them as being literal meanings which he finds indeed most puzzling."[64] Searles shows that "The deeply schizophrenic individual has, subjectively, no imagination" and perceives each new product of what we would call his imagination as "an actual and undisguised attribute of the world around him."[65]

"The 'concretization,' or contrariwise the seeming oversymbolization, of his communications . . . represents his having regressed, in his thinking (and over-all subjective experiencing), to a developmental level comparable with that of the young child. . . ."[66]

Searles explains that what *seem* to be metaphors in schizophrenics, just as what *seem* to be metaphors in children—when a word denoting one sensation is used to describe an unrelated sensation—are actually the undifferentiated *sensations* themselves.[67]

But children love nonsense rhymes, even if metaphor carries beyond them, and patients may enjoy poems without fully understanding their sense. To see what would happen, I decided to try with a few of my patients what Richards did with students. Brooks had assured that

. . . we can always abstract an "idea" from a poem—even from the simplest poem—even from a lyric so simple and unintellectual as

> Western wind, when wilt thou blow
> That the small rain down can rain?
> Christ, that my love were in my arms
> And I in my bed again!

But the idea we abstract—assuming that we can all agree on what that idea is—will always be *abstracted*. . . .[68]

I chose this little lyric to present to the patients, partly because Brooks considered it simple, but mainly because enough people have liked it to preserve it, despite its anonymous authorship, since around 1500.[69] It recently redemonstrated its ageless charm by being set to music in a popular recording.

Each patient was given the poem to read as "a short psychological test" and asked the following questions: *1.* What does this poem mean to you? *2.* Do you like this poem? *3.* Do you approve of using poems in therapy? Their answers follow.

Richard, an 18-year-old high school junior, whose poems we read above, his personality disorganized with catatonic traits:

1. Very good! Did you write that? I'm not very good at reading poetry. I don't know. The rain is there all the time, needs the west wind to blow. The rain is already in a state of being, not moving, and at the whim of the western wind. I don't get the last part. It's about his desire to be with his love in bed. The first two lines are a foundation for the statement; he draws a conclusion. I knew how it was connected, it was beautiful, but now I've forgotten. I'm sorry, I'm blocked.

2. Yes.

3. Yes, because I like poems and therapy, and it would combine two things I like with each other.

Lois, a 16-year-old high school graduate, whose poem we read above, with a schizoid and paranoid personality:

1. It's in the prairie states, the wind has to blow westward or the rain won't blow over the plain states. He wants to be in bed with his love, home.

2. Yes.

3. Yes. Is this therapy?

Darius, a 20-year-old college senior, with an obsessive and paranoid personality:

1. First of all, I don't believe that this is all there is to it. I've been

told too many times by psychologists, "You're going to earn $3," et cetera. I just see "the small rain down can rain" as little children being born. "My love" and "I" must be in bed so little children can be born. I see it very literally as a simple stanza, just a song. What does rain have to do with the second part? It's like those lines some people write that don't connect, like a farming song, where rain is important. If it rains, you have to go indoors, then you go to bed. I'm making a powerful attempt to see sexual imagery in this thing and can't. Now I can think the rain is like semen, but I'm forcing things. I don't have much respect for this because it's written on a scrap of paper.
2. It sounds nice.
3. It might make sense in my case because if you want me to project, I am good at reading things into words. A poem, especially an ambiguous one, leaves more to the imagination in my case than a picture, which may not look like the people it is supposed to remind me of. I can easily imagine that "I" in the poem is me and "love" is Sue.

Harry, a 22-year-old college graduate, with an obsessive and schizoid personality:

1. It doesn't make any sense at all to me. Just this? The second sentence doesn't mean anything, "the small rain down can rain." It's beyond me. I can't make heads or tails of it. I don't see how the two sentences, the four sentences, are tied together. This guy wants his love to be back with him in bed. I don't see how the western wind is going to do that. The second sentence throws me completely. I wish there was a different second sentence.
2. The first line has nice alliteration, it sounds nice.
3. It's supposed to be pretty good. Memorizing a poem gives you more self-confidence, but this one is 'way beyond me. This poem I think stinks; I don't understand it.

Diane, a 20-year-old night high school senior, with a passive-aggressive and hysterical personality:

1. The first thing that struck me is the last few words. Waiting for the wind to blow so it can rain. She's waiting for something to happen so she could have—right away I thought of sex, but it could also be going to sleep. Waiting for something to happen so she could be happy. Faith, the wind reminds me of faith. I don't get the small rain. The way the wind blows determines what's going to happen. Something you're wishing for will take place—nothing bad.
2. Yeah, I wish I could understand it more. It's pretty.
3. Poetry is good for anyone. It has many meanings, and people take it in different ways. It makes you—makes me think a little—let out deep inner feelings.

Diane was a neurotic patient and had never been hospitalized. The others had all had psychotic symptoms and were inpatients when they were shown the poem.

It appears that no patient abstracted a coherent, connected *prose sense* from the poem. This sense, to make the poem a unity, would have to account for the wind, if not the rain, as somehow bringing about the desired return to the loved one. The only way anyone is brought anywhere by wind is by sail at sea. Thus the speaker, who is clearly not at home, is by inference a sailor whose ship is stilled by a calm at sea, who longs for winds to prevail homeward. Winds also bring weather, and the fine rain is also associated in the poem (by paralogic) with being home with his love. Here *metaphorical possibilities* arise, and the rain may be associated with the woman paralogically in that both are small, delicate, gentle, etc. There are also *symbolic possibilities*, further removed, of associating the rain with fertility (cf. *Job* 38:28 "Hath the rain a father? or who hath begotten the drops of dew?" and Milton's ". . . fragrant the fertil earth/ After soft showers"[70]).

The patients' replies reflected their personalities, and made Darius' suggestion that poems be used as *projective tests* seem reasonable. Richard paralogically praised me as the poem's author, as I had handed it to him; then he showed his concern with metaphysics, states of being, and not committing oneself (being at the whim of the wind). Interference by his thought disturbance is evident. Lois cleverly found a setting for the poem on the prairie, but made or wished to make no connection of wind and being home. Darius in paranoid fashion suspected the whole business, then perceived symbolic senses of rain as "little children being born" and "like semen." He then "lost respect" for the poem, we may infer because of these associations, but paralogically blamed the cheap paper it was typed on. His connection of the rain allowing one simply to go indoors, thus permitting sex, is absurd, in view of the longing in the tone of the poem with its exclamation, "Christ . . . !" He did identify with the "I" of the poem (as Diane did). Harry was obsessed with fitting it all together and was angry that he couldn't, paralogically taking it out on the poem, but enjoying the sound nonetheless. Diane, interestingly the only neurotic, presented the best reading in that she perceived a coherent unity in the poem. It is not a *prose sense*, but a symbolic sense typical of her hysterical, wishful personality. She saw the wind as faith and the poem as a drama in which faith answered her wish for sex; but this had bad overtones, and she instead wished for sleep and happiness, like a good girl, avoiding those "deep inner feelings" that were let out for a moment.

All had something to say in favor of the poem and of poetry therapy. Richard would combine poems and therapy as two things he likes (but we have seen him willing to combine rapture and falling, fragrance and dust). Lois asked a pertinent question, "Is this therapy?" which also raises the question of the propriety of having shown her a love poem in view of her history of having indulged in too much loving too soon. Darius saw poems much as verbal Thematic Apperception Tests. Harry interestingly found self-confidence, a great lack of his, in memorizing a poem. And Diane said a poem lets one feel—a little. She wisely summarized for us: "It has many meanings, and people take it in different ways."

Because poetry is complex language, and because patients have problems with language, poems in therapy raise problems. Patients will tend to take the poem as written or intended by the therapist, rather than by the author or imaginary speaker of the poem. Because poetry is more difficult than prose or speech, they may take deleterious meanings from the poem unintended by the therapist and even the poet. Also because poetry is difficult language, patients often may feel stupid or crazy when they do not understand.

5. *Advantages of Poetry*

A. FOR THE PATIENT

1. Order and authority. To the disordered and unhappy patient, poetry offers the order of language in which authority may be granted for wish-fulfilling statements.

2. Portable brevity and memorability. A poem does not require the endurance that a book does. A poem can be carried on a scrap of paper and, better, committed to memory. The meter and rhyme and other kinds of phonetic and semantic order make poetry easy to remember, especially when concentrating abilities are impaired.

In these regards, poetry has an advantage over other things we say to patients. One patient has stated above that memorizing poems increases self-confidence—possibly that by mastering poems, one by paralogic masters the situations therein, or practices mastering them.

3. Conventions and patterns. Like rituals and prayers, poetry offers the individual a cultural solution to a situation. Arieti has described the need of the anxious precatatonic patient to fabricate his own rituals and watchwords with increasing speed.[71] Poetry could conceivably help support these crumbling defenses, and supplant autistic ideas with conventional ones. Conventional patterns of paralogical associations in poems could supplant autistic patterns, and in poetry paralogical and logical processes are reconciled for the patient to see—if he can.

4. Conflicted and covert expression. Ambiguity, conflict and ambivalence torment patients, and they welcome a chance to express these contradictory emotions, some of which they feel forbidden to reveal,[72] in complex and secret language. As Brooks and Empson have suggested above and my patients' poems illustrate, the imagery and sound of poems may modify or even contradict their overt meanings, thus allowing the patient what Ferreira describes in schizophrenic speech as "the much looked-after opportunity to say a piece of *his* mind about a relationship the nature of which he could not state publicly."[73] Barker has described in nonsense verse (by Edward Lear) this purpose that I am suggesting for poetry in general:

> In the first place, it was a way of expressing—of reliving—something forbidden, something traumatic, but which nevertheless had a considerable mischievous pleasurable component. . . . Secondly, the nonsense served a defensive function by blunting the original, raw affect, and by blunting the ideational content in such a way as to make it unobjectionable, even pleasurable. . . . Lear's nonsense appears to have had another, more generalized function—to divert him from the awareness of any painful affect, or even from boredom.[74]

5. Language as gesture and action. For the patient for whom words are not enough, who communicates in bodily language or acts, poetry offers something more than words and akin to action:

what Blackmur above called "the outward and dramatic play of inward and imaged meaning," what Cummings above said made 2 plus 2 equal 5. For the schizophrenic who believes in the magical omnipotence of words, that things are no sooner said than done, poetry is heady stuff and can be overindulged in.

6. *Appropriate tone.* Patients whose feelings are inappropriate to their thoughts may hear in poetry an expressive tone appropriate to the theme. Poetry has more affect than discursive statements, because of its bright images and strong phonetic order of harmony and rhythm. Patients with affective disorders may find a poem in sympathy with nearly any mood.

7. *Poiesis and metamorphosis.* Here we return to the similarities between poems and patients' thoughts. The process of poiesis and Arieti's process of metamorphosis discussed above are the literal concomitants, in the thought of schizophrenics and other patients, to the figurative processes of poetry and metaphor in language. *Poetry* is language made memorable by the establishment of linguistic order for the authority it may confer to wish-fulfilling statements, and *poiesis* is the same process believed in to such a degree that it is taken literally, so the wish said is considered done. *Metaphor* is one thing said in terms of another to suggest a likeness between them, and *metamorphosis* is the same process taken literally so the two things are considered identical or interchangeable. Thus both poiesis and metamorphosis involve word magic.

Searles has shown the recovering schizophrenic patient developing consensually validated metaphor [75] and has explained why "the mutual sharing of such metaphorical experience would seem, thus, to be about as intimate a psychological contact as adult human beings can have with one another."[76] It would seem that if one wishes to share metaphor with patients, one must be sure that metamorphosis is not occurring; correspondingly if one wishes to share poetry with patients, one must be sure that one is not promoting poiesis at the expense of the real world. We are not to miss the metamorphosis and poiesis of schizophrenics, for they are people whose thoughts must leap before they look. But we must not be in the position of *suggesting* leaps by giving poems to those for whom sentences are abysmal.

B. FOR THE THERAPIST

The advantages for the therapist himself reading poetry outweigh those for the patient. Poetry makes us think paralogically, and so increases our facility with the stuff of dreams and delusions, or the thoughts of patients. Poetry teaches economy and brief eloquence. Poetry offers us worlds rival to our own, and in experiencing such worlds we learn something of the life of those who live in them. And when we become complacent that poetic (or poietic) worlds are dreams and our workaday world is the real one, we may consult a poet:

> Which is real—
> This bottle of indigo glass in the grass,
> Or the bench with the pot of geraniums, the stained
>   mattress and the washed overalls drying in the sun?
> Which of these truly contains the world?
>
> Neither one, nor the two together.
>   —Wallace Stevens [77]

When I stated above that acceptance of the profoundly ill patient becomes less a suspension of judgment and more the "willing suspension of disbelief" of Coleridge, I meant to emphasize how difficult it is for most of us to wean ourselves from the comfortable framework and trappings of convention so as to understand people for whom conventionality and custom seem irrelevant or meaningless. In this difficult weaning, I have found my prior interest in poetry especially helpful, both in the suspension of disbelief when confronting the unique elements in such patients, and in the awakening of such a sympathy as

Mr. Wordsworth, on the other hand, was to propose to himself as his object, to give the charm of novelty to things of every day, and to excite a feeling analogous to the supernatural, by awakening the mind's attention from the lethargy of custom, and directing it to the loveliness and the wonders of the world before us; an inexhaustible treasure, but for which, in consequence of the film of familiarity and selfish solicitude we have eyes, yet see not, ears that hear not, and hearts that neither feel nor understand.[78]

If the movement to poetry in therapy does no more than get people in mental health themselves to read poetry, and get some of the many, many people who love poetry to listen to the mentally ill with the same love, then both groups will share inexhaustible treasures in human terms.

REFERENCES

1. Richards, I. A.: Science and Poetry, New York, Norton, 1926, pp. 70–71.
2. Blackmur, R. P.: Language as Gesture, New York, Harcourt, 1935, p. 6.
3. Cummings, E. E.: Poems 1923–1954, New York, Harcourt, 1954, p. [163].
4. Pound, Ezra: Treatise on metre, in Gross, Harvey, ed.: The Structure of Verse: Modern Essays on Prosody, New York, Fawcett World Library, 1966, p. 103.
5. Roethke, Theodore: What do I like? in Ibid., pp. 225–226.
6. Brooks, Cleanth: The Well Wrought Urn, New York, Harvest Books, Harcourt, 1947, p. 204.
7. Ibid.: p. 197.
8. Arieti has described the *matching* of secondary with primary process mechanisms as the process of creativity, and has termed this matching *tertiary process*. See Arieti, Silvano: Creativity and its cultivation, in Arieti, Silvano, ed.: American Handbook of Psychiatry, vol. 3, New York, Basic, 1966, p. 726. For an explanation of primary and secondary processes, see Freud, Sigmund: The Interpretation of Dreams, in Brill, A. A., ed.: The Basic Writings of Sigmund Freud, New York, Modern Library, 1938, pp. 535–536.
9. Storch, Alfred: The Primitive Archaic Forms of Inner Experiences and Thought in Schizophrenia, J Nerv Ment Dis Pub Co., 1924, p. 10.
10. Von Domarus, E.: The specific laws of logic in schizophrenia, in Kasanin, J. S., ed.: Language and Thought in Schizophrenia: Collected Papers, Berkeley (Calif.), Univ Calif Press, 1944, p. 111.
11. Forrest, D. V.: Poiesis and the language of schizophrenia, Psychiatry 28:1–18 (Feb), 1965, p. 2.
12. Arieti, Silvano: Interpretation of Schizophrenia, New York, Brunner, 1955, p. 203.
13. Johnson, Samuel: Life of Cowley, in Bate, W. J., ed.: Criticism: The Major Texts, New York, Harcourt, 1952, p. 218.
14. Forrest, D. V.: Ref. 11, pp. 2–3.
15. Eliot, T. S.: The Use of Poetry and the Use of Criticism, Cambridge (Mass), Harvard Univ Press, 1933, conclusion.
16. Forrest, D. V.: Ref. 11, pp. 6–7.
17. Bateson, Gregory, Jackson, Don D., Haley, Jay, and Weakland, John: Toward a theory of schizophrenia, Behav Sci 1:251–264, 1956.
18. Arieti, Silvano: See ref. 8, p. 735.
19. Blackmur, R. P.: *Op. cit.*, p. 3.

20. Pope, Alexander: An essay on criticism, part 2, lines 97–98, *in* Auden, W. H., and Pearson, N. H., eds.: Restoration and Augustan Poets, New York, Viking, 1950, p. 371.

21. *Ibid.*: Lines 162–165, p. 373.

22. Johnson, Samuel: *Op. cit.*, p. 218.

23. Pope, Alexander: *Op. cit.*, lines 142–143, p. 373.

24. Forrest, D. V.: Ref. 11, p. 9.

25. Aristotle: On the Art of Poetry, New York, Liberal Arts Press, 1948, pp. 3–11.

26. Ransom, John Crowe: Wanted: An ontological critic, *in* Williams, Oscar, ed.: A Little Treasury of Modern Poetry, New York, Scribner's, 1952, p. 805.

27. See ref. 12, p. 216.

28. Forrest, D. V.: Ref. 11, p. 4.

29. Noyes, A. P., and Kolb, L. C.: Modern Clinical Psychiatry, ed. 6, Philadelphia, Saunders, 1963, p. 73.

30. Forrest, D. V.: Ref. 11, pp. 5–6.

31. Fowler, H. W.: A Dictionary of Modern English Usage, Oxford (Eng.), Oxford Univ Press, 1950, p. 611.

32. Storch, Alfred: *Op. cit.*, p. 99.

33. Webster's Collegiate Dictionary, Seventh Edition.

34. Storch, Alfred: *Op. cit.*, p. 99.

35. McNeill, David: Speaking of space, Science *152*:875 (May), 1966.

36. Bleuler, Eugen: Dementia Praecox or the Group of Schizophrenias, trans. Zinkin, Joseph, New York, Internat Univ Press, 1950, p. 150.

37. Forrest, D. V.: Ref. 11, p. 6.

38. Potter, Simeon: Our Language, Baltimore, Penguin, 1950, p. 110.

39. *Ibid.*: p. 57.

40. Cummings, E. E.: *Op. cit.*, p. 413.

41. Bleuler, Eugen: The Theory of Schizophrenic Negativism, trans. White, W. A., J Nerv Ment Dis Pub Co., 1912, p. 155.

42. See ref. 36, p. 150.

43. Carroll, Lewis: Preface to The Hunting of the Snark, *in* Gardner, Martin, ed.: The Annotated Snark, New York, Pantheon, pp. 65, 34.

44. Forrest, D. V.: Ref. 11, pp. 14–18.

45. Kubie, Lawrence: Neurotic Distortion of the Creative Process, Toronto (Canada), Noonday Press, 1958, pp. 141–143.

46. See ref. 12, p. 219.

47. See ref. 17.

48. Searles, Harold F.: The differentiation between concrete and metaphorical thinking in the recovering schizophrenic patient, *in* Collected Papers on Schizophrenia and Related Subjects, New York, Internat Univ Press, 1965, p. 561.

49. Forrest, D. V.: Ref. 11, pp. 16–17.

50. Coleridge, Samuel Taylor: Biographia Literaria, *in* Bate, W. J., ed.: Criticism: The Major Texts, New York, Harcourt, 1952, p. 376.
51. Empson, William: Seven Types of Ambiguity, London, New Directions, 1930, pp. 192–193.
52. Cummings, E. E.: Personal communication, Feb 25, 1960.
53. Keyserling, Hermann: The Travel Diary of a Philosopher, translated by Reece, J. Holyroyd, New York, 1925.
54. Zimmer, Heinrich: *in* Campbell, Joseph, ed.: Philosophies of India, New York, Pantheon, 1951, p. 380.
55. Cummings, E. E.: *Op. cit.*, p. 398.
56. Thomas, Dylan: The Collected Poems of Dylan Thomas, New York, New Directions, 1939, p. 10.
57. Cummings, E. E.: *Op. cit.*, p. 358.
58. Mother Goose: Quoted *in* Roethke, Theodore, *op. cit.*, p. 218.
59. Roethke, Theodore: *Op. cit.*, pp. 218–219.
60. Richards, I. A.: Practical Criticism: A Study in Literary Judgment, New York, Harcourt, 1929, p. 292.
61. *Ibid.*: p. 4.
62. *Ibid.*: p. 12.
63. *Ibid.*: p. 308.
64. See ref. 48, p. 580.
65. *Ibid.*: p. 574.
66. Searles, Harold F.: Schizophrenic communication, *in* Collected Papers on Schizophrenia and Related Subjects, New York, Internat Univ Press, 1965, p. 401.
67. See ref. 48, p. 581.
68. Brooks, Cleanth: *Op. cit.*, p. 205.
69. Anonymous: *in* Auden, W. H., and Pearson, N. H., eds.: Medieval and Renaissance Poets, New York, Internat Univ Press, 1965, p. 426.
70. Milton, John: Paradise Lost, Book 4, lines 645–646, *in* Complete Poetry and Selected Prose of John Milton, New York, Modern Library, 1950, p. 184.
71. Arieti, Silvano: Some aspects of the psychopathology of schizophrenia, Amer J Psychother 8:396–414, 1954.
72. Ferreira, A. J.: The semantics and the context of the schizophrenic's language, Arch Gen Psychiat (Chicago) 3:128–138, 1960.
73. *Ibid.*
74. Barker, Warren J.: The nonsense of Edward Lear, Psychoanal Quart 35:568–586, 1966.
75. See ref. 48, p. 561.
76. *Ibid.*: p. 583.
77. Stevens, Wallace: Poems, selected and introduced by Samuel French Morse, New York, Vintage, 1959, p. 21.
78. Coleridge, Samuel Taylor: *Op. cit.*, p. 376.

CHAPTER 21

A Curriculum Proposal
For Training Poetry Therapists

KENNETH F. EDGAR, PHD   RICHARD HAZLEY, MA
Indiana State University of Pennsylvania

IN MAY OF 1963, J. J. Leedy and Eli Greifer read a paper at the meeting of the American Society of Group Psychotherapy and Psychodrama in Washington. It was concerned with the results and the potential of what was then a new approach to group psychotherapy, pioneered by the authors at Cumberland Hospital in Brooklyn. They had conducted an experiment in which they had used poetry as a therapeutic tool. The results obtained, and the enthusiasm of the patients, indicated that their technique, which Dr. Leedy called poetry therapy, could be profitably employed in the group process. Later experimental research, at Slippery Rock State College and Dixmont State Hospital in Pennsylvania, attempted a controlled evaluation of the technique and supported the hypothesis that poetry could be of value in a therapeutic situation. (See Chapters 2 and 9.)

The results at Dixmont in particular indicated that poetry therapy can achieve dramatic results where other approaches, both individual and group, have failed. Because of the growing interest in poetry therapy and the belief of the authors of this chapter that the technique, properly employed, can make a significant contribution to the mental health program it seems feasible now to propose the establishment of a graduate course of study to provide specialized training leading to certification in poetry therapy.

Such training, resulting in a more widespread employment of poetry therapy techniques, would represent a practical utilization of the significant relationship between literature and the psychic process that has been the subject of extensive comment for some time, by both psychologists and literary critics. It can be said that the theoretical basis for such application has long been present. In 1933, Jung noted: "What is of particular importance for the study of literature in these manifestations of the collective unconscious is that they are compensatory to the conscious attitude. That is to say that they can bring a one-sided, abnormal, or dangerous state of consciousness into equilibrium in an apparently purposive way."[1] More recently, S. I. Hayakawa has written in *Language in Thought and Action*[2]:

> The greater resources one has for achieving and maintaining adjustment, the more successful will the process be. Literature appears to be one of the available resources. . . . Even as one's physical health has to be maintained by food and exercise, it would appear that one's psychological health too has to be maintained in the very course of living by 'nourishment' at the level of affective symbols: literature that makes us feel that we are not alone in our misery; literature that shows us our own problems in a new light; literature that suggests new possibilities to us and opens new areas of possible experience; literature that offers us a variety of "symbolic strategies" by means of which we can "encompass" our situations. . . . The ordering of experiences and attitudes accomplished linguistically by the writer produces, in the reader, some ordering of his own experiences and attitudes. The reader becomes, as a result of this ordering, somewhat better organized himself. That's what art is for.

Kenneth Burke has referred to poetry as "equipment for living," and Robert Graves has called it a mental medicine. It would be the purpose of this curriculum to provide the poetry therapist with sufficient training in both literature and psychology to enable him to apply the healing powers that are in poetry to those who most gravely need them. In so doing, he would justify the proposed curriculum by providing a valuable service.

Resistances, Contemporaneity

Almost certainly, it can be assumed that such a proposal will meet with some resistance. One of the authors, himself a professor of English literature, is uncomfortably aware of the opposition, perhaps even scorn, that will be generated by some of his colleagues. In his profession, there is a formidable element that instinctively denies psychology any right in literary studies and that regards the possibility of profitable interdisciplinary study a violation. This element reacts to psychology with the same sense of affront and outrage with which many of the Victorians reacted to Darwin's propositions. The situations are analogous. Like the Victorians who felt that Darwin, in suggesting that man had evolved from lower life forms, was denying man as the ultimate creature creation of God, these literateurs feel that psychology attempts to deny the ineffable origin of poetry, reducing it to the expression of a neurosis. They believe that such a reduction destroys that sense of wonder and awe that they rightly think we should feel in the presence of art.

Their attitude, though it most often seems to spring from nearly instinctive suspicion and shallow knowledge, has some justification. Freud did propose that the origins of art were in neurosis and, in the first excesses following Freud's hypothesis, his disciples, like Darwin's, pushed his theories too far, assuming wrongly that the analysis of personal determinants could account for a work of art. As Jung has said, such a claim calls for a categorical denial. An analysis may have some validity for the artist as a person, but none at all for the man as an artist. It is *not* the purpose of this curriculum proposal to train people to the idea that the creative act can be accounted for by psychological analysis. That act, as Jung has said, will forever elude human understanding. It *is* the purpose to provide those interested with the tools by which they may be able to understand more profoundly and communicate more meaningfully to those who are disturbed or who function inadequately the important and permanent truths that are to be found in poetry.

One further observation, the authors feel, must be made. It is important that the future poetry therapist have a wide acquaintance with all of literature, but for therapeutic purposes, we are sure, relatively contemporary poetry will more consistently yield results. For this there are two reasons. First, in working with groups whose members have little acquaintance with literature, the presence of language difference found in the literature of earlier periods constitutes a barrier to understanding. Even where poems are relatively simple, the unfamiliar idiom diverts the patient's attention and diminishes the effectiveness of the poem. Second, to quote once again from Jung:

Every period has its bias, its particular prejudice and its psychic ailment. An epoch is like an individual; it has its own limitation of conscious outlook, and therefore requires a compensatory adjustment. This is effected by the collective unconscious in that a poet . . . allows himself to be guided by the unexpressed desire of his times and shows the way by word or deed, to the attainment of that which everyone blindly craves and expects. . . .[3]

Most of the time, the language of more recent poets, say those of the past hundred years, will speak most directly to the ills of the patient. This is of course a matter of emphasis. The authors themselves have found that Shakespeare, for example, has been, at the appropriate time and with the appropriate group, effective.

The program herein proposed would require the establishment of a new curriculum that would embrace training in both psychology and literature. While no departure from conventional training in clinical psychology would be necessary insofar as the standard courses are concerned, the courses in literature would need to be specifically designed not only to provide the necessary background but also to make the therapist aware of the symbolism and psychological themata in poetry. Because the selection of appropriate poems is critical, the therapist must have an extensive knowledge of the literature of poetry and the awareness of psychological themata that such training should provide.

The following proposal must of necessity be tentative. At the present time no such program exists; therefore, the courses listed and their descriptions are intended to be suggestive rather than prescriptive. Although the authors feel that the basic program as described is sound, it is not assumed to be all-inclusive. In practice, additions and alterations will suggest themselves, and in the process of preparing courses, assembling bibliographies, and the like, modifications may be found desirable.

Undergraduate Studies

It is proposed that, as an undergraduate, the student desiring certification as a poetry therapist may major in either of two disciplines, English or psychology, and minor in the other. The undergraduate program need not be other than the conventional one, though it should include, if possible, whatever courses in semantics or sociolinguistics that a particular institution offers to undergraduates. At least one course in literary criticism is also suggested. The range of courses, their content and approach, will of course be determined by the offerings of the particular institution. For this reason it is not felt that suggestions for a special undergraduate program would be practical or that course descriptions are necessary. It is suggested that the student include in his program as many of the following undergraduate courses as possible.

PSYCHOLOGY	ENGLISH
General Psychology	General Semantics
Developmental Psychology	Classical Literature
Abnormal Psychology	World Literature
Psychology of Personality	British Literature
Social Psychology	American Literature
Introduction to Clinical Practice	Shakespeare
	Poetry of the 17th Century
	The Romantic Movement
	Contemporary Poetry
	Introduction to Literary Criticism
	The Contemporary Novel

Graduate Studies

It is at the master's level that the proposed curriculum must be specifically designed. Initially, the problems of staffing the following program may be considerable. Unfortunately, few American institutions offer or permit interdisciplinary studies leading to postgraduate degrees. The success of the program, therefore, will depend on the ability of the institution to find or recruit personnel whose personal interests have led them from the particular field of either psychology or English to significant studies in the other area. Ideally, if the instructor's primary training has been in literature, he should have somehow acquired both academic and practical experience in psychology; if his training has been in psychology, then hopefully he will have had also an abiding interest in literature—in not only its psychological content but in literature qua literature. It may be desirable, in the early stages of the program, to employ team-teaching techniques in some of the courses to assure that they be not too heavily weighted in one direction. Such a program, once established, could accrue important side benefits for the sponsoring institution. The cross-fertilization by stimulating interest and valuable controversy should be instrumental in demonstrating the need and value of postgraduate work that transcends the narrow bounds of a particular discipline. As the program is presently conceived, the faculty resources of any institution presently offering a graduate degree in psychology will be adequate to that area of the program, and the student enrolling for the poetry therapy degree should be able to take the psychology courses required in already existing programs. The departures will occur in the courses that relate to literature and semantics. These will require the establishment of an entirely new curriculum. The recommended graduate courses in psychology are listed with standard course descriptions.

AREA OF PSYCHOLOGY: GRADUATE

1. *Developmental Psychology   3 credits*
   A comprehensive study of the principles of psychological development in the individual from conception to old age.
2. *Abnormal Psychology   3 credits*
   A systematic study of the full range of psychological functioning from the basic and accepted normal to the most extreme manifestations of pathology.
3. *Psychology of Personality   3 credits*
   A study of the significant experimental and clinical findings regarding the major theories and manifestations of personality.
4. *Social Psychology   3 credits*
   This course studies the interactions of people, the functioning human reacting to social pressure with his own biological and psychological make-up.
5. *Projective Tests   3 credits*
   The purpose of this course is to provide the therapist with a working knowledge of the major projective tests such as Rorschach, MMPI, *DAP*, etc. It is not designed to provide skill in administering these tests but simply to make the poetry therapist capable of understanding a diagnostic report submitted to him by the clinical psychologist.
6. *Techniques of Psychotherapy   3 credits*
   A survey of the various forms of psychotherapy including Freudian psychoanalysis, Rogerian nondirective therapy, Moreno's psycho-

drama, group therapy, etc. This course is intended to be as comprehensive as possible, giving the student a sense of the value inherent in all the forms of treatment.

7. *Group Psychotherapy   3 credits*
This course is designed to teach the student how to conduct a session in group psychotherapy. In addition to a text and outside readings, the student will observe group sessions and participate as an active member in group psychotherapy.

AREA OF LITERATURE: GRADUATE

The remaining, and significantly new, part of the program consists of courses in literature and semantics as they are specifically related to behavior and the expression of psychological themes. It is designed to provide the future clinician with the literary and psychological background and understanding necessary for him to function as a poetry therapist.

1. *Language as Behavior   3 credits*
A study of the social and psychological aspects of language as it relates to human behavior. The course will include considerations of the difference between appearance and reality, between self-concepts and actuality as expressed through language symbols. One of the purposes of the course will be to discover the ways in which the use of language may determine, change, or affect personality development, contact with the real world, and self-cognizance.

2. *Psychology and Literature   3 credits*
A study of psychology as it relates to literature. The course will include study and discussion of recent critical works that appraise and evaluate psychological themata in literature and the influence of psychology on literature. Primary materials that demonstrate significant psychological themes will be studied. Emphasis will be placed on literary works and studies that manifest and discuss specific characteristics of the conflicted personality.

3. *Psychological Themes in Poetry   6 credits (two semesters)*
An intensive analysis of poetry with a concentration on the general themata of specific writers. It is the aim of the course to make known to the students poems that could be used with certain psychological problems.

4. *Seminar   3 credits*
The concentration in this course will be on individual research in which the student will be presented with case studies and required to select poems appropriate for utilization in poetry therapy. There will be discussion and critique of the selections.

The two courses that follow are designed to provide the student with the clinical background necessary for successful practice. They represent a period of actual internship and, as such, the culmination in actual practice of his studies. As the two final courses in this program, they should provide the field where the student demonstrates his ability in the area for which the entire program has been designed. Every care should be taken at this point to see that the requirements of the internship are fully met and that the student demonstrate his capabilities in the clinical situation.

Clinical Practice in Group Poetry Therapy   6 credits
The purpose of the course is to provide clinical practice in the use of poetry therapy. The student will observe the use of poetry therapy in clinical situations during the first semester of this course. He will be required to submit written analyses of each observed session, evaluating group progress and making specific observations regarding the types of poems used and the rationale for their use. In the second semester, the student will act in an auxiliary capacity to the poet therapist and will be expected to submit his own selections of poetry for possible use and, also, to conduct the group on occasion, under the supervision of the poet therapist.

Internship in Group Poetry Therapy   3 credits
The student, under supervision, will conduct a poetry therapy group.

There is one physical requirement necessary to the success of the program. The university offering it will have to be located within reasonable distance from a hospital that can provide the opportunities for the required internship, and it must establish a working relationship with the staff of that hospital. The university, therefore, will have to convince the hospital personnel of the program's value. It is suggested that in attempting to do so, some of the studies reported in other chapters of this book will be of value. The authors' experiences indicate that with the use of a little diplomacy and much conviction this requirement can be met. There already exist programs for certification in music, art, and dance therapy. We believe that a program such as this is viable, and that when it is successfully established, it will make a valuable contribution to the overall mental health program.

REFERENCES

1. Jung, C. G.: Modern Man in Search of a Soul, New York, Harcourt, n.d., p. 165.
2. Hayakawa, S. I.: Language in Thought and Action, New York, Harcourt, 1964, pp. 149–155.
3. Jung, C. G.: *Op cit.*, p. 166.

CHAPTER 22

Postscript
Metamessages and Self-Discovery

S. I. HAYAKAWA, PhD
Acting President, San Francisco State College

I DON'T KNOW WHY it has taken the healing professions so long to discover the connection between poetry and the cure of souls. One reason, no doubt, is the fragmentation of knowledge, especially in our universities, resulting in the conviction that literature is literature and psychology is psychology, and never should the twain be permitted to meet. Another reason, I am sure, is the aloof mandarinism of all too many professors and critics of literature who believe that to find a *use* for literature is somehow to demean its character. Young scholars are not often encouraged to discover through reading, say, Emily Dickinson to mental patients what her poems can mean to those who need them for their soul's good. You can prove again and again that memorizing Henley's "Invictus" has helped troubled and overburdened people to endure intolerable conditions, but the literary mandarins will merely shudder in distaste and tell you that it is a thoroughly bad poem.

A poem communicates not in messages but in metamessages. Metamessage is of course an indispensable ingredient in all interpersonal communication. "Let's have lunch one of these days" may mean "I enjoy being with you." Or it may be, if said in a different tone of voice, merely a stylized way of saying good-bye. Or it may mean, in still another tone of voice, "I don't care if I ever see you again."

Many of the metamessages of spoken discourse are nonverbal: facial expression, gestures, body posture, warmth of handshake. Some are verbal but nonlexical: intonation, accent, loudness or softness of voice. Still other kinds of metamessage are conveyed by the choice of alternatives of vocabulary: "angry" or "indignant," "furious" or "hopping mad," "fit to be tied" or (I am writing this in Hawaii) "huhu." Or by the kind of metaphors you use. The difference between "I am growing old" and the following lines from Shakespeare are mostly a matter of metamessage:

> That time of year thou may'st in me behold
> When yellow leaves, or none, or few, do hang
> Upon those boughs which shake against the cold,
> Bare ruin'd choirs where late the sweet birds sang.

Good writing—writing that conveys not only ideas but how it feels and what it means to have those ideas—is that which confirms in metamessage what is said in the message. A well-written passage of prose, whether a love letter or a protest against tyranny, will express in its metaphors, in its rhythms and sounds, in its sentence structure and its pace, the sentiments lexically expressed. A writer does not have at his disposal the usual nonverbal components of metamessage, but he can with metaphor and sound and cadence convey the metamessages he wants to convey.

Metamessages strike at deeper levels of awareness than overt messages. This is so because we all learned to understand, as infants in our mothers' arms, that which is conveyed by tones of voice: love, concern, impatience, fear. Tones of voice tell us profoundly how others feel. Even as adults, we relate to each other as much by metamessage as by message, especially in interpersonal relations.

Poetry is that form of communication in which metamessage is all—or almost all.

> Loveliest of trees, the cherry now
> Is hung with bloom along the bough,
> And stands about the woodland ride
> Wearing white for Eastertide.

In an important sense, A. E. Housman is not talking about cherry blossoms at all, but mentioning them for their symbolic value in the course of saying something else altogether. He does not *tell* us what is on his mind. His rhythms *dance* his message.

The use of poetry in group therapy strikes me as an inspired idea. Because poetry says what it says in metaphor and symbol rather than in literal terms, in sound as much as in sense, it penetrates the patient's defenses and rationalizations and permits him to experience the feelings he is trying to deny. As Kenneth Edgar and Richard Hazley say in describing their therapeutic encounters in this volume, after a therapy group was formed and a certain amount of mutual trust had been established:

> It became increasingly apparent to the cotherapists and to the members of the group that when one individual reacted very strongly to a particular poem, the time had come for the entire group to focus on that person and sometimes to spend the entire hour discussing just a few lines of poetry as they related to that individual. It became increasingly clear to the cotherapists that these times constituted the precise moment "to communicate the repressed meaning of a series of symptoms or the hidden sense of some attitude of mind."

In short, the discussion of poetry often turns out for the patient to be the discussion—and the discovery—of himself.

I should think that a wide background of literary study and especially the reading of poetry should be part of a therapist's training. Such training should also include practice in reading aloud— what speech departments call "oral interpretation." The metamessages of poetry are often missed in silent reading because they are unheard; not every reader, going over a poem on the printed page, knows how it should be accented and phrased, how it should sound. But the therapist should be able to recreate the sound, so that he may reach by incantation, as well as by oblique, imaginative symbols, levels of response that cannot be reached by ordinary discourse.

"A well-chosen anthology [of verse]," said Robert Graves, "is a complete dispensary of medicine for the more common mental disorders, and may be used as much for prevention as cure."

I wonder if any of the contributors to this volume have ever thought of preparing an anthology of verse with the prevention and cure of emotional disorders specifically in mind? How would it be if the psychologists, psychiatrists, counselors, and English teachers who have contributed to this volume were to pool their experiences in order to make a list of poems that have proved especially effective in therapeutic work? What would we find? Much of Emily Dickinson, I am sure. And A. E. Housman? Walt Whitman? Matthew Arnold? William Blake? Robert Frost?

Edward Arlington Robinson? Auden? Spender? Dylan Thomas? If Robert Graves's "well-chosen anthology" were to be selected with therapeutic goals in mind, would it be very different from, or just the same as, one selected purely for literary enjoyment?

But I should think such an anthology should also contain poems written by patients—poems that have proved helpful not only to their authors, but also to other patients—and there surely must be many such poems in the files of the contributors. I wonder if they would be very different in quality from those written by acknowledged poets? The idea of a therapeutic anthology raises many fascinating questions about the relations between psychology and art. If the attainment of psychological self-insight (and therefore emotional health) is the same kind of integrative experience as that of artistic creation—and I believe that it is—it would not be altogether surprising to find among the writings of patients some poetry of a high order of artistic merit.

In Memoriam
Eli Greifer 1902-1966

PSYCHOTHERAPISTS ARE AWARE that volunteers are greatly valuable in treating the emotionally ill. Eli Greifer is a marvelous exemplar of the volunteer who, under guidance of the psychotherapist, can be of crucial help to patients. Although he was a lawyer and a pharmacist, his deepest lifelong interest was therapeutic poetry. His own poems are *Rhymes for the Wretched, Poems for What Ails You, Psychic Ills and Poemtherapy, Philosophic Duels* and several other volumes.

Forty years ago, in 1928, Eli began a campaign to show that a poem's didactic message, its quite explicit moral, has a specific healing power in itself. Like Alexander Pope, he castigated those for whom poetry is mere sound or esthetic experience, those "tuneful fools"

> Who haunt Parnassus but to please their ear,
> Not mend their minds; as some to Church repair,
> Not for the doctrine, but the music there.

He organized the Village Arts Center and the Messagists Club, at 37 West Eighth Street, and then the Remedy Rhyme Gallery, at One Charles Street, New York City.

He also became a volunteer, to document and test his principles, now far beyond theories with Eli. At Creedmoor State Hospital, he started a Poetry Group, and then, at my invitation, another at our Clinic, where our patients received it enthusiastically for six years. Then changing his *poemtherapy* to *poetry therapy*, with all the encouragement that I could give him, he formed Poetry Groups at Willoughby House Settlement in Brooklyn and at the Staten Island Aid for Retarded Children, Inc., where the Poetry Groups became a part of Sheltered Workshops for the children.

Sympathetic and enthusiastic, Eli was a generous humanitarian. He spent nearly all of his money furthering poetry as therapy. He gave the patients of his groups silver dollars for memorizing or writing poems, and each week brought them notebooks, pens, refreshments and prizes. He was also a devoted loyal friend. From 1959 till the very last minute of his life, on September 26, 1966, we often spoke together about the development of poetry therapy. Although Eli suffered many physical ailments, he ever enjoyed helping in adding a dimension in the treatment of mental illness.

They were exciting years. We tried new approaches to the use of poetry in or as therapy; we went on tours; we participated in meetings and conventions. Our aim was to stimulate members of the mental health professions, teachers and educators, the clergy and penologists, nurses and others to explore the uses of poetry in the alleviation of mental suffering.

I wish that Eli could have lived to see more of his dream coming true, *Poetry Therapy* a portion of it—though Eli had countless other ideas, too.

JJL

A POET WANTS A SEPULCHER IN THE FORM OF A BOOK FOR HIS WORKS *

Oh, buy me not a tombstone,
   Squander not your gold
For a home to house my body,
   When my limbs are hopeless cold!

I have scorned my throbbing flesh
   When it glittered warm and young,—
To minister unto the Muse!
   I breathed each breath for Song!

I starved for food and beauty,
   And homeless roamed the earth,—
Since Love and Home, beside my poems,
   Had such little worth!

But yet I failed to pierce
   The granite wall, that throngs,
Sweet patrons, and salt critics
   Raised against my songs.

In Memoriam

  I hurled my flesh so painful,
   I battered with my bones,
  I clutched away with frozen hands
   At their stolid, cynic stones!—

  But failed to see my message
   Break through to reach mankind,—
  Now, will ye, who so pity me,
   Rather see confined

  In a home,—what now is careless clay,
   Yet homeless leave my shivering verses?
  I charge you! house my words in print
   With the gold ye'd pour for graves and hearses,
   Lest I give thanks to you in curses!

* *From* Eli Greifer: *Philosophic Duels*, Brooklyn, NY, Academy Publications, 1938, p. 89—with the kind permission of Bernard Tassler, Executor.

A List of Poems

Suitable for Use in Poetry Therapy

ONE SUPPOSES that a therapist who knows the great body of English and American poetry (not to mention one acquainted also with the poetry of other nations), and has lived with it for some years, could find a thousand, possibly even five thousand, poems suitable to his therapeutic needs and purposes. But vast numbers are unnecessary: a practicing therapist might be hard put to use more than fifty or a hundred poems in a year; and excellent large anthologies and smaller paperbacks are available to the searcher, in many good bookstores and probably many college classrooms. This List does not intend to be complete in any way. It derives from either *Poetry Therapy* (when it shows page numbers) or from suggestions by its authors.

ANONYMOUS
   Alysoun
   Sumer is Icumen in
   Western Wind, when wilt thou blow? 250
BIBLE
   Ecclesiastes, 78
   Psalms, 1, 23, 91, 134, 137, 138, 139
WILLIAM BLAKE
   Cradle Song
   A Little Boy Lost
   A Poison Tree, 232
   The Fly
   The Lamb
   The Little Black Boy
   The Tyger
ROBERT BROWNING
   Epilogue, *Asolando*, 173
   Home-Thoughts, from Abroad
   Meeting at Night
   Prospice
   Rabbi Ben Ezra
   From *Paracelsus*, 176
   Song from *Pippa Passes*, 173
KENNETH BURKE
   Alky, Me Love, 105
ROBERT BURNS
   A Man's a Man for A' That
   My Luve
   The Banks o'Doon
   To A Mouse
THOMAS CAMPION
   There Is a Garden in Her Face
THOMAS CARLYLE
   Today
LEWIS CARROLL
   Beware the Jabberwock, 61
   The Hunting of the Snark, 231
JOHN CLARE
   I Am
   Young Lambs
ARTHUR HUGH CLOUGH
   Say Not the Struggle Naught Availeth
SAMUEL TAYLOR COLERIDGE
   Dejection: An Ode

List of Poems

Kubla Khan
The Ancient Mariner
Work without Hope
WILLIAM COWPER
Light Shining Out of Darkness
STEPHEN CRANE
The Wayfarer
E. E. CUMMINGS
Buffalo Bill's
dying is fine) but Death
no man, if men are gods
one's not half two, 241
voices to voices, lip to lip
what if a much of a which of a wind
will you teach a/wretch to live, 246
you shall above all things be glad and young
WALTER DE LA MARE
The Listeners
EMILY DICKINSON
A Prison Gets To Be a Friend
A Triumph May Be Several Kinds
Because I Could Not Stop For Death
I'm Nobody, 90
I Never Saw a Moor
I Went to Heaven
Magnanimous as Bird, 33
Not With a Club, The Heart is Broken
The Mountains Grow Unnoticed
There Is No Frigate Like a Book, 46
JOHN DONNE
Death, Be Not Proud
Holy Sonnets
Song (Go and catch a falling star)
Song (Sweetest love, I do not go)
The Ecstasy
The Good-Morrow
The Sun Rising
JOHN DRYDEN
To the Pious Memory of the Accomplist Young Lady Mrs. Ann Killigrew, 68

ALAN DUGAN
Love Song: I and Thou
T. S. ELIOT
Four Quartets, 131
The Cocktail Party, 79
RALPH WALDO EMERSON
Give All To Love, 175
The Problem
FRA GIOVANNI, 127
ROBERT FROST
Birches
Mending Wall
Stopping by Woods on a Snowy Evening
The Road Not Taken, 22
The Secret Sits, 222
Tree at My Window
Two Tramps in Mud-Time
SISTER PAUL GABRIEL, *in*
I'm a lean dog, a keen dog, 58
It's hopperty, skipperty, 60
One, two, three, four, five, 56
'Tis all the way to Toe-Town, 56
ISABELLA GARDNER
That Craning of the Neck
KAHLIL GIBRAN
The Prophet, 78, 80-81, 126, 127, 128, 129
LOUIS GINSBERG
Hunger and Thirst, 48
GEORGE GORDON, LORD BYRON
Maid of Athens, Ere We Part
She Walks in Beauty
When We Two Parted
JULIA GREEN
I Knew Not That We Counted Little
ELI GREIFER
A Poet Wants a Sepulcher in the Form of a Book for His Works, 274
A Song of Emancipatory Renaissance
Creative Smiling
Life Triumphs
THOMAS HARDY
Afterwards

The Darkling Thrush
WILLIAM E. HENLEY
  Invictus
GEORGE HERBERT
  The Altar
  The World
ROBERT HERRICK
  Grace for a Child
  The Argument of His Book
  To Daisies, Not to Shut So Soon
RALPH HODGSON
  Time, You Old Gypsy Man
HOMER
  The Illiad
  The Odyssey
GERARD MANLEY HOPKINS
  God's Grandeur
  Pied Beauty
A. E. HOUSMAN
  Loveliest of Trees, 270
  When I Was One-and-Twenty
  Terence, this is stupid stuff, 80
BEN JONSON
  Oak and Lily
  To Celia
JOHN KEATS
  Bright Star, Would I were Stedfast
  Ode on a Grecian Urn
  Ode to a Nightingale
  On First Looking into Chapman's Homer, 9
  When I Have Fears That I May Cease To Be, 6
EDWARD LEAR
  The water it soon came in, it did, 55
HENRY WADSWORTH LONGFELLOW
  Hymn To The Night
  The Day Is Done, 72
  The Rainy Day
  The Tide Rises, The Tide Falls
RICHARD LOVELACE
  To Althea, from Prison
AMY LOWELL
  Patterns
GUSTAV MAHLER
  They melt, the shadows of the night, 7

EDWIN MARKHAM
  Outwitted
CHRISTOPHER MARLOWE
  The Passionate Shepherd to His Love
ANDREW MARVELL
  The Garden
  To His Coy Mistress
JOHN MASEFIELD
  Sea-Fever
EDNA ST. VINCENT MILLAY
  Renascence
  The Return
JOHN MILTON
  On His Blindness
MOTHER GOOSE
  Hinx, minx, the old witch winks, 247
ARTHUR O'SHAUGHNESSY
  Ode
PATIENTS' POEMS
  AFTLI is a blithe spirit, 221
  As an old friend, you walk in, 186
  As out the flowers bloom deathwards, 243
  As petals open one by one, asserting, 198
  Bad dreams/What do they mean? 95ff
  Because you have paved the way, 184
  Creation adorns the earth with flowers, 101
  Did you ever shiveringly tinkle? 82
  Environment, heredity, 195
  Give me your little hand, 101
  God is Godot, and God is time, 198
  Had you not the greater beauty, 242
  Harold—Your heart is as big, 152
  Hope—Haven for children and innocents, 127
  How came such poisoned pap from so excellent an udder? 146
  How can one bear the awful loneliness, 194
  I bounce in late, 150

List of Poems

If the world were my oyster, 150
I have taken flight from preoccupation with man, 187
I like trees because they are green, 182
I never say/What I want to say, 153
In my heart/Where cold winter reigns, 101
In this interior decoration, 36
I sank into a well, 195
It is Love that shows me how, 186
I wanted to ask Nancy, 152
Like the child waiting in the night, 143
Move and change, 196
My day of innocence is past, 245
My dreams/Yellow leaves, lifeless, dead, 100
My universe is small, you see, 150
No man is an island, 151
No one cares, I think, 243
Of wounded times the grave bird wails, 145-146
Perhaps if I tried to communicate, 93
Remember/The bright sunsets in the bamboo of your youth, 101
She has new leaves, 71
She reminded me that your eyes were made for tears, 101
Short sleek and witty sits this gravid owl, 147
. . . the arching goddess/a silken lure, 120
Then sleep, your dark head warm, 197
There is a dark place where sometimes, 195
There once was a fisherman who lived at sea, 181
The sun has arrived in the sky, 102
Today I meet a stranger, 39
Today I poisoned my life, 216
To mine own execution/Be true, 144
To walk the virgin snow alone, 71
We sat in a room, 149
What a sweet repast, 185

What is it to care, 83
What is next? 93
what's it like? 246
Will someone/Tell me who I am? 186
You shine on my bitter days/Like a sky full of stars, 103
Your embraces were created to hold me, 102

ALEXANDER POPE
JOHN CROWE RANSOM
  Essay on Criticism, 235, 273
  Lady Lost
RICHARD REALF
  The World, 176
CHRISTINA ROSSSETTI
  A Birthday
  Does the road wind uphill all the way? 178
CARL SANDBURG
  The People Will Live On
  The People, Yes
WILLIAM SHAKESPEARE
Plays (passim)
  Alas, that love (*R & J.* I, i), 175
  . . . but man, proud man (*Meas.* II, ii), 177
Sonnets
  29. When, in disgrace with Fortune and men's eyes, 174
  30. When to the sessions of sweet silent thought
  33. Full many a glorious morning have I seen
  73. That time of year thou mayst in me behold, 270
  116. Let me not to the marriage of true minds
  130. My mistress' eyes are nothing like the sun
PERCY BYSSHE SHELLEY
  Love's Philosophy
  Ode to the West Wind, 179
  The Cloud
  To a Skylark
CHRISTOPHER SMART
  A Song to David, 73
STEPHEN SPENDER
  I think continually of those

WALLACE STEVENS
  Tomorrow
  Which is Real—, 256
ROBERT LOUIS STEVENSON
  Resurgence, 171
  Romance
  The Celestial Surgeon
SIR JOHN SUCKLING
  Why So Pale and Wan
ALGERNON CHARLES SWINBURNE
  In Harbour, 172
  Love at Sea, 173
  The Garden of Proserpine, 173
ALFRED LORD TENNYSON
  Locksley Hall
  Ulysses, 177-178
DYLAN THOMAS
  Fern Hill
  If I were tickled by the rub of love
FRANCIS THOMPSON
  In No Strange Land, 63
THOMAS TRAHERNE
  Wonder
HENRY VAUGHAN
  The World
EDMUND WALLER
  Go, lovely rose
  On a Girdle

JOHN HALL WHEELOCK
  The Black Panther
WALT WHITMAN
  A Child Went Forth
  I Celebrate Myself
  I Hear America Singing
  Song of Myself
  Song of the Open Road
JOHN GREENLEAF WHITTIER
  My Soul and I
  The Eternal Goodness, 125
  The Light That is Felt
WILLIAM WORDSWORTH
  A Slumber Did My Spirit Seal
  Intimations of Immortality From Recollections of Early Childhood
  It Is a Beauteous Evening, Calm and Free
  My Heart Leaps Up When I Behold
  She Dwelt Among the Untrodden Ways
  The World is Too Much With Us
  Tintern Abbey
WILLIAM BUTLER YEATS
  Dialogue of Self and Soul
  The Lake Isle of Innisfree

Index

THE READER WILL FIND THE POEMS IN *Poetry Therapy* LISTED NOT IN THIS GENERAL INDEX BUT IN A LIST OF POEMS SUITABLE FOR USE IN POETRY THERAPY BEGINNING ON PAGE 276.

A.

Abbe, George, 157, 166, 169
Achievement, in writing poetry, 228
Addison, Joseph, 189
Adler, Gerhard, 11, 124, 132
Adolescents, 88-103, 223-230
AFTLI, 212-222
AFTLI — A Sequel, 221
Alcoholics, poetry for, 80
Alger, I., 154
Altschuler, Ira M., 41
Ambiguity, 240

Ambivalence, 254
American Foundation of Religion and Psychiatry, 171
American Psychiatric Association, 21
American Society of Group Therapy and Psychodrama, 260
Anger, dispelling of, 177
Anthology, of poems for therapy, 271
Anxiety, 178
Arieti, S., 234-236, 257, 259

Index

Aristophanes, 105
Aristotle, 39, 51, 258
Arnold, Matthew, 271
Aronov, B. M., 114, 123
Art, therapeutic aspects, 108
Art therapy(ies), 9, 19, 38, 167
Asklepios, 11
Auden, W. H., 258, 259, 272
Autism, rhythmic sign language in, 58
Awareness, poetry and, 124-132

B.

Barasch, Julius, 169
Barker, Warren J., 254, 259
Bate, W. J., 257
Bateson, Gregory, 235, 257
Beethoven, Ludwig van, 158, 159, 170
Behavior, rhythmic, embryonic, 55-56
Bereavement, 171
Berger, Milton M., 15, 75, 81
Berne, Eric, 147, 154
Bion, W. R., 160, 169
Blackmur, R. P., 232, 235, 254, 257
Blake, William, 157, 232, 233, 271
Blanton, Smiley, 16, 41, 70, 74, 171
Blends, 238-239
Bleuler, Eugen, 238, 239, 258
Bonime, Walter, 114, 122
Bortz, E. L., 51
Breast-feeding, rhythm in, 56
Brill, A. A., 257
Brooks, Cleanth, 233, 249, 250, 254, 257, 259
Browning, Robert, 173, 174, 176
Bruch, Hilde, 240
Bryn Mawr Hospital, 188
Burke, Kenneth, 12, 15, 104, 110, 261
Burrow, T., 65
Butcher, S. H., 39, 51
Byron, George Gordon, 41, 70

C.

Calabria, F., 157, 169
Cammer, L., 170
Carlyle, Thomas, 68
Carrier, W., 86
Carroll, Lewis, 65, 231, 238, 258

Case histories and examples, 82-85, 125-128, 131; of adolescents, 89-103; of patient Barbara, 92-94; Darius, 250-252; Diane, 251-253; Esther, 84; Francisco, 94-99; Glenda, 149-153; H., 34; Mrs. H., 23-28; Harold R., 84; Harry, 251-253; Jean, 216-218; Joan, 85; Katina, 99-103; Lewis, 145-149; Lois, 246-248, 250, 252; Lorene, 89-91; M., 34; Mollie, 85; R., 32-34; Richard, 241-246, 250, 252, 253; Richard N., 19; S., 33-34; Sam, 85; Sybil, 143-145; V., 36
Catharsis, 36, 39, 64-65, 158, 160-161, 193
Censorship, 106
Center for Creative Living, 142
Chaucer, Geoffrey, 39
Child, autistic, rhythmic sign language for, 58
Clare, John, 73
Clark, Robert A., 113, 122
Clock, biologic, 54
Clough, Arthur Hugh, 73
Coates, Samuel, 19
Cohen, D. A., 141
Coleman, M. L., 160, 169
Coleridge, Samuel Taylor, 70, 157, 164, 240, 256, 259
College, group therapy at, 111-115
Committee for the Education of Pregnant School Age Girls, 12
Com-motion, 61
Communication, archaic, definition, 61; poetry as, 35, 38, 70, 142-154; rhythm and, 53, 59-60
Concretization, 249
Conflict, 241
Contagion, mental. See *Mental contagion.*
Contradictory emotions, 254
Cooscillation, 60, 61
Counseling center, poetry therapy in, 184-187
Cowper, William, 68
Crane, Robert S., 74
Creativity, 46, 51, 108, 109, 158-159, 180, 184, 187, 192, 193, 214, 215, 219, 220, 224

Creedmoor State Hospital, 40
Crootof, Charles, 15, 38
Crownville State Hospital, 11
Cumberland Hospital, 12, 13, 40, 67, 155, 260
Cummings, E. E., 232, 238, 239, 241, 247, 254, 257, 258, 259
Curriculum, for poetry therapists, 260-268

D.

Dahlstrom, W. G., 122
Dance, rhythm in, 89
DAP, 113, 117
Darwin, Charles, 54, 262
David, 134
Davison, A., 141
Daydreaming, 224
Decision making, by emotionally fragile persons, 22
Defense mechanisms, 192, 193
Dependency needs, 148
Depression, 68, 172
Despair, 217
Desymbolization, 249
Dewey, John, 225, 230
Diamond, Edwin, 45, 51
Dickinson, Emily, 32, 33, 46, 90, 91, 157, 269, 271
Discouragement, 177, 179
Discussion, of poetry, 35
Diseases, periodic, 54
Dixmont State Hospital, 29, 33, 34, 71, 260
Donne, John, 72, 76, 86, 157, 248
Doodling, 100
Dostoevski, F. M., 80, 87
Draw-A-Person test, 113, 117
Dreams, 45, 114, 119
Drew, Elizabeth, 103
Drug addiction, 128
Dryden, John, 68, 74
Dylan, Robert, 39, 223, 226
Dysrhythmia, 60

E.

Edgar, Kenneth, 15, 16, 29, 37, 69, 111, 162, 165, 169, 260, 271
Ego intactness, in group therapy, 165-166

Eichmann, Adolf, 226
El Camino Hospital, 11, 12
Eliot, T. S., 41, 79, 87, 89, 132, 141, 154, 234, 257
Emerson, Ralph Waldo, 174
Emotion(s), definition, 61; expression through poetry, 154
Empathy, 159-160
Empson, William, 240, 254, 259
Engle, P., 86
Erotic feelings, breathing rhythm and, 64
Esthetic illusion, 161
Euripides, 105, 175
Expression, 160-161; of repressed, 104
Externalization, 31, 35, 36, 45, 94, 158
Ezriel, H., 160, 167

F.

Fantasy, 224, 226
Feelings, expression of, 35
Ferreira, A. J., 254, 259
Fetterman, David, 225, 226
Figures of speech, 233
FitzHerbert, J., 65
Fleischl, Maria, 38
Fontaine, Elizabeth, 13
Form, psychodynamics of, 104
Forrest, David, 12, 16, 231, 257, 258
Fowler, H. W., 46, 237, 258
Fox, Emmet, 138, 141
Frank, Anne, 203
Frankl, Viktor, 141
Franklin, Benjamin, 19
Free association, 183
Freud, Sigmund, 5-7, 11, 156, 169, 192, 193, 199, 224, 225, 230, 257, 262
Friedlander, M., 141
Frost, Robert, 22, 39, 70, 73, 74, 89, 104, 110, 214, 222, 271
Fultz, A. F., 165, 169

G.

Gabriel, Sister Paul, 55, 65
Galt, John M., 20
Gangs, street, 98
Gelberman, Joseph H., 16, 133, 184
Gesture, poetic language as, 232, 235,

Index

254-255
Gibran, Kahlil, 78, 80, 81, 87, 126, 132
Ginsberg, Louis, 48, 51, 92, 226
Giovanni, Fra, 132
Gleason, R. J., 230
Gould, M., 215
Gounod, Charles, 215
Graves, Robert, 261, 271, 272
Greenberg, Samuel Alvin, 16, 212
Greenwald, Harold, 16, 142
Greifer, Eli, 12, 34, 37, 41, 51, 67, 72, 111, 112, 122, 155, 167, 260, 274
Group(s), variability of, 162-163
Group interaction, 44, 49
Group poetry therapy, assumptions, 161-163; clinical practice in, 267; cohesiveness in, 35; discussion in, 166; ego intactness in, 165-166; elimination of warm-up in, 35, 45, 164; emotional climate for, 165; goals, 166-167; group variability and, 162-163; in college students, 115-116; individual therapy and, 167-168; insight provided, 167; interaction in, 163; internship in, 267; poem selection in, 73, 112, 116; principles, 163-168; problems, 202-207; resolution of resistance in, 167, 168; state of flux in, 166; strategy in, 161-168; training individual in, 164; validation, 111-123
Group recitation, 71
Guilbert, Yvette, 5
Guthiel, Emil A., 37, 114, 122

H.

Habits, rhythms and, 60
Haley, Jay, 257
Hallucinations, 34
Hammer, Emanuel, 122
Happiness, search for, 81, 151
Hardy, Thomas, 248
Harker, Anne, 215
Harris, Marguerite, 212, 214
Hathaway, S., 122
Hayakawa, S., 16, 261, 268, 269
Hazley, Richard, 15, 16, 29, 37, 69, 111, 162, 165, 169, 260, 271
Headbanging, 57, 58

Henley, W. E., 34, 41, 73, 269
Herrick, Robert, 72
Hillel, Rabbi, 76, 86
Hillside Hospital, 200-211
Hippocrates, 54
Hitchings, W. Douglas, 16, 124
Hitler, Adolf, 57
Hogan, P., 154
Holmes, O. W., 68
Homer, 39, 98, 237
Hood, Thomas, 215
Hooker, D., 65
Hopelessness, in patient's poem, 151
Hopkins, Gerard Manley, 73, 248
Horney, Karen, 76, 118, 123
Hospitalized Veterans Writing Project, Inc., 13
Hostility, in patient's poem, 150
Housman, A. E., 80, 270, 271
Humor, 193
Hypnotic effects, 59, 60, 70

I.

Identification, 120
Image production, movement exercises and, 167
Imagery, 157, 233
Indiana State University of Pennsylvania, 69, 111, 192, 260
Individual poetry therapy, 23-28, 137-139, 171-179; group therapy combined with, 167-168
Infantilism, 120
Inman, W. S., 65
Inner Light, 124
Insight, poetry and, 159-160; in group therapy, 167
Institute of the Pennsylvania Hospital, 11, 19, 23, 188, 223, 225
Institute of Theopsychosophy, 212
Institutions, poetry therapy in, 11
Intellectual defense, 147
Interaction, postnatal, rhythm in, 56-57
Isoprinciple, 41, 67-68, 112

J.

Jackson, Don D., 257
James, William, 222
Jazz, rhythm in, 56

Jeffers, Robinson, 68
Jochum, Eugen, 157, 160, 169
Johnson, Julia, 228
Johnson, Samuel, 235, 257, 258
Johnson, Thomas H., 90
Jones, Robert, 15, 16, 19, 223
Jung, Karl, 11, 114, 120, 122, 123, 153, 167, 261, 262, 268

K.
Kandinski, Vasili, 125
Keats, John, 6, 9, 70, 84, 100, 204, 229, 230
Kennedy, John F., 111
Kenneth E. Appel Award, 21
Kenny, Nick, 209
Kerouac, Jack, 92
Keyserling, Hermann, 241, 259
King, E. G., 141
Kirkbride, Thomas S., 21
Klages, L., 65
Klee, Paul, 124
Klein, Melanie, 160
Kobak, Dorothy, 16, 133, 180
Kolb, L. C., 236, 258
Korngold, Erich, 215
Kraepelin, Emil, 239
Kramer, Aaron, 12, 16, 200
Kris, E., 157, 161, 169, 193
Kronmeyer, Robert, 87
Kubie, Lawrence, 258

L.
LaForge, J., 215
Landor, Walter Savage, 68
Langer, S. K., 65
Langley Porter Institute, 11
Language in Thought and Action, 261
Lawrence, D. H., 248
Lear, E., 65, 254, 259
Ledwith, Nettie H., 113, 123
Leedy, Jack J., 3, 5, 7, 15, 37, 41, 51, 67, 111, 112, 123, 155, 164, 165, 169, 260
Levit, Herbert, 15, 29, 165, 169
Lieberman, M., 170
Lincoln, Abraham, 222
Literature courses, for poetry therapists, 264, 266

Longfellow, Henry W., 39, 41, 68, 70, 72, 74, 248
Loomis, H. W., 215
Lowell, James Russell, 172
Lundlin, W. H., 114, 123
Lyttleton, Lucy, 215

M.
Machover, Karen, 123
Magidoff, Robert, 170
Mahler, Gustav, 6, 7
Mallarmé, Stéphane, 92
Manic-depression dysrhythmia, 60
Mann, Joseph B., 13
Manning, Henry E., 12
Marc, Franz, 125, 157
Margalith, Helen, 171
Married couples, poetry for, 81
Masefield, John, 73
Masserman, J. H., 59, 65
Masturbation, compulsive, 58
McGinley, Phyllis, 195
McMurray, Georgia, 12
McNeill, David, 258
Meerloo, Joost A. M., 15, 52, 66
Memorization, of poems, 34-35, 69, 112
Mendelssohn, Felix, 159, 215
Menninger, Karl, 114, 123, 222
Mental contagion, 62-64
Mental health center, poetry therapy in, 38-51
Mental hospital, newsletter in, 189; poetry therapy and workshop in, 200-211; recital at, 200-202
Mental retardation, 71
Metamessages, 269-272
Metamorphosis, in poetry, 255
Metaphor, 229, 235, 249, 255
Metonymy, 237
Metropolitan Institute for Psychoanalytic Studies and Community Guidance Service, 142
Mid-Way Counseling Center, 180
Milieu therapy, 21
Milk dance, 56
Mill, John S., 222
Millay, Edna St. Vincent, 91, 197, 248
Miller, Joaquin, 41

Index

Milton, John, 65, 72, 252, 259
Minkowski, M., 66, 68
Mintz, Elizabeth E., 116, 123
Mittleman, B., 57, 66
MMPI, 113, 117
Moreno, J. L., 11
Morrison, Morris R., 12, 15, 88
Morse, Samuel, 259
Movement exercises, image production and, 167
Mowbray, Jean K., 16, 188
Mowrer, O. Hobart, 123
Murray, H. A., 123
Music, rhythm in, 56, 63, 64; therapy, 41

N.

Nash, Ogden, 195
National Association for Poetry Therapy, 69
Naumberg, M., 165, 167, 169
Nelson, B., 160, 169
Nelson, M. C., 169
Neurosis, poetry as substitute for, 192
Newsletter, in mental hospital, 189
Nicolai, C. O. E., 215
Nonsense poems, 254
Northampton County Asylum, 73
Novalis, 52
Noyes, A. P., 236, 258

O.

Objectification of feelings, 35
OEO, 11
Onions, C. T., 170
Order, from chaos, 65, 76
Overprotectiveness, 80

P.

Pain, 127
Paleologic, 234
Pan Tadeusz, 201
Paradigmatic technique, 160
Paralogic, 234, 235
Paranoid schizophrenic reaction, 23-28
Parapathy, personification of, 114
Parker, Rolland, 16, 155, 162, 170
Patient(s), desire to write poetry, 192; differences between poets and, 239-240; poems by, 20, 21, 93, 95-98, 101-103, 181, 182, 184-187; selection of, for poetry therapy, 137

Pearson, N. H., 258, 259
Personality, integration of, 191
Personification of the parapathy, 114
Philosophies of India, 241
Piersol, G. M., 51
Pinza, E., 170
Poe, Edgar A., 70, 157
Poem(s), anthology of, for therapy, 271; as objectification of illness, as substitute for headbanging, 58; by mental patients, 20, 21, 93, 95-98, 100-103, 127, 143-153, 240-248; choice of, criteria for, 41, 43, 67, 73, 114, 116; definitions, 70, 226; discussion of, 44, 49; emotional theme of, 44; for anxiety, 178; for bereavement, 171; for depression, 68, 172; for discouragement, 177, 179; for patients, 248-253; for tension, 173, 215; for therapist, 256-257; for unrequited love, 173; memorization of, 34-35, 69, 112; multiplicity of feelings about, 44; nonsense, 254; patient's sense of, 231-259, thoughts and, 235-239; presentation and questions of, 43; significance of, 31-33; to encourage meeting responsibilities, 173; to express feelings, 35; to express love, 175; to show what life is, 176; unsuitable, 41, 47, 68; written by patients, 71, 82-85, 114, 142, 181, 182, 184, 187, 194-198, 208-209, 228, 272
Poet(s), changes in, during writing of poem, 107; defense mechanisms used by, 192, 193; differences between patients and, 239-240; emulation of, 211; professional, in poetry therapy, 190, 202, 207; therapeutic, 72-73
Poetic expression, schizophrenic expression versus, 235-239
Poetic language, as gesture and ac-

tion, 232, 235, 254-255; extra force of, 232; figures of speech in, 233
Poetry, ambiguity in, 157; appropriate tone in, 255; as meaningful language, 231; as substitute for neurosis, 192; as therapy, 75-87; as therapeutic art, 155-170; awareness and, 124-132; brevity and memorability of, 253-254; communication through, 35, 38, 70, 142-154; conflicted and covert expression in, 254; conventions and patterns in, 254; creativity in, see *Creativity*; definitions of, 155, 210, 270; didactic, 47; discussion similar to free association, 183; dissimilar images in, 234; dreams versus, 45; effects of, 39, 89; empathy and, 159-160; esthetic illusion of, 161; expression and, 154, 160-161; extrapsychic aspects of, 236; for alcoholics, 80; for married couples, 81; for non-fulfillment in family life, 79; for parental overprotectiveness, 80; insight and, 159-160; integration of personality and, 191; in workshop sessions, 210; misunderstanding of, 249; of therapeutic value, 72-73; oral interpretation of, 271; order and authority in, 253; ordinary language versus, 232-235; patient's writing of, 36-37; philosophy of life and, 40; rhythm in, 62, 232; self-censorship in, 106; self-discovery and, 271; self-judgments in writing, 107; sense of well-being from, 47; subconscious sources of, 157; subject material for, 86; success of, 207-211; symbolic qualities of, 157; types used in therapy, 41; writing of, 107, 192
Poetry recital, at mental hospital, 200-202
Poetry seminars, 225
Poetry therapist, 68-69; clinical experience for, 267; curriculum for, 260-268; literature courses for, 264, 266; poems for, 256-257; psychology courses for, 264, 265-266; training for, 168, 271; two, 33, 113, 140
Poetry therapy, advantages, 253-257; anthology of poems for, 271; brief history, 39; certification in, 260; classroom atmosphere in, 207; curriculum for, resistance to, 261-263; effectiveness of, 88; evaluation methods, 29-30; for adolescents, 88-103, 223-230; for groups, see *Group poetry therapy*; for individual, see *Individual poetry therapy*; for psychoneurotics, 38-51; freedom of discussion in, 208; graduate studies in, 264-267; in AFTLI, 212-222; in private mental hospital, 200-211; in self-help group, 212-222; institutions using, 11; principles, 67-74; procedures used, 29-30; professional poet in, 190, 202, 207; psychoanalytic theory and, 156; requirements, 89; results, 30-31; teacher used in, 228; undergraduate studies in, 263-264; voluntary participation, 208; with hospitalized schizophrenics, 29-37
Poetry therapy group, 12, 71; room, 12
Poetry workshop, in mental hospital, 202-211; poetry selected for, 210
Poiesis, in poetry, 236, 255
Polysemia, 238
Pope, Alexander, 235, 236, 258
Portmanteau words, 238-239
Postgraduate Center for Mental Health, 11, 38, 42, 124
Potter, Simeon, 258
Pound, Ezra, 232, 257
Project Teen Aid, 11, 12, 67
Prothero, R. E., 141
Psalms, The, as psychological and allegorical poems, 133-141; classification of subject matter, 134; emotional reactions from, 133; selection of patients for therapy, 137; therapeutic applications of, 137, 140; therapeutic characteristics of, 136

Index

Pseudostatements, 232
Psychoanalytic theory, poetry therapy and, 156
Psychograft, 34, 112, 167
Psychologic tests, in evaluation of poetry therapy, 29
Psychology courses, for poetry therapists, 264, 265-266
Psychoneurosis, 38-51
Psychoses and neuroses, cyclic, 54
Psychosomatic disease, dysrhythmia and, 60
Psychotherapy, lengthiness of, 161; poetry and, characteristics of, 39; religion and, 220

R.

Ransom, John Crowe, 236, 258
Rawlins, Winifred, 125
Read, Herbert, 66
Realf, Richard, 176
Reality testing, suspension of, 46
Reconstructive therapy, 131
Regression, in rhythm, 62
Reich, Wilhelm, 156, 168, 170
Reik, Theodor, 7, 11, 15, 112, 115, 118, 123
Reiman, H. A., 66
Relaxation, 173
Religion, 220
Repressed, expression of, 104
Resistance, overcoming, 163-164, 167, 168
Responsibilities, meeting of, poem to encourage, 173
Rhythm, 52-66; abnormal expression of, 57-59; biologic, 53-55; catharsis and, 64-65; communicative function of, 53, 59-60; creativity and, 51; hormonal, 54; in dance, 89; in hypnosis, 59, 60; in jazz, 56; in music, 63, 64; in poetry, 62, 232; in postnatal interaction, 56-57; in rock and roll, 62; language of, 60-61; mental contagion and, 62-64; natural, technologic contamination of, 61; of breathing, erotic feelings and, 64; repression in, 62; tidal, 54; transfer from person to person, 60

Richards, A., 232, 249, 257
Richards, I. A., 248, 259
Rimbaud, J. N. A., 92
Robbins, B. S., 154
Robinson, Edward Arlington, 272
Robinson, S. Sue, 16, 188
Rock and roll rhythm, 62
Rocking, rhythmic, 58
Roethke, Theodore, 232, 233, 247, 257, 259
Rorschach, Hermann, 123
Rorschach test, 113, 117, 162
Rosenblatt, Louise, 88, 103
Rosetti, Christina, 178, 248
Rubenstein, C. Robert, 224
Rush, Benjamin, 19

S.

Sandburg, Carl, 39
Schiller, J. C. F. von, 158
Schizophrenia, 29-37; verbilization in, 236
Schizophrenic expression, similarity of poetic expression to, 235-239
Schlauffler, R. H., 159, 170
Schlegel, Friedrich, 159
School, 600, poetry therapy in, 180-184
Schubert, Franz, 215
Schulberg, Budd, 164, 165, 170
Schwartz, E., 170
Searles, Harold F., 249, 255, 258, 259
Self-discovery, 271
Self-knowledge, 126
Self-realization, 36
Service, Robert, 43
Shakespeare, Wm., 39, 41, 72, 73, 79, 162, 174, 177, 204, 207, 208, 214, 215, 238, 263, 270
Sharpe, E. F., 51
Shelly, Percy B., 68, 100, 179
Shieman, Joy, 12
Sinsheimer, H., 162, 170
Slippery Rock State College, 36, 71, 111, 260
Smart, Christopher, 73, 74
Smith, L. H., 40, 51
Socrates, 105
Solace, 171
Solberger, A., 66

Song(s), Shakespeare's, 215; to stimulate poetry therapy group, 69
Sonne, John C., 228-230
Sonnet(s), Shakespeare's, 73
Sophocles, 107
Spector, Samuel, 12, 155, 170
Spender, Stephen, 272
Statements, discursive versus poetic, 232
Staten Island Aid for Retarded Children, 71
Steele, Richard, 189
Stekel, Wilhelm, 114, 123
Stevens, Wallace, 256, 259
Stevenson, R. L., 68, 171, 172
Stock, D., 170
Storch, Alfred, 237, 257, 258
St. Paul, 171
Strauss, Richard, 215
Street gangs, 98
Suicidal tendencies, 68
Swineburne, Algernon C., 172, 173
Symbolic parallelism, 114
Symptoms, in patient's poem, 145
Synecdoche, 237-238

T.

Talmud, 76, 134
TAT, 113, 117, 253
Tatler, 188-193, 198, 227
Teacher, in poetry therapy, 228
Tennyson, Alfred, 39, 73, 177
Tension, poetry for, 173, 215
Theopsychosophy, 219
Therapy, as poetry, 75-87; definitions of, 75, 155
Thomas, Ambroise, 215
Thomas, Dylan, 244, 259, 272
Thompson, Francis, 63, 68, 110
Thoughts, similarity of poems to, 235-239
Timing, in psychotherapy, 77
Togetherness, 182
Transference, 33-34, 185, 244; in group therapy, 165; in patient's poems, 147, 152

Travel Diary of a Philosopher, The, 241
Tschaikowsky, Peter I., 215
Turner, Walter James, 215
2:00 AM, 197
Twyeffort, L. H., 40, 51
Tyson, F., 170

U.

Ulysses, 177
Unconscious, communicating with, 229; effect of poetry on, 47

V.

Van Der Post, L., 66
Verbalization, 31, 35, 45, 236
Verdi, Giuseppi, 215
Von Domarus, E., 234, 257

W.

Walter, Bruno, 159, 170
Ward, Aileen, 229, 230
Warm-up, elimination of, 35, 45, 164
Weakland, Jean, 257
Well-being, sense of, 47
Welsch, G. S., 122
Werner, Alice, 237
White, Glenn, 194, 195, 199
Whitman, Walt, 39, 73, 271
Whittier, John G., 68, 125
Wiederlight, Melvin, 169, 170
Williams, Oscar, 258
Williams, William Carlos, 226
Winston, S., 167, 170
Wolberg, Lewis, 10, 15
Wolf, A., 170
Wordsworth, William, 157, 233, 256
Writing, poetic versus schizophrenic, 239

Y.

Yale Psychiatric Institute, 228

Z.

Zimmer, Heinrich, 241, 259